THE LONGMAN COMPANION TO
THE FORMATION OF THE EUROPEAN EMPIRES, 1488–1920

LONGMAN COMPANIONS TO HISTORY

General Editors: Chris Cook and John Stevenson

The following Companions to History *are now available*:

Renaissance Europe, 1390–1530
Stella Fletcher

The European Reformation
Mark Greengrass

The Tudor Age
Rosemary O'Day

The Stuart Age, 1603–1714
John Wroughton

*Britain in the Eighteenth Century,
1688–1820*
Jeremy Gregory and John Stevenson

European Nationalism, 1789–1920
Raymond Pearson

European Decolonisation
Muriel E. Chamberlain

The Middle East since 1914
(Second Edition)
Ritchie Ovendale

America, 1910–1945
Patrick Renshaw

Nazi Germany
Tim Kirk

Britain since 1945
Chris Cook and John Stevenson

Germany since 1945
Adrian Webb

The European Union since 1945
Alasdair Blair

Imperial Russia, 1695–1917
David Longley

Napoleonic Europe
Clive Emsley

*Britain in the Nineteenth Century,
1815–1914*
Chris Cook

The Labour Party, 1900–1998
Harry Harmer

Russia since 1914
Martin McCauley

Britain, 1914–45
Andrew Thorpe

*America, Russia and the Cold War,
1941–1998* (Second Edition)
John W. Young

THE LONGMAN COMPANION TO

THE FORMATION OF THE EUROPEAN EMPIRES, 1488–1920

Muriel E. Chamberlain

An imprint of **Pearson Education**

Harlow, England · London · New York · Reading, Massachusetts · San Francisco · Toronto · Don Mills, Ontario · Sydney
Tokyo · Singapore · Hong Kong · Seoul · Taipei · Cape Town · Madrid · Mexico City · Amsterdam · Munich · Paris · Milan

Pearson Education Limited

Edinburgh Gate
Harlow
Essex CM20 2JE
England

and Associated Companies around the world

Visit us on the World Wide Web at:
www.pearsoneduc.com

First published in Great Britain in 2000

ISBN 0-582-36979-7 LIMP
ISBN 0-582-36980-0 CASED

British Library Cataloguing-in-Publication Data
A catalogue record for this book is available from the British Library

Library of Congress Cataloging-in-Publication Data
A catalog record for this book can be obtained from the Library of Congress

10 9 8 7 6 5 4 3 2 1
05 04 03 02 01 00

Typeset by 35
Produced by Pearson Education Asia Pte Ltd.
Printed in Singapore

CONTENTS

LIST OF MAPS

PREFACE

Whatever one may think of the morality of empire, it is undeniable that the European empires, created between the late fifteenth and the early twentieth centuries, have shaped the modern world, certainly in its political and economic aspects and often culturally as well. They began not in strength but in weakness, when Europe itself was still in retreat from the forces of Islam, but by the late nineteenth century Europe seemed invincible. The watershed was the First World War, although this was not immediately apparent. Some empires, like the British, actually grew larger after 1918 with the acquisition of 'mandated' territories. But the creation of the League of Nations and the establishment of the mandate system marked the beginning of a change in world opinion. The smash and grab tactics of the nineteenth and earlier centuries were no longer acceptable.

In one sense the present book is Volume One to the author's *European Decolonisation in the Twentieth Century,* setting the scene for the developments of that century. As in the earlier work only certain aspects could be covered. Only the European maritime empires are included. The equally large and important land empires of Russia and the United States are not. Very important controversies about the reasons for European expansion and the reactions of the non-European peoples could only be hinted at.

My thanks are due to my successor as the Head of the History Department in the University of Wales Swansea, Professor David Eastwood, who readily allowed me to continue to use departmental facilities to enable me to finish this book.

Professor M.E. Chamberlain
July 2000

CHRONOLOGY

1 THE FOUNDATIONS

THE AGE OF DISCOVERY

The effects of the conflicts between Christendom and Islam

The Age of Discovery was in part a response to the pressures of Islam at a time when Europe itself was still contracting. Consequently it always had elements of a crusade, including the hope of linking up with Christians left behind by the advance of Islam, such as the mysterious Prester John.

Conflicts

632	Death of Muhammad.
637	Arab conquest of Jerusalem.
640	Arab conquest of Egypt.
711–15	Arab (Moorish) conquest of whole of Visigothic Spain.
732	Battle of Poitiers. Charles Martel defeated Arabs near Tours. Henceforth Islamic forces remained south of the Pyrenees.
827	Arab invasion of Sicily.
Late 10th cent.	Venice took advantage of political decline of Byzantine empire to become the rising power in the Eastern Mediterranean. Began to conquer Dalmation coast. Genoa too tried to replace Byzantium (Constantinople) in Mediterranean trade.
11th cent.	Rise of Seljuk Turks.
1071	Seljuk Turks defeated Byzantine forces at battle of Manzikert and gained control of Asia Minor.
1096	First Crusade launched in response to Constantinople's pleas for help from the West.
1096	Pope extended the crusade to the struggle against the Moors in Spain. Reconquest (*Reconquista*) of Iberian Peninsula took several centuries.
1157	Christians had regained control of most of modern Portugal and northern half of modern Spain.
13th cent.	Rise of Ottoman Turks in Asia Minor.
1204	Fourth Crusade turned aside to sack Constantinople. For a short time the Greek empire was replaced by a Latin empire there. Venice acquired Crete and part of Greece from the Byzantine empire.

1249	Silves, the last Moorish stronghold in the Algarve, captured. Portugal became a nation state.
1270	Portuguese began exploration of African coast.
1308	Ottoman Turks entered Europe.
1389	Turks defeated Serbs in Kosovo.
1415	Portuguese took Ceuta, an important strategic harbour on the southern shores of the Straits of Gibraltar. Learnt more about African trading routes.
1453	Constantinople itself fell to the Turks.
1462–71	Venice lost much of Greece to the Turks.
1489	Venice acquired Cyprus by purchase from Byzantines.
1492	Spanish monarchs, Ferdinand and Isabella, gained control of Granada and finally expelled the Moors from the Iberian Peninsula. (Christopher Columbus commissioned to undertake his first voyage of discovery.)
1523	Turks captured Rhodes, defeating the Knights of St John, who re-established themselves in Malta.
1526	Turks occupied much of Hungary but failed to take Vienna.
1565	Great siege of Malta. Turks failed to take it.
1571	Turks captured Famagusta (a major Eastern Mediterranean port since fall of Acre in 1291).
	Turks defeated in great sea battle of Lepanto.
1664	Turks took Crete from the Venetians.
1683	John Sobieski defeated Turks in second siege of Vienna and regained Hungary.
1687	Turks captured Athens.
1714	Peace of Passarowitz. Venice surrendered remaining claims in Greece to the Turks.

Intellectual factors

Although the political relations between Christendom and Islam were frequently those of conflict, the intellectual relations were often fruitful. The European Renaissance was, as the name implied, a rediscovery of the rich inheritance of classical learning, but it developed over a long period and owed a substantial debt to Arab, and Jewish, sources and learning. When the Arabs conquered Syria in the eighth century they became familiar with many Greek texts, lost to the West during the period of the barbarian invasions. Some of these found their way back to the West through Arabic translations. Avicenna (Ibn Sina) and Averroes (Ibn Rushd) were key figures in restoring knowledge of Aristotle to the West.

Contacts occurred in southern Italy and Sicily, but Spain was the most important centre for this interchange of ideas, scientific as well as philosophical.

4

Some of the scientific advances made there underlay the development of the technology that made the Age of Discovery possible. The fall of Constantinople in 1453, although a less important trigger of the Renaissance than was at one time believed, did bring Greek scholars and manuscripts to the West.

Mathematics and astronomy

Arab scholars drew on Indian, as well as Greek, sources. Maslama of Madrid (d. *c.*1007) founded a school of astronomers based on Ptolemy's *Algamest.* Leonardo Fibonacci (Leonardo of Pisa) travelled in the Arab world. His *Liber abaci* (1202) introduced the western world to Indian numbers (miscalled Arab numbers) including the zero, which replaced the clumsy Roman system.[1] His *De Practica Geometrica* (1220) directed them to geometry and trigonometry. Latin scholars travelled to Toledo and produced new translations of classical works, e.g. Gerard of Cremona (1147–87) and Adelard of Bath translated Ptolemy's *Algamest* and Euclid's *Elements* respectively. Islam required accurate astronomical information for religious purposes and elaborate astronomical tables were produced and precision instruments like astrolabes, quadrants and globes of the heavens developed. Pope Sylvester II (Gerbert d'Aurillac, d. 1003), himself a mathematician, brought back an astrolabe from Spain.

Navigation and ships

Early sailors were reluctant to venture out of sight of land because of the difficulties of navigation. Arab seamen had always made some use of the stars. New technology, like the astrolabe and the quadrant, which made it possible to determine latitude from the position of the sun, made Renaissance sailors bolder in ocean navigation. In ship design too, much was learnt from the Arabs. The square-rigged European ships of the late Middle Ages, although they had considerable carrying capacity, had limited ability to manoeuvre. In the late fifteenth century, Portuguese and Spanish shipbuilders found a way to combine the European square rig with the Arab lateen sail. The result was the *caravela redonda.* These caravels, light manoeuvrable vessels, were the main ships employed in the voyages of discovery. At the same time, the heavy merchant ships, the carracks, developed in northern Europe, were important in the new carrying trade with the East.

Cartographic knowledge

By the early fourteenth century, Italian traders from Venice and Genoa knew something of trade routes in both Asia and Africa. The most famous medieval traveller, Marco Polo, had published the account of his travels (1271–95) in which he had reached China.

A very important school of Jewish cartographers developed in Majorca (Jews had some degree of entrée to both Islamic and Christian societies). In 1375 it

---

1. Although some earlier use is recorded, e.g. in a Latin ms in a monastery in northern Spain in 976.

produced the Catalan map, which showed both the outlines of Asia and the trade routes between North and West Africa (the Guinea coast).

Some knowledge also filtered back from Constantinople. In 1407 a copy of Ptolemy's *Geography* reached the West. Ptolemy provided information about Africa and also drew upon the work of an important classical geographer and astronomer, Eratosthenes. By the fifteenth century, educated people were well aware that the earth was spherical, not flat, but calculations of distance were often erroneous and the American continent was unknown. Ironically it was their underestimation of the circumference of the globe and their ignorance of the existence of the American continent which made a westward route to Asia seem feasible to them.

Printing

This invention meant that knowledge circulated much more quickly. Marco Polo's *Travels* and Ptolemy's *Geography* were printed in 1483 and 1462 respectively. The printing of maps and charts (particularly in Antwerp, Bruges and Dieppe) made it impossible to keep the new discoveries secret for long.

Economic pressures

Western trade with Asia stretched back to classical times and before. Luxury goods like silk had always been prized. Paradoxically, the Crusades had given the West even greater knowledge of the riches of the East. *Spices*, especially pepper, were not only desirable but near essential when livestock had to be slaughtered in the autumn and the meat kept over the winter. Some trade routes had been disrupted by the advance of the Ottoman Turks, although Arab trade continued and the important route through Egypt had actually improved when the Turks replaced the decrepit Mameluke regime there in 1517. The Mediterranean end of the trade was monopolised by the Venetians, whose position was resented by other powers. Alternative routes to the source of the spices in Asia had come to seem highly desirable. A shortage of *bullion* also played a part, especially in Portugal. It is likely that Henry the Navigator's explorers were initially seeking gold from West Africa, about which something was known, rather than a route to India.

THE FIRST EMPIRES

The Portuguese empire

Early voyages of discovery

1341	The Portuguese visited the Canary Islands. (These had been known in classical times and rediscovered by the Genoese the previous century. A Genoese, Lanzoretto Malocello, conquered Lanzarote in the 1330s.)
1415	Portugal captured Ceuta.

1419	Henry the Navigator, a younger son of King John I, founded an important school of navigation at Sagres in southern Portugal and, from 1420, began to send out exploring expeditions down the west coast of Africa.
1420	Portuguese settled in Porto Santo and subsequently on the main island of Madeira. Planted sugar cane and Malvoisie grapes (from which Madeira wine was later made).
1425, 1427	Tried to settle on Gran Canaria but beaten off by existing inhabitants, the Guanches.
1430s	Systematic exploration of, and first settlements in, the Azores.
1434	Gil Eannes successfully rounded Cape Bojador, 100 miles south of the Canary Islands, in a caravel, thus breaking through superstitious dread of what lay beyond the Cape, which had inhibited earlier explorations.
1441	A caravel brought home gold dust and Negro captives from south of Cape Bojador.
1441–6	Portuguese ships brought home nearly 1000 captives. They were instructed in the Christian faith but in practice were slaves and were used as interpreters in later explorations.
1456–60	Discovered and settled the (uninhabited) Cape Verde islands.
1460	Death of Henry the Navigator.
1479	Treaty of Alcacovas with Spain. Confirmed Portugal in monopoly of trade, settlement, and exploration of west coast of Africa and in the possession of all the Atlantic Islands except the Canaries.
1481	Succession of King John II, an enthusiatic patron of exploration. By now the Portuguese were actively seeking a route to Asia.
1487–93	Pedro da Cavilha explored a land route to the East, visiting Cairo, Suakim, Aden, Calicut, Goa, Hormuz, Sofala, Mecca and Abyssinia. At least some of his reports reached Portugal.
1487–8	Bartolomeu Dias rounded the Cape of Good Hope (which he originally called the Cape of Storms) and landed at Algoa Bay.

International arrangements

1493	Papal Bull *Inter Caetera* divided newly discovered world between Portugal and Spain by drawing a line 100 leagues west of the Azores, Portugal to have the new lands east of the line, Spain those to the west.
1494	Treaty of Tordesillas between Spain and Portugal moved dividing line 250 leagues further west. (Later interpreted to mean longitude 54.37 West.) This ultimately allowed Portugal to claim Brazil. It left authority over the all-important Spice Islands, which it was later discovered could be approached

from either east or west, uncertain at a time when longitude could not yet be measured satisfactorily.

1497–9 Vasco da Gama sailed to India in the hope of opening up trade. Touched at East African ports, including Malindi, where he picked up a Muslim pilot, Ibn Majid. Reached Calicut on the Malabar coast of India. Unenthusiastically received by Arab traders but acquired cargo of pepper and cinnamon.

Asia

1500 Pedro Álvarez Cabral sailed for Calicut. Quarrelled with Hindu authorities in Calicut and moved further south to Cochin.

1502 Third Indies fleet sailed under Vasco da Gama. Also quarrelled with Calicut authorities and bombarded the town. Won important naval battle against the Arabs.

1505–9 Francisco d'Almeida first Portuguese Viceroy of the Indies. Established trading bases in Cochin, Ceylon and Sumatra.

1509 Portuguese won decisive victory over combined Egyptian and Gujerati fleets off Diu. Portuguese fleets now able to operate freely.

1510 Almeida killed in skirmish with Khoikhoi near Cape of Good Hope while returning to Portugal.

1510–15 Affonso d'Albuquerque second Viceroy of the Indies. Forbade spice trade except to ships carrying certificates from the captain of a Portuguese port. Determined to disrupt Arab–Venetian spice trade by the Red Sea route.

1510 Conquered city of Goa and made it principal Portuguese base in the East.

1511 Took Malacca.

1513 Failed to take Aden but temporarily held Socotra.
Defeated Javanese fleet off Malacca.

1514 Reached Moluccas. Subsequently allowed by Sultan of Ternate to build fortified warehouse. (Important as a source of cloves.) Voyaged to Canton. First European contacts with China by sea.

1515 Captured Hormuz.
Albuquerque died at sea off Goa.

1521 & 1522 Portuguese fleets defeated by Chinese.

1540 Portuguese ordered destruction of all Hindu temples in Goa.

1542 Francis Xavier arrived in Goa. Jesuits selected Goa as their second headquarters outside Rome.

1543 Sailors sighted Japan (by accident).

1560 Inquisition arrived in Goa.

| 1571 | Portuguese established a base in Nagasaki (Japan). |
| 1575 | Driven out of their base in Ternate. |

(Portuguese position significantly affected by events in Europe and in India in latter part of sixteenth century.)

1580	Philip II of Spain succeeded to Portuguese throne. Although Portuguese in the Indies retained some autonomy, became subject to attack from Philip's Protestant enemies in Europe, i.e. the English and the Dutch. Spanish and Portuguese thrones remained united until 1640.
1565	Battle of Talikot marked effective end of the Hindu kingdom of Vijayanager in south India. Nothing now to check rising fortunes of Islamic Mughal empire in northern India. Although Portuguese regarded Muslims as their hereditary enemies, had done little to help Hindus. But (in 1535) had received Diu from Gujerat in return for promise (not fulfilled) to assist Gujeratis against the Mughals.
1556	Akbar became Mughal Emperor. Exceptionally tolerant in religious and other matters.
1573	Akbar allowed Portuguese to retain their position in Diu.
1578	First Portuguese ambassador accredited to Akbar's court.
1580	First Jesuit mission visited Akbar's court.
1599	Synod of Diamper denounced all Nestorian (St Thomas) Christians as heretics.
1622	Portuguese lost Hormuz.
1641	Portuguese lost Malacca to the Dutch.

Africa

1448	First European trading factory overseas: fort and warehouse for reception of slaves built on Arguim Island in modern Mauritania. Portuguese end of the trade was in Lagos, near Sagres, which became first African slave market in Europe.
1482	Built fortress and warehouse at Elmina in the Bight of Benin. Became in effect the Portuguese capital in West Africa and centre of trade in slaves, ivory and gold dust.
1483	Diogo Cão explored the mouth of the Congo. Established friendly relations with Nzinga Nkuwu, the Manikongo or King. At his request, the Portuguese sent out priests and technical experts, including, in 1492, printers. Nzinga Nkuwu converted to Christianity in 1490. His son, who succeeded in 1506, was educated in Portugal but there was a backlash of traditionalist forces in the Congo at the same time that the Portuguese

9

	were losing interest in Africa in favour of Brazil and India. The territory became the prey of speculators and a centre of the slave trade.
1505–7	Established forts on east coast of Africa at Sofala and Mozambique and gained influence at Malindi.
1526	Embassy reached Abyssinia.
1541–3	Helped Abyssinians to fight off Turkish attack.
c.1550 onwards	Trade in slaves greatly increased to meet Brazilian demand.
1575	Luanda (Angola) founded.

Brazil

1500	Cabral, taking a westerly course through the Atlantic *en route* for Calicut, sighted Brazil. Claimed it for Portugal. Originally known as Vera Cruz but name changed to Brazil after the dyewood (*caesalpinia echinata*) which was its first export.
1521	Exploring expedition (which included Amerigo Vespucci) sent to Brazilian coast.
1531	Established system of *capitanias* to keep out French interlopers. Men of substance were granted territories at intervals round the coast and given authority to govern and organise settlement. Limited success.
1549	Thomé de Souza sent out as first royal governor. Built San Salvador (Bahia), which became the capital.
c.1550 onwards	Sugar displaced brazilwood as principal export. Required labour force. Amerindians unwilling to work as bondservants and (1570) Crown forbade their enslavement except in certain specific circumstances (e.g. as prisoners of war). Amerindian populations declining in part as result of European diseases such as smallpox. Began to import slaves from Africa, at first from Senegambia and Niger delta, later mainly from Congo and Angola.
1565	Expelled French from Rio de Janeiro area.
1598–1640	Dutch acquired northern part with capital at Recife (Pernambuco). Expelled with difficulty after 1640.
Late 16th cent. onwards	Missionaries (often Paulistas, men of mixed blood) followed rivers into the interior. Often clashed with Spanish Jesuits.
1699	Important gold desposits found at Minas Geraes. Later diamonds also discovered.
1762	Capital moved to Rio de Janeiro.

Government and society in the Portuguese empire

Both the explorations and the establishment of factories and settlements were, from the beginning, state enterprises. After 1503 all imports of spices from the East were channelled through the *Casa da India* in Lisbon. The factories, in Asia, were usually self-contained, heavily fortified, enclaves. The system of government was authoritarian and often military.

Partly because of the continuing crusading tradition, the Portuguese eruption into the Indian Ocean was a violent one. Subsequent English commentators (not entirely impartial) regarded it as little short of piratical and attributed its lack of long-term success to this factor.

Religious zeal was genuine and soon influenced by the Counter-Reformation. Jesuit influence was particularly strong. After initially friendly contacts, the Portuguese came to regard the Nestorian Christians (by tradition first converted by St Thomas the Apostle) as heretics to be extirpated. At first the Portuguese believed the Hindus to be some strange kind of Christians (mistaking Hindu shrines for Christian ones) but quickly realised their mistake. In Portuguese-controlled territory, such as Goa (or Brazil), mass conversions, voluntary or coercive, took place.

The belief that the Portuguese were less colour-conscious than the northern Europeans has been revised in recent years. There were few Portuguese women in the colonies despite the scheme known as the 'Orphans of the King', by which girls from orphanages in Lisbon and Oporto were shipped to the colonies to marry officials. Marriages between Portuguese and non-Europeans were comparatively rare. Sexual relations were not, and large mixed-race populations were created in all Portuguese colonies. The situation was particularly complex in Brazil, giving rise to the *mamelucos* and *mesticos* of mixed European and Amerindian parentage (although *mestico* was also used of Eurasians) and the *mulattos* (of mixed European and African parentage).

The Spanish empire

Background

1344	Castile obtained title to Canary Islands from the Pope. Attempts to settle there brought Spanish into conflict with the inhabitants, the Guanches.
Early 15th cent.	Canary Islands contested between Spain and Portugal. Began to cultivate sugar, vines and wheat.
1469	Marriage of Isabella of Castile to Ferdinand of Aragon.
1479	Union of kingdoms of Castile and Aragon.
	Treaty of Alcacovas. Portugal abandoned claims to Canary Islands.
1490	Finally subdued Palma and (1493) Tenerife. Possession of Canary Islands complete.
1492	Moors expelled from Granada, last stronghold in Spain.
	Christopher Columbus commissioned (in Granada) to seek western route to Asia.
1493	Spain obtained four Bulls from Pope Alexander VI (a Spaniard) conferring exclusive rights on them. The most important was

Inter Caetera, which granted Spain the right to all discoveries west of a line drawn 100 leagues west of Azores.

1494   Bull modified by Treaty of Tordesillas between Spain and Portugal, moving the line 250 leagues further west.

1519–58   Emperor Charles V ruled not only over Spain but also over Germany, the Low Countries and most of Italy.

1580–1640   Crowns of Spain and Portugal united.

Principal voyages of discovery

1492–3   Columbus sailed from Spanish port of Palos to Canary Islands and thence westwards across the Atlantic. Touched land in Bahamas and also reached Hispaniola and Cuba. Believed he had reached outer islands of Asia.

1493–4   Columbus given title of Admiral of the Ocean Sea and Viceroy of the Indies. Provided with fleet of 17 ships carrying 1500 men and instructed to convert the Indians and establish a trading port. Revisited Hispaniola and Cuba, which he believed to be Japan.

1498–1500   Columbus' third voyage. Discovered Trinidad and mouth of the Orinoco.

1499–1500   Ojeda and Amerigo Vespucci explored coast of Guiana and discovered River Amazon. Realised they were dealing with a new continent.

1501   Coelho and Vespucci explored coast of South America, possibly nearly to the River Plate.

1502–4   Columbus' fourth voyage. Touched Honduras, Nicaragua and Isthmus of Panama. Still believed had reached Asia and that Honduras was probably Indo-China.

1507   Name 'America' first appeared on a map.

1519–21   First circumnavigation of the globe by Victoria, initially commanded by Ferdinand Magellan, who discovered passage round South America (Magellan Straits), the vast size of the Pacific Ocean and the Philippine Islands, before being killed in the Moluccas. Voyage completed by Elcana.

Development of the Spanish empire in the Americas

When the Spaniards arrived, the peaceful Arawak population of the Caribbean islands was already under attack from the much fiercer Caribs from the mainland. The Spaniards originally concentrated on the islands under Arawak control and avoided the Caribs, but this eventually left a toehold for European rivals. In the end both Arawak and Carib populations were virtually wiped out.

1493   Columbus began second settlement in Hispaniola. (Men left behind on first expedition having disappeared.) Hoped to find gold and open up trade with China, which was believed to be close. Columbus was unable to control the colonists. Turned on the, previously friendly, inhabitants, the Tainos, demanded tribute of gold dust, hunted them down with dogs and enslaved many as 'prisoners of war'.

1496–7	Settlers on Hispaniola began to build town of Santo Domingo, which became capital of Spanish Indies for fifty years.
1499	Francisco de Bobadilla appointed to replace Columbus.
1502–8	Frey Nicolas de Ovando was Governor. Arrived with 30 ships and 2500 colonists – marked real beginning of Spanish colonisation. By 1520s alluvial gold almost exhausted. Spanish landowners began to grow sugar. Needed labour. Tainos dying out and not considered good labourers. Began to import negro slaves on small scale at first.
1509	Juan de Esqivel began settlement of Jamaica.
1511	Ovando's assistant, Diego Velázquez, began the settlement of Cuba and subdued the island within three years.
1512	Settlement of Puerto Rico began. First Governor, Juan Ponce de Leon, was also interested in Florida.
1513	Vasco Nunez de Balboa joined expedition to Darien and on 25 September was the first Spaniard to sight Pacific Ocean (or 'South Sea') and claimed it for Spain. Soon realised how narrow the isthmus of Panama was and hoped for channel through it.
1518	Velázquez, Governor of Cuba, sent Hernando Cortés to Mexico to trade and explore.
1519–21	Cortés ignored his instructions, struck out on his own and conquered Aztec empire, which was still expanding at this time, with tiny force of 400 infantry, 16 horsemen and a small force of artillery. The Emperor, Montezuma II, died a Spanish captive. Helped by divisions among Amerindian population, as well as by some superiority in technology. Mexico City became capital of Spanish empire in Central America.
1519	Settlement in Panama, first settlement on Pacific coast.
1530	Spaniards becoming aware of Inca empire, then seriously split by civil war. Atahualpa had just seized crown from Huascar.
1531	Francisco Pizarro landed in Peru with even smaller force than Cortés. Took Atahualpa prisoner and later executed him. Here too local divisions prevented effective resistance.
1533	Pizarro's forces entered capital, Cuzco.
1535	Pizarro founded new capital, Lima. Rest of Inca empire slowly conquered. Viceroy at Lima ruled what is now Bolivia and Peru and had authority over most other Spanish governors in South America.

1536	War with France. French privateers began to attack Spanish in Caribbean.
1542	Spaniards organised convoy system for ships to and from the Caribbean.
1545	Conquered Yucatán Peninsula, the territory of the Maya.
1559	Treaty of Cateau-Cambresis settled outstanding questions between Spain and France.
1564–5	'Spanish Manila Galleon' inaugurated regular trans-Pacific trade between Mexico and the Philippines. American silver exchanged for Chinese silk.
1570	Deterioration of relations with England. Thereafter Spanish subject to English attacks in Caribbean. (For details, *see* under British empire.)

Government and society of the Spanish empire in America

Despite the important role of individual adventurers, sometimes largely out of control, in the early days, the Spanish empire soon became a state (royal) enterprise, organised and controlled from metropolitan Spain. The bureaucratic headquarters were in Seville. The *Casa de Contratación* (1503) regulated trade and related matters. *The Real y Supremo Consejo de las Indias* (the Council of the Indies), established 1524, was the key body, advising the King on legislation and acting as the court of last resort in judicial matters.

Until 1714 the King maintained direct relations with each colony through a Viceroy or Captain-General. The Viceroyalty of New Spain (Mexico) was established in 1535 and that of Peru in 1543. There were originally three captaincies-general: Santo Domingo (1492), Guatemala (1543) and New Granada (1598). New Granada became a Viceroyalty in 1739 and the Viceroyalty of La Plata was created in 1776. New Captaincies-General were created in Havana (Cuba), 1630, Caracas (Venezuela), 1742, and Chile, 1776.

Viceroys and Captains-General were appointed by the Council of the Indies and were usually from metropolitan Spain. They were assisted (and checked) by *audencias*, primarily judicial bodies but which also acted as advisory councils.

Spanish legislation applied in the colonies. In 1681 the *Recopilación de los leyes de las Indias* codified 11,000 laws which applied to the Indies.

Trade was tightly controlled. Until 1720 it was channelled through Seville. (For further details, *see below* pp. 33–4.) The colonies were also taxed for the benefit of metropolitan Spain. Apart from the duties on trade, the Crown had royal monopolies in the colonies and levied the *quinto* (originally one fifth of the value) at assay offices in the colonies when bullion was converted into stamped bars. Other colonial taxes went first to pay colonial expenses but any surplus was remitted to Spain.

Settlement was encouraged and organised. A new Spanish colonial aristocracy emerged. The old aristocracy of Spain was not inclined to go to the colonies. The new aristocracy was drawn from the middle and even the lower classes, who went to seek their fortunes. Significant numbers of women emigrated and there was less mixing with non-European women than in the Portuguese colonies. The government experimented with the *encomienda* system, which had been successfully employed during the *Reconquista* and in the Canaries, where individuals were given authority over groups of Indians, but it was allowed to die out and replaced by the development of *haciendas* or estates.

Hopes of vast quantities of gold were quickly dashed but silver emerged as a major resource. By the 1540s silver mines had been discovered in both Mexico and Peru. Those at Potosi, then in Upper Peru (now in Bolivia), proved to be the world's biggest source of silver. Spanish America did export other goods to Spain, among them cochineal, hides, tallow and sugar, but these were unimportant compared with the silver. The vast silver exports had a number of consequences. They caused monetary inflation in Europe and they tempted attacks from other European powers. The Spanish had to build strongly fortified harbours at Cartegena, Vera Cruz, Havana and San Juan del Puerto Rico. From 1564 the silver was transported to Europe in the twice-yearly treasure fleets, guarded by warships.

Like the Portuguese, the Spanish wanted a labour force. In 1542 the enslavement of the Amerindians was forbidden but the enactment was evaded by the use of the traditional Aztec and Inca systems of forced labour. However, the Amerindians were never regarded as satisfactory labourers and, as in Brazil, their numbers were dramatically reduced by the importation of European diseases, to which they had no immunity. African slaves were increasingly imported. In 1586 the *asiento* system was introduced; contractors undertook to deliver a stipulated number of slaves each year, either to the New World or to Europe.

Spanish thinking was influenced not only by the crusading spirit but also by the vigour of the Counter-Reformation. The conversion of any non-Christians with whom they came into contact was central to both their practice and their justification of empire. It had been enjoined by the papal Bull *Inter Caetera*. In the Americas the lead was taken by the Dominicans. They produced subtle legal justifications for the conquest but also, not infrequently, championed the Indians against exploitation.

The Spanish empire which eventually extended over virtually the whole of South and Central America, apart from Brazil, was a homogeneous one, with a common language (Spanish), a common religion (Catholicism) and, basically, a common legal and governmental system.

The British empire

(Strictly speaking the English empire until 1707, *see below* p. 27)

The British empire was founded more by private enterprise and less by government direction than either the Portuguese or Spanish empires. But government intervention was important in a number of respects.

1. The creation of an effective navy under the Tudors, especially by Henry VIII. This gave greater security to British ports and trade and led to technical innovations, including ship design.
2. Government regulation of trade. This reached back into the Middle Ages when merchants sought royal charters. The important Merchant Adventurers (of London) received a charter from Henry IV in 1407. The most important trading company of all, the English East India Company, was incorporated in 1600. Trade was also regulated by a series of Navigation Acts, viz. those of 1382, 1430, 1485, 1540 and 1559. The Acts differed in detail but had the common purpose of ensuring that, as far as possible, trade to and from British ports was carried in British ships.
3. A colony of settlement (commonly called a Plantation) required a royal patent or charter. The most important grants included those to the Virginia Company in 1606 and to the Massachusetts Bay Company in 1629.

The Americas

Northern Europeans had reached the American continent before John Cabot voyaged from Bristol in 1497. The Vikings had established settlements in Iceland and Greenland, and had visited Newfoundland (e.g. Anse aux Meadows) and 'Vinland', the location of which is still unknown but which must have been on the North American coast. Almost certainly fishermen from Brittany and Bristol had become familiar with the Grand Banks off Newfoundland. Columbus, as well as Cabot, had thought it worth approaching the King of England for patronage. After 1494 England sought alternative routes to Asia not subject to Spanish or Portuguese control, hence the quest for the North-West (or, more occasionally, the North-East) Passage.

1485	Henry VII became King.
1496	Henry authorised John Cabot to make an exploring voyage to the west to seek a route to China.
1497	Cabot, with his son Sebastian, sailed from Bristol in the *Matthew*, reached Newfoundland and touched at unidentified points on the mainland.
1498	John Cabot undertook a second voyage, in which he may have made further discoveries, but was lost at sea.
1509	Sebastian Cabot probably reached the Strait leading to Hudson's Bay. Henry VIII became King.
1534	Henry VIII broke with Rome, and England no longer felt bound by papal decrees.
1547	Succession of Edward VI.
1553	Succession of Mary Tudor, who married Philip II of Spain.
1558	Succession of Elizabeth I.

1562	John Hawkins' first voyage to West Indies, on which he carried some slaves. English and French Huguenots established a settlement on the Florida coast. (Destroyed by Spanish in 1565.)
1564	John Hawkins' second voyage, in which began slaving as commercial operation. Took cloth and other goods to West Africa, purchased slaves, sailed to Caribbean to trade for sugar, hides and silver. Beginning of lucrative 'Triangular Trade' between Britain, Africa and the Americas.
1567	John Hawkins' third voyage, on which Francis Drake was present. Hoped to establish peaceful trading relations with the Spaniards in the Caribbean but ended in bloodshed at San Juan de Ulua when Spaniards attacked British ships as interlopers.
1570	Relations between Catholic Spain and Protestant England deteriorated when Pope Pius V excommunicated Elizabeth I and released her subjects from allegiance to her. Situation aggravated by English sympathy for Dutch (Protestant) rebels against Spain. No official state of war but privateering and deliberate encroachment on Spanish claims in the Caribbean, summed up in the phrase 'No peace beyond the line', i.e. the Tordesillas line, unrecognised by England.
1572	Spectacular exploit by Drake, who, with two ships and seventy men, took Nombre de Dios and captured three mule trains crossing Isthmus of Panama, loaded with treasure from Peru.
1576–8	Martin Frobisher's attempts to find a North-West Passage to the Pacific Ocean.
1577–80	Francis Drake circumnavigated the world in *Pelican*, renamed *Golden Hind*. Mission undertaken in great secrecy with aim of exploring the Pacific and the Spice Islands and searching for North-West Passage from Pacific side. In course of it landed on western coast of North America and claimed it under name 'New Albion'.
1578	Sir Humphrey Gilbert secured patent from Elizabeth I authorising him to found colonies in any land 'not actually possessed of any Christian prince or people'.
1583	Gilbert took formal possession of Newfoundland but failed in his attempt to establish colony there.
1584	Open war with Spain. After Gilbert's death, his brother-in-law, Sir Walter Ralegh, obtained new patents for colonisation and began preparations for establishment of colony at Roanoke, in territory about to be called Virginia. (The name 'Virginia' was originally applied to the whole coast. Even in 1606 it was defined as stretching

	from the 34th to the 45th degree of latitude. Roanoke Island is in the modern state of North Carolina.)
1585	Fleet of seven ships sailed for Roanoke under command of Sir Richard Grenville. Colonists found conditions difficult to cope with and quarrelled with Indian tribes. Drake made major assault on Spanish position in the Caribbean. Hoped to take and hold Havana and Cartegena, so disrupting whole Spanish system. Successfully attacked but could not hold Santo Domingo and Cartegena. Abandoned plans to attach Havana.
1586	Drake visited Roanoke and colonists persuaded him to take them off. Grenville returned with supplies to find settlement deserted.
1587	Second attempt to found colony at Roanoke also failed.
1588	Defeat of Spanish Armada relieved Britain of immediate fears of invasion.
1595	Last Indies campaign by Drake and Hawkins, in the course of which Drake died.
1595	Ralegh secured patent to open up Guiana, the land between the Orinoco and the Amazon. Produced further tales of marvels and hopes of wealth (the legend of El Dorado) but war with Spain took priority over further development.
1602	Captain Batholomew Gosnold explored substantial part of coast of what later became New England.
1603	Death of Elizabeth I and accession of James VI of Scotland as James I. Ralegh accused of treason and imprisoned in the Tower of London.
1604	Treaty of London ended the war with Spain.
1605	Captain George Waymouth explored New England coast, sponsored by Sir Ferdinando Gorges and Sir John Popham, who were interested in colonising the coast of Maine.
1606	Merchants, who had helped to finance Ralegh's projects, founded new Association, the Virginia Association, and took over Ralegh's patents. Functioned in two parts: the Virginia Company of London (London Company) was to colonise the southern half of the territory, the Virginia Company of Plymouth (Plymouth Company), the northern half. (December) London Company sent out three ships, *Susan Constant, Goodspeed* and *Discovery*, with 100 colonists. Began settlement at Jamestown, 60 miles up the James River, a bad site, swampy, mosquito-ridden and in the territory of the generally hostile Indians, the Powhatans. Captain John Smith

emerged as the strong man. According to tradition his life was saved by Pocahontas, the daughter of the Powhatan chief, and relations became more friendly, but the colony nearly perished in the 'starving time'.

1607   Plymouth Company established a small settlement, Popham Plantation, near the mouth of the Kennebec River but lasted only one year.

1608   Group of Puritans, who wished to 'separate' from the official Church of England, migrated to Leiden, led by William Brewster.

1609   London Company sent out Lord De la Warr as Governor of Jamestown with reinforcements. (Effective control in fact in hands of Thomas Dale.)

1610   Company of Adventurers founded in London and obtained grants of land in Newfoundland.

1611–12   Henry Hudson sailed into bay that was to bear his name but died after his crew mutinied.

1612   John Rolfe developed a new cash crop, tobacco, in Jamestown. The economy began to boom. Soon exporting 500,000 pounds of tobacco a year. Began to acquire negro slaves to work plantations. Stockholders in the Virginia Company were given large land grants along the James River to grow tobacco. Encroached on Indian land. The Indians counter-attacked (1623) and killed 347 of the 3000 settlers. Indian power in the region was destroyed by superior European force over next twenty years.

1615   Somers Island Company received charter to colonise Bermuda.

1616–17   Ralegh allowed to mount a new expedition to Orinoco. Results unsatisfactory. Spanish ambassador protested. On his return Ralegh was executed.

1617   A Welshman, William Vaughan of Golden Grove, founded Cambriol settlement on the Avalon Peninsula in Newfoundland. Failed but survivors probably moved to nearby Ferryland settlement (1621) founded by George Calvert (later Lord Baltimore).

1619   House of Burgesses (elected assembly) established in Virginia.

1620   Sir Ferdinando Gorges and others reconstituted moribund Plymouth Company as Council for New England.
(16 September) Voyage of the Puritan Fathers. Puritans from Leiden (with others) sailed from Plymouth in the *Mayflower* to establish their own settlement in Virginia. Blown off course and landed at Cape Cod in what became New England. Founded settlement of Plymouth. Leaders signed 'Mayflower Compact' to establish form of government. Climatic conditions

very difficult and nearly half the colonists died in the first winter.

Concluded friendly treaty with neighbouring Indians (1621) who taught them suitable methods of agriculture and helped them to survive.

1624 Government of Virginia changed when made a royal colony by James I with a Governor appointed by the King.

First permanent English settlement in the West Indies, on St Kitts.

1625 Settlement in Barbados, followed by Nevis (1628), Antigua and Montserrat (1632) and some unsuccessful attempts elsewhere. Marked by disorderly scramble for patents among entrepreneurs in London.

1628 John Endicott brought out 60 colonists to Salem.

1629 Puritan Providence Company incorporated to settle Santa Catalina (Providence) Island off coast of Nicaragua. Expelled by Spaniards in 1641.

John Winthrop obtained charter for Massachusetts Bay Company from Charles I. Did not specify (as was usual) that headquarters of the Company must be in London. Winthrop took advantage of this to establish it in America.

1630 Winthrop brought out nearly 1000 settlers to Massachusetts. Chose Boston as seat of government. Company unusually successful. By 1640 had 10,000 settlers and had established 15 towns.

1632 Williamsburg founded. More healthy position and later (1692) replaced Jamestown as the capital of Virginia. Lord Baltimore obtained a grant of land on Chesapeake Bay to settle Catholics (subject to civil disabilities in England). Baltimore died but project pursued by his heirs, who founded state of Maryland.

1636 Some Puritans felt oppressed even in new colonies, where religious toleration was generally not practised. Roger Williams fled with his supporters to found new settlement at Providence (later became Rhode Island) and Thomas Hooker travelled down the Connecticut River to settle at Hartford.

1637 Colonists killed 600–700 Indians after alleged murder of a colonist.

1642–60 Civil war in Britain. Although royalists and parliamentarians contended for power in the West Indies, the colonies were often left largely to their own devices and became used to managing their own affairs. Although after the Restoration the Crown tried to return to pre-war situation, this was often not possible.

1653 Oliver Cromwell became Lord Protector.

1654	Cromwell's 'Western Design'. Military expedition to attack the Spaniards in the West Indies. Only success was the capture of Jamaica.
1660–3	The restored monarchy tried to regain complete control of colonial trade. This resulted in a number of key measures – the Navigation Act (1660) provided that no goods should be imported into or exported from any colony except in English or colonial ships and that the 'enumerated articles' (all the most important West Indian products, including sugar, tobacco and cotton) should be shipped only to England or another English colony; the Staple Act (1663) provided that almost all goods, English or foreign, intended for the colonies, must be shipped from English ports.
1662	Connecticut chartered.
1663	Rhode Island received new charter (replacing one granted to Roger William in 1644).
1664	Systematic settlement of Jamaica began. Sugar was the main crop and estates were very large. (Change from small freeholders to plantation farming also underway in Barbados and elsewhere.)
1667	Treaty of Breda at the end of the Second Dutch War temporarily settled the division of the West Indian islands between England, France and Holland.
1672–8	Third Dutch war, in which England was allied with France against Holland, saw much fighting in the West Indies.
1675–8	War with Indians. Group of New England tribes attacked Massachusetts settlements. Full-scale war resulted. A thousand colonists were killed and 12 towns destroyed.
1680	New Hampshire received charter.
1689–97	King William's war, in which English and Dutch were allied against French, saw further fighting in the West Indies. Frequency of wars between European powers encouraged the growth of the 'buccaneers', who gained effective control of large parts of the Caribbean.
1691	Massachusetts government absorbed Plymouth community.

Africa and Asia

1549	Sebastian Cabot created Grand Pilot of England and presided over Company of Merchant Adventurers to Russia, formed to seek north-east passage to China.
1553	Voyage of Willoughby and Chancellor. Willoughby died but Chancellor reached Moscow by way of Archangel. William Hawkins began regular voyages to West Africa.

21

1579	Thomas Stevens, a Jesuit priest, sailed from Lisbon to Goa. An Englishman by birth, it seems likely that he kept in touch with his father, a London merchant.
1581	Levant Company formed.
1582	Edward Fenton sailed from Southampton for the Spice Islands but did not reach the Indian Ocean.
1583	John Newbery, Ralph Fitch, William Leedes and James Storie set out for India, travelling overland via Aleppo. Fitch alone returned to England (in 1591) to give an account of his travels. (Storie died, Newbery became a shopkeeper in Goa, Leedes entered the service of the Mughals.)
1584	The war with Spain, which then ruled Portugal, led to the capture of Portuguese merchantmen, who often carried maps and charts as well as rich cargoes.
1591	Expedition under George Raymond. One ship, commanded by James Lancaster, reached India and Malayan archipelago. Profitable cargo but only 25 of his 198 men returned.
1599	(22 September) Eighty London merchants, including Ralph Fitch, met at Founders' Hall, under the chairmanship of the Lord Mayor, and agreed to form an association to trade directly with the East.
1600	(31 December) English East India Company incorporated under royal charter. Had 125 shareholders and, initially, a capital of £70,000.
1601	First East India Company voyage sailed for the Spice Islands, under command of James Lancaster.
1607	Third East India Company voyage. Instructions incidentally mentioned opening up trade on west coast of India. William Hawkins, a former Levant merchant, impressed the Mughal Emperor, Jehangir, with his ability to speak Turkish. But Portuguese secured the cancellation of his permission to trade at Surat.
1612	British fleet defeated Portuguese fleet in Swally Roads, off Surat.
1613	British permitted to establish a factory at Surat.
1615	Sir Thomas Roe, first British ambassador, arrived at Mughal court. Secured general permission to trade but not the desired commercial treaty.
1657	Oliver Cromwell granted East India Company a new charter.
1661	Charles II confirmed East India Company's charter in return for large loan. Charter had to be renewed at intervals – usually 20 years.

1663	Company of Royal Adventurers of England trading into Africa formed. Mainly a slaving concern. Were to supply English sugar colonies with 3000 slaves a year at average price of £17, or one ton of sugar per slave.
1672	Royal Africa Company incorporated (superseded Company of Royal Adventurers to Africa).
1684	Bermuda became Crown colony.

Government and society in the British empire

Systems of government

Central administration

There was no coherent central administration of the empire under the Tudors or the early Stuarts. Authority was vested in the monarch, assisted by the Privy Council, and arrangements were usually *ad hoc*. The Privy Council operated through its Committee of Trade and, intermittently, through a Plantation Commission. In 1623, when the House of Commons attempted to discuss the Virginia Company, it was told that it had no role. In 1634 a Commission for Plantations was created, headed by Archbishop Laud, mainly to curb the Puritan colonies, but it was abolished in 1641. During the Civil War, Parliament established a new Commission of Plantations under the Earl of Warwick. During the Protectorate, Oliver Cromwell set up a Colonial Board.

The restored government of Charles II tried various experiments after 1660.

1660	(4 July) A Committee of the Privy Council was established by Order in Council 'for the Plantacions'.
	(1 December) A separate 'Council of Foreign Plantations' was created by Letters Patent.
1672	These two committees were united as the 'Council of Trade and Plantations' but suppressed a few years later as inefficient and responsibility reverted to the Privy Council.
1695	The Board of Trade and Plantations was reconstituted and began to act as an embryonic colonial office. Its first two secretaries, Robert Southwell and William Blathwayt, were particularly important. But its main function was to advise the Secretary of State for the Southern Department. Other departments such as the Admiralty also maintained direct relations with the colonies.

English policy in the empire at large was equally *ad hoc*.

Colonies of settlement

Colonies were usually founded by Companies or 'proprietors' (a powerful man or group of men). Although practice was originally diverse (and remained so in details), a norm emerged for the government of a British colony of settlement, consisting of a Governor (usually nominated by the King, the

23

Company or the proprietor, although elected in the case of Rhode Island), a council (similarly nominated) and an assembly, elected by the 'freemen' (usually the free-holders) of the colony. The assemblies came to regard themselves as miniature parliaments with the rights and privileges that that implied.

Company colonies
Virginia, 1606 – became royal colony 1624
Massachusetts, 1629, and its offshoots, Connecticut and New Haven. Rhode Island (Providence) was dissident offshoot, which escaped company control.

Main proprietary colonies
Barbados (Earl of Pembroke/Earl of Carlisle), 1627
Maryland (Lord Baltimore), 1632
Surinam (British Guiana) (Lord Willoughby), 1654/1663
Carolina (Earl of Clarendon and others), 1663
Delaware (Duke of York), 1664
New Jersey (Lord Berkeley and Sir George Carteret), 1664
Pennsylvania (William Penn), 1681
Georgia (General James Oglethorpe), 1732

Development of representative government (examples)
Virginia. In 1619 (in accordance with resolution of the Company the previous year) a representative assembly was summoned consisting of two burgesses from each of the 11 settlements that made up the colony. The assembly (House of Burgesses) adopted parliamentary procedures, elected a Speaker and enacted laws for the colony. In 1624 Virginia became a royal colony. In 1625 a new charter invested appointment of governor and council in the Crown. Did not mention the assembly but left it undisturbed in the exercise of its powers.

Massachusetts. By the 1629 charter the election of the governor and officials lay with 12 stockholders or freemen of the company. In 1631 the status of free-man was extended to colonists who met approved religious tests.

Maryland. Governor originally summoned all the 'freemen', to accept or reject, but not to initiate, proposed legislation. Developed into representative system with more powers. Assembly sat as separate body (1647).

Connecticut. In 1639 townships devised a constitution of a Governor, six officials and a number of deputies.

New Haven. In 1639 drew up its own constitution.

Rhode Island. In 1643 its founder, Roger Williams, obtained a parliamentary charter and, in 1647, the colony adopted a constitution, enfranchising all householders.

Jamaica. In 1662 a constitution established by royal proclamation provided for a Governor, a nominated council and an elected assembly of thirty.

Carolinas. In 1667 the Fundamental Constitution of Carolina was drawn up by John Locke and Lord Ashley (Shaftesbury) but never implemented. However, in that year, a constitutional government, including elected representatives, was operating in North Carolina.

Pennsylvania. In 1681 William Penn drew up elaborate *Frame of Government*, providing for an elected council of 72 to draft laws and a further elected assembly of 200 to approve them. All landowners and taxpayers would have the franchise. Only put into operation in a modified form. In 1683 there was a council of 18 and an assembly of 36.

Society and religion in colonies of settlement

There were considerable variations in Britain's American colonies.

Virginia. This came to be characterised by large estates. Society was stratified between landowners and capitalists, poorer white immigrants (including ex-indentured servants) and black slaves. Most, at least of the upper classes, adhered to the established Church of England and, generally, tried to replicate the lives of English gentlemen.

Maryland. Here there were more small free-holders. It had been founded by a Roman Catholic peer, partly as a refuge for his co-religionists, but many colonists were not Catholics and generally a policy of religious toleration was pursued, even when it meant curbing Jesuit zeal.

New England. These colonies had a specifically religious base, founded by Puritan separatists from the established Church of England. The franchise was sometimes confined to members of acceptable Protestant churches.

West Indies. These were at first regarded as colonies of settlement. The settlers (mainly small free-holders with indentured servants) grew subsistence crops with a little tobacco and cotton. Indentures usually lasted three to seven years and at the end of it men expected a grant of land. Initially the population grew rapidly, e.g. in Barbados from 4000 in 1631 to 30,000 in 1640; St Kitts had 20,000 in 1640. The white population predominated, although there were some negro slaves.

After the Restoration, the plantation system developed, producing cash crops of tobacco, cotton and, especially sugar. Required labour. Government began to send out convicts – some political dissidents, Irish after the siege of Drogheda, royalists in the Civil War, parliamentarians after the Restoration, those involved in the Monmouth rebellion; others ordinary criminals. But came to be believed Europeans could not labour in the tropics. Increasingly imported negro slaves. This resulted in a complete change in the balance of the population. By 1700 there were only 12,000 white colonists in Barbados, compared with 46,000 negroes.

Economic systems

Much was achieved by individual entrepreneurs. The sixteenth century saw increasing sophistication in the organisation of trade. The older 'regulated' companies were replaced by joint-stock companies, where the risk was spread among the subscribers.

The British government never exacted 'tribute', direct taxation, from its colonies, but it expected them to be financially self-sufficient. Financial responsibilities were an important element in the growing powers of the colonial assemblies.

The government did expect to regulate trade and it was axiomatic that colonies existed to benefit the metropolitan power, but only towards the end of this period did the system which came to be called 'the Old Colonial System' (*see below* pp. 34–5) become coherently organised. Earlier decisions were usually *ad hoc*. From an early date colonies like Virginia, which produced export crops like tobacco and willingly accepted British manufactures, fitted conveniently into the system. New England did not.

The West Indies were at this time regarded as much more valuable than the mainland colonies. The famous 'Triangular Trade' took cheap manufactured goods from Britain to West Africa, slaves to the West Indies, and sugar, rum and molasses from the West Indies to Britain.

Asia

British enterprise in Asia differed radically from that in America. Here the goal was trade and there was no serious suggestion of settlement.

The East India Company's charter gave it monopoly rights against other Englishmen east of the Cape of Good Hope. Although both James I and Charles I allowed breaches of this, the Company's rights were restored by Cromwell in 1657.

The real prize was the trade with the Spice Islands and the Company's main competitors were the Dutch. The most notorious incident was the massacre of 10 Englishmen and 9 Japanese in Amboina in February 1623. Although the English persisted for some time after 1623 in attempting to establish a foothold in the islands, the Dutch proved too strong.

India was therefore a consolation prize. When Francis Day established a station at Fort St George (Madras) on the east coast of India in 1639 it was to keep a watchful eye on the Spice Islands. The British also obtained permission from the Mughal emperor to establish a base on the Hugli River, from which Calcutta developed. Their third base was to be Bombay, obtained from the Portuguese. But in the seventeenth century the East India Company saw themselves only as merchants seeking privileges from the powerful Mughal empire. In Professor Harlow's words, they no more expected to rule India than the Muscovy Company expected to rule the Russias.[2]

---

2. V. Harlow, *The Founding of the Second British Empire, 1763–1793* vol. 2 (1964), p. 7.

Scotland

Despite the union of the crowns when James VI of Scotland became James I of England in 1603, England and Scotland remained separate countries until the Union in 1707. Scottish-based enterprises were excluded from the colonial trade by the Navigation Acts – although there was Scottish settlement in British North America in the seventeenth century.

1695	An Act of the Scottish parliament established the Company of Scotland, trading to Africa and the Indies.
1698	Ship with 1200 persons sailed from Leith to plant a settlement at Darien in the Isthmus of Panama. Abandoned after many starved or died of yellow fever.
1699	Second Darien expedition compelled to surrender to the Spanish in 1700.

The French empire

The Americas

Breton and Norman fishermen (like the Bristol men) almost certainly knew of the Newfoundland Grand Banks before John Cabot. Later the French, like the English, sought a route to China and Asia which would not encroach on established Spanish and Portuguese rights, that is, they too looked for the North-West Passage.

1534–5	Jacques Cartier reached Newfoundland and the Gulf of St Lawrence (although without finding the entrance to the river). Having anchored off the Gaspé Peninsula and traded with the Micmac Indians, he claimed the territory for France and returned with two captives.
1535	Cartier was commissioned to discover whether the St Lawrence River (of which he had learnt from his captives) was the North West Passage. He sailed up the St Lawrence to the Huron village of Stadcona, roughly the site of Quebec City, and learnt that the name of the country was Canada. He sailed further up the St Lawrence in his ship's pinnace and reached Indian village of Hochelaga, where he climbed the mountain which he named *Mont Réal* (Royal Mountain). Rapids, which in disgust he called Lachaine (Chinese) rapids, blocked his further progress.
Late 16th century	Official patronage of exploration was interrupted by the Wars of Religion between Catholics and Huguenots. But the fur trade was developed rapidly by private enterprise. Some fur traders were offered monopoly privileges in return for settling colonists in what was now called New France but devoted little time to it.

27

1604	Samuel Champlain's second voyage to New France. Planted a small colony near the mouth of the St Croix river (later transferred to Port Royal in Acadia). In subsequent years he explored as far south as Cape Cod.
1608	Champlain established a trading post at the future Quebec City.
1609	Champlain became involved in Indian conflicts. Agreed to help the Huron against the Iroquois. In an incident near the site of the later Fort Ticonderoga, Champlain and two companions ensured Huron victory by use of firearms – but made the Iroquois the enemies of France and therefore later the allies of the British in later contests.
1615–35	Further explorations by, or sponsored by, Champlain (who settled his family in Quebec in 1620). Explored Great Lakes and reached the Mississippi. *Coureurs de bois* developed inland trade along the rivers. Missionaries, both Franciscan and Jesuit, attempted to convert the Indians and, incidentally, explored the country.
1627	War between Britain and France.
1629	Quebec captured by the English.
1632	Treaty of St Germain-en-Laye restored Quebec and Port Royal to France.
1663	Crown assumed full responsibility for Canada.
1665	Colbert became Controller-General of Finance (and also Minister of Marine in 1669). Responsible for the economic reconstruction of Louis XIV's government in which intended colonisation was to play a part. Planned 'systematic colonisation' of New France, sending out balanced groups of men and women, *seigneurs* (landowners), professional men, agricultural labourers and artisans. By 1700, there were 15,000 colonists in Quebec, which created a 'distinct society', which has endured. Colbert also established a *Compagnie des Indes*, intended to operate like the Dutch East India Company.

Government and society in the French empire

France had two quite distinct empires in the western hemisphere:

1. The valuable Caribbean colonies. Martinique, Guadeloupe, Grenada, part of San Domingo, as well as Cayenne (later French Guiana). These were all plantation colonies, relying on slave labour, and supplying sugar and tobacco.
2. On the North American mainland. New France (Canada), which was less valued than the islands, although it was important for the fur trade and gave rise to much more extensive French claims extending down the

Mississippi Valley. Between 1712 and 1721 an attempt was made to foster colonisation and commerce there through the Mississippi Company established by Antoine Crozart and John Law, but it ended in financial ruin.

The French, like the British, empire had been founded by individuals and chartered companies, but they had usually enjoyed government encouragement and the existence of an absolute monarchy in France and the monopoly position of the Roman Catholic church ensured differences in development. In 1683, in line with policy in metropolitan France, religious uniformity, i.e. Roman Catholicism, was imposed in the colonies. Jews and Huguenots were denied freedom of worship.

Before 1660 the companies had enjoyed ownership of land, a monopoly of trade and varying degrees of administrative autonomy. The Crown assumed direct responsibility in the 1660s and 1670s under Colbert's centralising policy.

In each colony there was to be a governor (normally a noble and a soldier), assisted by an *intendant* (a lawyer and an administrator). The *intendants* were assisted in both legal and administrative matters by a *Conseil Souverain* or *Conseil Supérieur*, consisting of officials and nominated colonists. There was no tradition of elected assemblies as in the British colonies, although representative assemblies were convened in Martinique and Guadeloupe in 1715 to agree to exceptional taxation.

The Dutch empire

1565	Dutch revolt against Spain began.
1580	Union of Spanish and Portuguese Crowns under Philip II.
1581	William of Orange and the States-General of United Provinces of Holland, Zeeland, Utrecht, Guelderland, Overjissel, Groningen and Friesland formally renounced their allegiance to Philip II.
1585	Spanish embargo on Dutch shipping.
1588	Defeat of Spanish Armada.
1590–1600	Great expansion of Dutch seaborne trade in Mediterranean and to West Africa.
1595	First trading voyage to Spice Islands.
1595–1601	Fifteen Dutch fleets sailed for the East.
1600	First Dutch ship reached Japan.
1602	Dutch East India Company founded, with strong government backing and capital of over £500,000.
1605	Dutch expelled Portuguese from the Moluccas.
1606	Spanish reclaimed part of Moluccas. Dutch attacks on Mozambique and Malacca unsuccessful.
1609	Factory in Japan at Hirado established. Truce with Spain.

29

1610–12	Founded settlements in Guiana and Amazon region, latter destroyed by Portuguese.
1612	Founded Fort Mourée on Guinea coast.
1614	Fur traders become active on Hudson River.
1618	Outbreak of Thirty Years War.
1619	Coen seized Jakarta (in Java) from Portuguese. Built castle and fortified town of Batavia. Marked the beginning of a serious Dutch presence in the region.
1621	Dutch West India Company established.
1623	Massacre of Amboina.
1624–5	Established New Amsterdam on Manhattan Island. Failed to take Puerto Rico from Spain or Elmina (West Africa) from Portuguese. Temporarily took Bahia (Brazil) from Portuguese.
1628	Captured silver fleet.
1630	Began conquest of north-east Brazil.
1637	Took Pernambuco (Brazil). Van Diemen made alliance with Raja Sinha of Kandy against Portuguese in Ceylon.
1638	Began conquest of coast of Ceylon. Captured Elmina.
1641	Captured Malacca and Luanda. Concluded truce with Portuguese. Dutch the only Europeans allowed in Japan with recognised trading base at Nagasaki.
1644–5	Lost position in north-east Brazil to Portuguese.
1648	End of Thirty Years War. Spain recognised Dutch independence. Portuguese regained Angolan ports of Luanda and Benguela from the Dutch.
1652	Van Riebeeck founded settlement at Cape of Good Hope as 'refreshment station' for Dutch fleets on the way to and from the East Indies. Finally lost Brazilian territories to the Portuguese.
1652–4	First Anglo-Dutch War. Dutch defeated in North Sea but did well in Mediterranean and the East Indies.
1654–8	Conquered large part of coast of Ceylon.
1661	Chinese successfully invaded Formosa, where Dutch had established considerable influence.
1663	Displaced Portuguese on stretches of Malabar coast of India. Spaniards finally evacuated Moluccas.

1664	British took Dutch North American colony of New Netherlands on banks of Hudson River and also some Dutch forts on the Gold Coast in West Africa.
1665–7	Second Anglo-Dutch War. De Ruyter penetrated British naval defences on the Medway.
1669	Final conquest of Macassar.
1677	Mataram recognised Dutch suzerainty over Java.
1684	Conquered Bantam but finally lost Formosa to the Chinese.
1685	Revocation of the Edict of Nantes, which had granted toleration to French Protestants. Many Huguenots emigrated to Holland and some to Cape Colony.
1697	Introduction of coffee tree into Java provided valuable cash crop but development of the area interrupted by a series of wars which occupied most of first half of eighteenth century.

Government and society in the Dutch empire

The Dutch East India Company (VOC) was an amalgamation of six companies, those of Amsterdam, Hoorn, Enkhuizen, Rotterdam, Delft and Middelburg, which not only remained in existence but played a major role in the work of the company. The 17 members of the Court of Directors (the *Heeren Zeventien*) provided the central administration. The Company was extremely powerful. The initial capital of 6.5 million guilders was 10 times that of the English East India Company and the Directors had close links with the Dutch government. Its charter gave the Company the national monopoly of trade east of the Cape of Good Hope, empowered it to make treaties with Asian states, to take possession of territory in full sovereignty and to wage war.

Although the Dutch captured Portuguese forts in key strategic places, their intention was to acquire trading bases and to avoid territorial responsibilities. By about 1700 they only exercised direct political control at the Cape of Good Hope and in Ceylon, the Banda Islands and Amboina. They enjoyed, however, a virtual trading monopoly in the Spice Islands, controlling the Malay Straits from Malacca, Sumatra from Padang and the Celebes from Macassar, buttressed by alliances with local rulers. They also had factories in India, on the Malabar coast (Calicut and Cochin), the Coromandel coast (Negapatam and Pulicat) and at Masulipatam; as well as in Cambodia, Siam, Tonking, Mokja and Japan.

The government was based in Java, at Batavia, where the Governor-General resided, assisted by a Director-General, who controlled trade and finance, and by a council of officials. The Council of Justice had jurisdiction over the Company's servants but not over Asians. Where the Company did hold sway, it governed indirectly through the indigenous authorities.

Settlement was not encouraged. The Cape of Good Hope was a partial exception. Time-expired servants of the Company were permitted to settle there and, after the Revocation of the Edict of Nantes, French Huguenots were also accepted (although deliberately dispersed among the Dutch population). The normal pattern was that officials would be recruited in Europe and then serve the Company for the rest of their career before returning home. Dutch officials were not permitted to marry Asians.

The Company was generally profitable both to the Dutch state and to its members. Dividends (usually about 12 per cent) were regularly distributed throughout the seventeenth century.

2 EIGHTEENTH-CENTURY COMPETITION FOR EMPIRE

The first empires had been forged largely in war, in the continuation of the struggle against Islam, and then in wars between the European powers themselves. The great division of Europe between Catholic and Protestant powers as the result of the Reformation had played a part, but from the beginning the conflicts had also had an economic dimension. The eighteenth century too was a period of European war in which the colonies were important pawns. Economic competition, rather than religious conflict, was now the driving force.

Mercantilism

The prevailing economic theory of the time was mercantilism. This could be variously interpreted in its details (how far, for example, was the objective to amass bullion, which would serve as a 'war chest' to pay mercenaries?), but its general thrust was clear. Each sovereign state must strive to be self-sufficient and maintain a favourable trade balance. Imports should generally be discouraged by high duties or outright prohibitions. Tightly controlled colonies, which existed only to help the economy of the 'mother country', were desirable because they supplied raw materials (and, in some empires, paid 'tribute', i.e. special taxes) and bought manufactured goods. As destinations for emigrants, their role was less clear. Such emigrants established territorial rights, but at a time when populations were thought (probably wrongly) to be falling and when population itself was regarded as a measure of wealth, emigration was an ambiguous benefit.

THE ECONOMIC SYSTEMS OF THE MAJOR EMPIRES

Spain

The *Casa de Contratación* in Seville regulated colonial trade. Until 1720 all colonial trade was channelled through Seville. Even in Seville the right to trade with the Americas was confined to the members of the *Consulado*, a closed merchant company. From 1720 until 1765 the trade passed through Cadiz. Certain other ports were allowed to trade after 1765, and from 1789 trade could be conducted from any Spanish port.

Foreigners were excluded from the colonial trade. No foreign ship could enter a colonial port or sail from Spain to the Indies. Until the middle of the eighteenth century even Spanish sailings were tightly regulated. An annual fleet went out. Half, the *flota*, sailed to Vera Cruz; the other half, the *galeones*, went to Cartegena and Puerto Belo. After wintering in the Americas, the fleets met at Havana to return to Spain.

The development of industries, and even of wine production, was severely restricted in the colonies to safeguard the market for Spanish products. For the same reason little inter-colonial trade was allowed.

Imports of negro slaves were restricted by the *asiento* clauses, which laid down the number of slaves any company might import.

France: the *pacte colonial*

In the early days of the empire, chartered companies had monopoly rights against other Frenchmen but were not prohibited from trading with foreigners. However, under Colbert, the system was tightened up. Colbert's West Indian Company excluded foreign ships from its ports.

The regulations of 1670, 1695 and 1717 excluded foreigners from the colonial ports and forbade direct trade between the French colonies and foreign states.

In theory, the advantages were reciprocal. Apart from protecting the colonies, the French government gave the colonists tariff advantages, paid bounties and supplied technical help to develop the colonies' economy, where it did not directly compete with metropolitan interests (although, for example, the export of rum was forbidden to protect French brandy).

Britain: the 'Old Colonial System'

Royal regulation of trade went back to the Middle Ages. Arrangements in the early days of colonisation were generally *ad hoc*, but, after the Stuart Restoration in 1660, attempts were made to tidy up the system. The key measures were as follows:

1. The Navigation Act (1660) incorporated measures passed during the Commonwealth. All trade to and from the colonies had to be carried in English ships (this was amended to 'British' in 1707, after the Union with Scotland). The 'enumerated articles', i.e. the most important colonial products (e.g. sugar, tobacco, cotton, indigo, ginger and dyewoods), could only be shipped to England or other English colonies.
2. The Staple Act (1663) prohibited the introduction into English colonies of goods not of English origin, unless they were shipped to England and then taken out in English ships.

The Navigation Act was amended at various times up to 1696. A loophole was closed in 1673 when the Plantation Duties Act prevented the New England colonies from buying sugar and tobacco from the southern colonies and shipping them direct to Europe with the fish they could legally export.

The growth of industries in the colonies was discouraged. In 1699 they were forbidden to export manufactured woollens. In 1719 heavy duties were imposed on the colonial export of iron and, famously, in 1731, they were forbidden to export hats.

In return the colonists had protected markets in Britain and, importantly for the future, their defence was paid for by the British taxpayer since the colonies were never taxed for this purpose.

COLONIAL WARS

Portugal's decline

Portugal was a declining power in the seventeenth century. Some Portuguese enterprises were simply allowed to crumble. Others were taken over by more enterprising powers, especially the Dutch.

Brazil

The Dutch made considerable inroads into northern Brazil, even establishing a capital at Recife, but were expelled after about 1640.

Africa

The Portuguese also regained Luanda and Benguela (basis of later colonies of Angola and Mozambique) from the Dutch at the end of the Thirty Years War in 1648.

India

The Dutch displaced the Portuguese on the Malabar coast in the 1660s.

Spice Islands

The Dutch displaced the Portuguese, e.g. 1605 expelled Portuguese from Moluccas (though temporarily regained by Spanish); 1619 seized Jakarta; 1641 captured Malacca; 1669 conquered Macassar.

Ceylon

In 1637–58 the Dutch displaced the Portuguese in Ceylon.

In addition to her losses in war, Portugal ceded Bombay and Tangiers to England by treaty in 1660 as part of the marriage settlement between Charles II and Catherine of Braganza.

Anglo-Dutch wars

In the seventeenth century, England and the Netherlands were both rising commercial powers, with developing navies and trade. Their common Protestantism and their suspicions of French, as well as Spanish, power made them allies in some European conflicts. But this was interspersed by what were essentially trade wars. The main conflicts were as follows:

1652–4

This was mainly provoked by the English Navigation Acts of 1650 and 1651, which restricted trade with the colonies (some of which were royalist in sympathy), although the immediate cause of the rupture was Admiral Tromp's refusal to salute Admiral Blake's flag. Tromp defeated Blake off Dungeness in November 1652 but was himself killed in a battle off the Texel in July 1653. Peace was concluded in April 1654. The Dutch accepted the Navigation Acts and paid compensation for the Amboina massacre of 1623.

1664–7

The Dutch were antagonised by the new Navigation Acts of the Restoration and felt threatened by the English acquisition of Bombay and Tangiers. English and Dutch colonies were confronting one another in Guiana and North America (i.e. Connecticut and New Amsterdam). Unusually, the Dutch were allied with the French. Fighting took place as follows:

1. In *Africa*, where Admiral de Ruyter seized six stations belonging to the African Company on the Guinea coast.
2. In *South America*. Surinam (of which Francis, Lord Willoughby was proprietor) several times changed hands.
3. In the Caribbean. St Kitts, Antigua and Montserrat were for a time in French hands, although Nevis was successfully defended.
4. In *North America* Charles II gave his brother, the Duke of York, permission to attack New Amsterdam, which, with other adjoining lands, he was then to hold as proprietor. Colonel Richard Nicolls took New Amsterdam and Delaware in 1664.
5. In *European waters*. Fortunes fluctuated but the Dutch admiral De Ruyter carried out a celebrated exploit in June 1667 when he sailed up the River Medway and bombarded the British naval depot at Chatham, capturing or destroying a number of ships. The Treaty of Breda (July 1667) ended the war. The Dutch gave up New Amsterdam (renamed New York), New Jersey and the Delaware estuary. The British gave up Dutch Surinam and Acadia (which had been captured from the French in 1655).

1672–4

This arose from European politics. By the Treaty of Dover of 1670 Louis XIV offered Charles II financial and military support in return for help against the Netherlands. The Dutch re-occupied New York. The alliance was never popular in England, where the people suspected the King of allying with France to reimpose Roman Catholicism, and it was ended by the Treaty of Westminster of February 1674, which restored New York to England.

GENERAL EUROPEAN WARS WITH A COLONIAL DIMENSION

War of the Grand Alliance, 1689–97 (popularly called King William's War)

Anglo-French contest in North America

England, under James II, had allied with the Five Nations (the Iroquois) against the French.

1690	Forces from Massachusetts captured Port Royal in Acadia, but failed to capture Quebec and Montreal.
1691–7	Port Nelson, the key to the control of Hudson's Bay, continually changed hands.
1697	Treaty of Ryswick largely restored the status quo in North America but left Port Nelson in French hands.

War of the Spanish Succession, 1701–13

England and Holland were anxious to prevent the Spanish Netherlands (Belgium) and the Spanish empire falling into French hands.

1704	Sir George Rooke and Sir Cloudesley Shovell captured Gibraltar.
1708	Britain took Minorca.
1710	Force from Massachusetts retook Port Royal (Annapolis) and Acadia.
1711	Britain failed to take Quebec.

Treaty of Utrecht (1713)

Confirmed Britain in possession of Acadia (Nova Scotia), Newfoundland, Hudson's Bay and whole of St Kitts. But the French retained fishing rights on the western shore of Newfoundland; the boundaries of Nova Scotia were not defined and did not include Cape Breton Island, on which the French subsequently built the fortress of Louisbourg; and the boundaries between French Canada and the territories of the Hudson Bay Company were also left for further discussion – they ultimately agreed on the 49th parallel west of the Great Lakes.

Britain retained Gibraltar and Minorca.

Spain transferred the *asiento*, or right to supply slaves to the Spanish colonies, from a French company to Britain. Britain was allowed to send one ship a year to Puerto Bello.

The treaty of Utrecht was accompanied by a commercial treaty, which would have made trade between Britain and France freer but, being a commercial treaty, it required parliamentary consent (unlike the main treaty) and vested interests secured its defeat.

War of Jenkins' Ear, 1739–41

In reality a trade war between Britain and Spain. The Treaty of Utrecht had allowed some legitimate trade with Spanish America and a good deal of illicit trade also went on, which was fiercely and sometimes brutally repressed by the *guarda costas* (themselves freelances rather than official coastguards). In 1731 an Englishman, Captain Robert Jenkins, was detained off Havana, half-hanged from his own yard-arm and had his ear cut off. Jenkins gave evidence before a parliamentary committee in 1738, and in 1739, the government of Sir Robert Walpole reluctantly authorised war with Spain.

The main British objective was to break into the Spanish trading monopoly. The war merged into the more general conflict of the War of the Austrian Succession.

1739	Admiral Vernon captured Puerto Bello, now the main Atlantic port for the shipment of treasure and Asiatic goods crossing the Isthmus of Panama, but was unable to hold it.
1740–4	Commodore George Anson was sent to attack the Spanish colonies on the Pacific coast of South America and to encourage them to break with Spain. His force was insufficient but he did capture the Manila galleon.
1742	The British tried, unsuccessfully, to take Cuba.

War of the Austrian Succession, 1740–8

Although this war originated in European issues, primarily the right of succession to the Habsburg lands, it quickly spilled over into disputes about rights in other parts of the world. France formally declared war on Britain in March 1744.

Naval war

1747	Anson defeated a French fleet, taking reinforcements to the French garrisons overseas, off Finisterre. Hawke defeated another French fleet, bound for the West Indies. These two victories tipped the war overseas in Britain's favour.

North America

1744	A combined French and Indian force from Louisbourg invaded Nova Scotia but failed to take Annapolis. A force from Massachusetts, aided by the West Indian squadron, captured Louisbourg after a long siege (1745).
1748	Treaty of Aix-la-Chapelle. Britain exchanged Louisbourg for Madras.

India (*see also* pp. 42–4)

Both the British and the French governments would have preferred to have maintained the peace in India but they were thwarted by ambitious local officials.

1746	Admiral Labourdonnais, the Governor of Mauritius, captured Madras. Dupleix, the Governor of Pondicherry, refused to return it to the British according to an agreement made by Labourdonnais.
1748	The Treaty of Aix-la-Chapelle restored Madras to Britain.

The Seven Years War, 1756–63

This confirmed Britain's claim to be a European great power. The French withdrew from the contest with Britain in North America and, for practical purposes, in India.

Naval war

1756	The French captured Minorca.
1759	The British took Gorée and Guadeloupe.
	The French began preparations for the invasion of Britain.
	Boscawen defeated the Toulon fleet in Lagos (Portugal) Bay.
	Admiral Hawke defeated the Brest fleet at Quiberon Bay.
1760	A French attempt to involve Ireland failed.
	Essentially Britain had won the naval war and all danger of invasion had passed. France had difficulty in reinforcing her overseas stations.
1762	British captured Martinique.
	British took Havana.
	British took Manila and gained control of the Philippines.

North America

Fighting pre-dated the outbreak of war in Europe. The contest centred on the Ohio basin. Britain claimed it as the hinterland of the Thirteen Colonies; France as part of the Mississippi river system and properly belonging to Louisiana.

1754	Duquesne, the new Governor of Quebec, defeated a British force under George Washington at Fort Ohio.
1755	A four-fold British attack on Acadia, Crown Point, Niagara and Fort Dusquesne was planned. Only the attack on Acadia was successful.
1756	Montcalm captured Oswego and built Fort Ticonderoga.
1757	British failed to take Louisbourg.

1758	The British took [Fort] Duquesne and Louisbourg. The further capture of Frontenac and Oswego cut communications between Canada and Louisiana.
1759	The British took Fort Niagara, Ticonderoga and Champlain. Wolfe defeated Montcalm on the Heights of Abraham on 13 September. Wolfe and Montcalm were both killed. On 18 September Quebec surrendered to the British.

India (*see also* pp. 42–4)

Dupleix had been recalled in 1754 but Robert Clive determined to root out French influence by defeating their Indian allies.

1757	Clive took Chandernagore.
1758	General Lally reached India with French reinforcements but recalled the Marquis de Bussy from Hyderabad, where the Nizam had supported France. Lally failed to take Madras.
1759	A British force took Masulipatam, and the Nizam of Hyderabad threw in his lot with the British.
1760	Sir Eyre Coote defeated Lally at Wandenash. Lally retired to Pondicherry.
1761	British took Pondicherry.

Peace of Paris (10 February 1763)

Britain, France and Spain signed peace treaty. Colonial clauses:

North America

France ceded to Britain: Canada, Nova Scotia (Acadia), Cape Breton and all the disputed lands east of the Mississippi, except New Orleans. French fishermen retained fishing rights in the St Lawrence and off Newfoundland. France retained the small (demilitarised) islands of St Pierre and Miquelon to provide facilities for the fishermen.

India

France regained the stations she had held in 1749, including Pondicherry, on condition that they were used for trading, not military, purposes.

West Indies

Britain retained Grenada, St Vincent, Dominica and Tobago, but returned Martinique, Guadeloupe and St Lucia to France.

Africa

Britain kept Senegal but returned Gorée to France.

Spain

Spain ceded Florida to Britain but received Havana in exchange. Britain restored Manila and the Philippines to Spain. Spain ceded all rights to fish off Newfoundland, allowed the British to cut logwood in Honduras, and agreed to refer disputes as to 'prizes' (vessels captured at sea) to the British courts.

THE WEST INDIES

These were the most prized of the European colonies. Many thought that Britain had been foolish to retain Canada rather than the rich sugar colony of Guadeloupe in 1763.

The most important changes of ownership were as follows:

Antigua

Colonised by the British in 1632; attacked by the French but declared British by the Treaty of Breda of 1667.

Bahamas

Settled by the British in 1629; expelled by Spanish, 1641; re-colonised by the British, 1657; French and Spanish forces took them in 1703; became centre of piratical activity; British surrendered them to Spain in 1781 but regained them in 1783.

Dominica

Conquered in 1756 by the British, who were challenged by the French until 1806, when it was finally conceded to Britain.

Grenada

French established colony about 1650. Ceded to Britain in 1763. Re-taken by French in 1779 but restored to Britain in 1783.

Jamaica

Spain took possession in 1509. Captured by expedition sent by Oliver Cromwell in 1655. Ceded to Britain by Treaty of Madrid in 1670.

Montserrat

Colonised by Britain in 1632. Taken by France in 1664. Restored to Britain in 1668. Taken by France, 1782. Restored to Britain, 1783.

St Christopher (St Kitts)

Treaty of Utrecht (1713) eliminated the French presence from part of the island.

41

St Lucia

French took possession in 1635. In 1639 brief British settlement but the settlers were killed by the Caribs. In 1642 became a possession of the French West Indies Company. Control frequently contested between Britain and France, 1663–1803. Ceded to Britain in 1803.

Tobago

British flag first planted in 1580. Claimed by Spain in 1608. Finally ceded to Britain in 1803.

Trinidad

Settled by Spain in 1588. In 1676 French took it but later returned it to Spain. In 1797 Britain captured it. Ceded to Britain in 1803.

THE GROWTH OF EUROPEAN INFLUENCE IN INDIA

France

1664	Colbert founded the *Compagnie des Indes Orientales*, a state corporation to take over from a number of private enterprises. In particular, he wished to stop the drain of bullion involved in buying luxury goods from Dutch and English intermediaries. The Company was a commercial failure.
1719	Colbert's company was submerged in John Law's *Compagnie des Indes*, which also had monopoly rights in Louisiana, San Domingo and West Africa. But it continued to have a quasi-official character. It developed bases in the Île de France (Mauritius), Île de Bourbon, in the Carnatic and Bengal, at Surat and on the Malabar coast. Its capital was at Pondicherry on the Coromandel coast.
1741–54	Governorship of Dupleix. Dupleix was an ambitious man whose schemes, particularly to eject the British from the Carnatic, went beyond his government's wishes.
1749	Battle of Ambur. French auxiliaries helped Chanda Sahib in his bid to displace Anwar-ud-Din Khan as the nawab of the Carnatic. Also secured succession of French protégé Salabat Jang as nizam of Hyderabad.
1754	Dupleix recalled.
1763	Most of the French bases captured in the Seven Years War were returned by the British and continued as trading bases.
1769	*Compagnie des Indes* went bankrupt and (1770) lost its charter. (But French continued to hold several trading stations, including Pondicherry, Chandernagore, Yanaon, Karikal and Mahé, until Indian independence in 1947.)

Britain

1600	English East India Company incorporated. (For early voyages, *see above* p. 42)

(For early voyages, *see above* p. 42)

1639   Francis Day obtained a grant from the Rajah of the Carnatic which enabled him to build a small fortified station, Fort St George, around which grew up the town of Madras. Madras became (1658) the headquarters of the Company's activities on the east coast.

1650   Company permitted to establish a base on the Hugli River, from which Calcutta developed.

1661   Charles II confirmed Company's charter. All stockholders holding £500 worth of stock were members of the Court of Proprietors, who elected the 24 members of the Court of Directors. It held the exclusive rights of trade between Britain and the East (i.e. east of the Cape of Good Hope), although not of the 'country trade', i.e. trade between different centres in the East. It was periodically challenged by 'interloper' companies. It was accused both of draining bullion from the country and of ruining Britain's textile industry since its main imports were now not spices but silks and cottons.

Charles II received Bombay as part of Catherine de Braganza's dowry. Passed to the Company (1668) and (1687) superseded Surat as the headquarters of British trade on the west coast.

1707   Death of Emperor Aurungzabe. Although the Mughal empire had reached its greatest geographical extent under his rule, it was beginning to disintegrate. Governors appointed by the emperor began to assume the rights of hereditary rulers in their provinces.

1739   The Persians under Nadir Shah sacked Delhi and carried off the peacock throne.

1749   British alarmed by outcome of battle of Ambur.

1751   Robert Clive captured Arcot, the capital of the Carnatic.

1752   Chanda Sahib defeated and succeeded by British candidate, Muhammad Ali.

1756   Siraj-ud-daula, the nawab of Bengal, accused the Company of exceeding the privileges granted to it by the Mughal Emperor and marched on Calcutta, which he captured in June. Incident of the 'Black Hole of Calcutta'.

(October) Clive sailed for Calcutta from Madras.

1757   Clive defeated Siraj-ud-daula in battle of Plassey. Mir Jafar became Nawab of Calcutta.

1761	Battle of Panipat. Afghans, external contenders for succession to the Mughal throne, defeated the Marathas, the strongest internal contenders.
1763	End of Seven Years War. The French effectively withdrew from contest for political power in India. Britain now had no serious European rival for influence.
1765	Emperor granted the Company the *diwani* of Bengal – essentially the responsibility for collecting the revenue for the Emperor but carrying with it wide administrative and judicial powers. The British government became alarmed by the power of the Company and rumours of its corruption. The first official British intervention in Indian affairs was primarily to restrain the Company.
1773	North's Regulating Act. This raised the Governor of Bengal to the status of Governor-General with some (ill-defined) authority over Madras and Bombay. The Governor-General was to share authority with a council of four.
	The Act also established a Supreme Court of four judges in Calcutta to try cases involving British subjects. Indian employees of the Company were sometimes held to come within that definition and the Court represented the first introduction of English concepts of law into India.
	Clive, who had returned to England with a large private fortune, was accused of financial misconduct but the outcome of a parliamentary inquiry was indecisive.
	Warren Hastings, the President of the Council in Bengal, was named Governor-General. Quarrelled with his council, led by Philip Francis, a political enemy.
1780	Hastings and Francis fought a duel, in which Francis was wounded.
1783	Fox's India Bill represented the first attempt of the British government to assume any direct responsibility for the management of Indian affairs. Rejected by the House of Lords because it was argued it gave the government too much patronage.
1784	Pitt's India Act inaugurated the 'Dual Government' of the British Crown and the East India Company in those parts of India under British control. The Court of Directors remained but was to be supervised by a Board of Control, consisting of six privy councillors under a President.
1785	Hastings recalled to London.
1786–91	Impeachment of Hastings before the British parliament. Hastings was acquitted but during the trial Edmund Burke had formulated important principles for the proper government of an alien people.

EXPLORATION AND ENTERPRISE IN THE PACIFIC

1642–3   Abel Tasman discovered Tasmania (originally called Van Diemen's Land after the Dutch Governor of the East Indies). Also discovered New Zealand.

1697   Publication of William Dampier's *New Voyage round the World* aroused considerable interest in the possibilities of the South Sea (Pacific Ocean).

1711   South Sea Company founded by Robert Harley with government sponsorship in anticipation of increase in trade in the South Sea after the Treaty of Utrecht. The Company was promised a monopoly of trade with South America in the Pacific. Proved largely illusory since the Treaty of Utrecht did not include the expected concessions. But made a modest profit on first voyage (1717) and the king became the Governor of the Company (1718) Led to wild speculation which ended in ruin for most of the investors (the South Sea Bubble) in 1720. (But the Company remained in existence until 1853.)

1768–71   Captain James Cook sailed in command of a scientific expedition (which also included the naturalist Sir Joseph Banks), financed by the British government and sponsored by the Royal Society, to observe the transit of Venus from Tahiti (discovered 1767) but also to explore the Pacific. Circumnavigated New Zealand, reached Australia (previously called New Holland) and named eastern coast New South Wales.

1772–5   Cook's second expedition. Explored widely in Australasia.

1774   Spaniards sailed up coast of California to 56 degrees, discovering Nootka Sound (Vancouver Island).

1776   Cook sailed by way of the Cape of Good Hope and the Sandwich Islands (Hawaiian islands) to Vancouver Island and Alaska. Killed in the Sandwich Islands on his return voyage in 1779.

1785   British began trade in furs from Nootka Sound to China in exchange for tea.

1789   Spanish expelled British from Nootka Sound and seized ships.

1790   Nootka Sound crisis nearly brought war between Britain and Spain (allied to France). The British Prime Minister, William Pitt the Younger, maintained that effective occupation was the only valid title to land. Spain, unable to fight because her potential ally, France, was embroiled in the revolution which had broken out the previous year, conceded the principle.

3 LOSS AND CONTINUITY

THE BRITISH EMPIRE

The American War of Independence

The Thirteen Colonies in 1776

Massachusetts (including Maine); New Hampshire; Rhode Island; Connecticut; New York; Pennsylvania; New Jersey; Delaware; Maryland; Virginia; North Carolina; South Carolina; Georgia.

Background factors

1. *Social.* The population of the Thirteen Colonies had increased from about 265,000 in 1700 to just over 2,000,000 in 1770. Emigration (not all of it from the British Isles) had run at a modest level throughout the eighteenth century and consequently an increasing proportion of the colonists had been born in America and had no close ties with Britain.

2. *Economic.* As the American economy expanded, it began to break out of the strait-jacket of the Old Colonial System, although this was more true of the New England colonies, which had never fitted comfortably into it, than of the southern colonies, which still valued protected markets for their staple products such as tobacco. The colonists accepted the metropolitan power's right to regulate trade, although they evaded the regulations as far as possible by a flourishing contraband trade.

3. *The effects of the Seven Years War.*
   (a) Britain's victory relieved the colonists of any fear of French attack. In particular the Puritans of New England no longer feared being overwhelmed by Catholic France.
   (b) The colonists expected to be able to expand into the Mississippi Valley. The British government did not want colonies straggling across America and feared conflict with the native Americans. 'Pontiac's Conspiracy' of 1763 (in reality an attempt by an alliance of Indian tribes to protect their lands) alarmed them. They set the limits of British colonisation at the Alleghenies (Proclamation Line, 1763)
   (c) British taxpayers (particularly the powerful landed gentry) resented the fact that they had to pay the bill for the defence of the American colonies both during the war and afterwards, while the colonists had contributed little either financially or militarily for their own defence.

   The British government tried to raise more money from the colonies. The colonists resented, but accepted as legal, British attempts to raise more revenue from customs duties etc. They rejected attempts to impose other types of taxes as an unacceptable constitutional innovation.

Events

1763–5   George Grenville, the new Prime Minister, tried to reform the British financial system (the National Debt had risen to £140 million as a result of the war) and, more particularly, provide for strong garrisons in the colonies as a safeguard against French revenge. In 1764 he considerably extended the list of 'enumerated articles'. He also tried to enforce more strictly existing legislation which his predecessor, the Duke of Newcastle (1756–62), had allowed to become a dead letter. The trade between the Thirteen Colonies and the French West Indies was a particular case in point. The Molasses Act of 1733 had tried to kill such trade by imposing prohibitive duties on French-produced rum, molasses and sugar but it had been virtually ignored until the Seven Years War. Grenville now replaced it with the Sugar Act, with lower duties, meant to raise revenue. In 1764 Boston merchants resolved not to import ('embargo') British manufactures until their grievances were redressed. Merchants from New York and Philadelphia supported them.

1765   The Stamp Act. This extended to the colonies the requirement that certain legal documents be validated by the attachment of an official stamp. It was expected to raise £60,000 towards the annual cost of £350,000 to maintain 10,000 regular troops in North America. It was rejected by the colonists on the grounds that it was a direct revenue tax, voted by a House of Commons in which they had no members. The cry 'No taxation without representation' was born. Riots followed.

1766   The Stamp Act was repealed by the Rockingham administration, which had come into office in July 1765, but it also passed the Declaratory Act, asserting the British government's right in principle to tax the colonies.

1767   Townshend Duties. Charles Townshend, as Chancellor of the Exchequer, proposed to impose new duties on glass, lead, paper and tea (expected to raise about £40,000 per annum), arguing that these were traditional customs duties. Protests and threats of more embargoes against British goods resulted.

1770   'Boston massacre'. Massachusetts was the centre of resistance and more British troops were sent there. A sentry was set upon, his comrades fired and five people were killed.
Lord North became Prime Minister.
All the Townshend Duties, except that on tea, were repealed.

1773   Boston Tea Party. The East India Company complained that the Americans were buying all their tea from smugglers. North's government permitted the Company to ship its tea direct to America, thus undercutting the smugglers' prices. New York and Philadelphia refused to allow the tea to be landed. In Boston a party, disguised as Indians, boarded the tea ships and threw 342 chests of tea into the harbour.

1774	The Quebec Act (see p. 53) was perceived as a threat by the American colonists.

Boston harbour was closed until the tea had been paid for and the customs house moved to Salem. The Massachusetts constitution was altered. British officials were to be tried in England not in the colony for certain offences. Together the Americans regarded these as the 'Intolerable Acts'.

(August) The first Continental Congress met in Philadelphia.

1775   (19 April) Skirmish at Lexington. General Gage, the Governor of Massachusetts, sent a force from Boston to Concord to destroy military stores being collected there. The column was attacked by armed farmers at Lexington.

(May) Second session of Continental Congress met in Philadelphia and voted to raise a colonial army.

Vermont leader, Ethan Allen, seized Fort Ticonderoga, commanding the route to Montreal by Lake Champlain.

(15 June) Congress appointed Colonel George Washington of Virginia to command colonial forces.

(16 June) Americans occupied Brend's Hill overlooking Boston.

(17 June) Battle of Bunker Hill. Gage sustained heavy losses trying to regain control.

(Autumn) Americans held St Lawrence. British garrison, under Sir Guy Carleton, besieged in Quebec City.

1776   British fleet arrived in St Lawrence and Americans withdrew from Canada.

(March) British forces left Boston for Halifax.

(4 July) American Declaration of Independence.

(September) Sir William Howe defeated Washington in battle of Long Island and regained New York.

1777   (26 September) Howe took Philadelphia but British offensive ill coordinated and (17 October) General Burgoyne surrendered to General Gates at Saratoga.

1777–8   Washington's army wintered in bad conditions at Valley Forge.

1778   (6 February) France signed an alliance with the Americans. The British navy was henceforth distracted by having to defend the West Indies too.

(December) British occupied Savannah.

1779   (April) Spain entered the war on the American side.

1780	Holland began hostilities in protest at British seizures of contraband of war from neutral ships.
	(August) Cornwallis defeated Gates in South Carolina and came close to regaining Virginia.
1781	(19 October) Cornwallis forced to surrender to Washington at Yorktown (a French fleet having cut off any possibility of reinforcements from the sea).
1782	(February) Lord North resigned as Prime Minister.
	(November) Preliminary peace treaty signed in Paris.
1783	(3 September) Final peace treaty signed. Britain recognised the independence of the Thirteen States as the United States of America. Ceded sovereignty over a vast area between the Allegheny Mountains and the Mississippi.

Comments

1. Although the assemblies in the Thirteen Colonies had long acted like miniature parliaments, they had been slow to move to demands for complete independence. Various federal solutions were suggested in which the colonies, although independent of the British parliament, would still owe allegiance to the king. (Hancock suggested that this was the solution arrived at with the dominions in the reign of George V but was unacceptable in the reign of the ambitious George III.[1])

2. There were deep divisions in the colonies. Entrenched oligarchies feared the radicals. Many remained loyal to the British connection. Approximately one third joined the rebels, one third remained neutral and one third actively supported the British. The 'Loyalists' were discriminated against after 1783 and often emigrated, the largest number going to Canada.

3. There were also divisions in Britain. Commercial interests had sometimes restrained British policy, e.g. in pressing Rockingham to repeal the Stamp Act. Radicals sympathised with the American demands for representation. The most eloquent defence of the American position came from the Whig Edmund Burke, who held that the British government, not the Americans, had departed from the constitutional norms.

4. According to mercantilist theory, the loss of her American empire should have reduced Britain to the status of a third-rate power, and some expected that to happen. With increased trade after independence, and Britain's rise to become a leading industrial power, mercantilist beliefs, already under attack on the theoretical level, now seemed discredited on the practical level too.

---

1. W.K. Hancock, 'The Old Empire: The Logic of the Schools', in *Survey of British Commonwealth Affairs*, vol. 1, pp. 6–13 (Royal Institute of International Affairs, 1937).

The British empire after the loss of the Thirteen Colonies

British North America – Quebec (the former French Canada), Nova Scotia, Prince Rupert's Land (the sphere of the Hudson Bay Company).
Newfoundland.
Caribbean – Antigua, Bahamas, Barbados, Bermuda, Dominica, Grenada, Jamaica, Montserrat, St Kitts, St Vincent, Virgin Islands (British).
Africa – The Gambia, Cape Coast Castle.
India – The 'Presidencies' of Bengal, Madras (the Carnatic) and Bombay.
Europe – Gibraltar.

(Losses to other European powers; Tobago and Senegal to France; Minorca and Florida to Spain. Most conquests during the war were returned to their original owners.)

British gains in the Napoleonic wars

Britain established a remarkable measure of command of the high seas by battles such as Aboukir Bay (1798) and Trafalgar (1805). The first prevented France from gaining control of the Middle East and rendered impracticable any ambitions to re-establish her position in India; after the second, Britain was not seriously challenged at sea by another European power until after German unification in 1871. She was thus able to capture the colonies of other powers almost at will.

1795	Capture of Trincomalee (Ceylon) and Cape Colony (South Africa) from the Netherlands (then a French satellite).
1797	Capture of Trinidad from Spain. Britain also took Martinique, Tobago and St Lucia from France and Malacca and Dutch Guiana from the Dutch.
1800	Captured Malta, which Napoleon had seized from the Knights of St John in 1798.
1802	Peace of Amiens. Britain returned Cape Colony, Malacca and Guiana to the Dutch, and Martinique, Tobago, St Lucia and Gorée to France. She promised to return Malta to the Knights of St John but, suspicious of French intentions, did not do so. The failure contributed to the further outbreak of war.
1803	Britain again took Tobago, St Lucia, Demarara and Surinam (Dutch Guiana).
1806	Britain again took Cape Colony.
1807	Captured Malacca from the Dutch.
1808	Captured Moluccas from the Dutch.
1810	Captured Mauritius, Réunion and the Seychelles from France.
1811	Captured Java from the Dutch. Sir Stamford Raffles became the Governor.

1814–15   Vienna Settlement. Significantly, at the end of the Napoleonic wars, although she used the captured colonies as important bargaining counters, Britain was not very interested in retaining any except those which seemed desirable for the security of her Indian empire, such as the Cape of Good Hope and Ceylon, along with Mauritius and the Seychelles. She also retained British Guiana (part of Dutch Guiana), Tobago and St Lucia. But she returned Java, Malacca and the Moluccas to Holland and Martinique, Guadeloupe, Gorée, Senegal, Réunion and the French stations in India to France (as well as French fishing rights on the Newfoundland coast).

Continuity of the British empire

The loss of the Thirteen Colonies (sometimes referred to as 'the First British Empire') was initially greeted with despair in many quarters in Britain. It was widely believed that Britain would be ruined economically and would be reduced to the status of a second-class power. Many became disillusioned with the idea of empire. 'Separatist' and 'Pessimist' ideas became fashionable. The former believed that an empire was a burden and that the remaining colonies should be abandoned. The latter held that empire was always a transient state and that ways should be found of managing its dissolution peacefully. In fact the remaining empire was not discarded. Indeed the British empire continued to increase in size (although at a modest rate) in the early and mid-nineteenth century. Factors behind these changing attitudes were as follows:

Changing economic theories

Mercantilism had dominated eighteenth-century thinking, but it was challenged:

1. on the theoretical level by:
   (a) the French physiocrats, such as Turgot, who held that national wealth should be measured by other criteria than bullion reserves, e.g. by the prosperity of agriculture;
   (b) most powerfully by the Scottish economist Adam Smith in his *Wealth of Nations* (1776), in which he argued that artificial restraints on international trade benefited no one;
2. on the practical level:
   (a) by the fact that Britain prospered and increased her trade after the loss of the Thirteen Colonies;
   (b) by changing economic circumstances, such as the industrial revolution in Britain, which required new thinking.

Population growth

The realisation that the population was growing rapidly (revealed by regular censuses after 1801) led others to fear new stresses in society and to believe that emigration was a necessary safety valve. (Even Jeremy Bentham, otherwise

51

a committed anti-colonialist, hesitated on this point.) One peculiar manifestation of this was the transportation of criminals, mainly to Australia. Some radicals, such as Edward Gibbon Wakefield and the Colonial Reformers, advocated the reform of empire through 'systematic colonisation'. What they believed to be the surplus population and surplus capital at home should be fruitfully united with the surplus land to be found in the colonies.

Strategic considerations

World-wide British trade continued to need the protection of the Royal Navy, and this necessitated the maintenance of bases round the world. As steam slowly began to replace sail from the 1840s, this implied more elaborate coaling and repair facilities.

British attitudes to empire

But attitudes did change. The underlying belief that empire was a temporary state and that the colonies would all one day be independent, combined with domestic examples of diversity (e.g. the fact that Scotland retained her own legal and ecclesiastical system) and practical problems of distance, meant that the British empire moved in the direction of devolution, not centralisation. All the colonies of settlement gained more and more control of their domestic affairs. (Independence in foreign affairs did not come until the twentieth century.)

Central administration

This had always been *ad hoc* and frequently seemed confused. It did not become less so in the aftermath of the American war.

The Privy Council acting through its Committee for Trade and Plantations, as reconstituted in 1695, continued to exercise jurisdiction.

1748–84	The affairs of India also came under the Privy Council's jurisdiction. (Board of Control for India created in latter year.)
1768	Third Secretary of State created for the American, or Colonial, Department.
1782	The Third Secretaryship was abolished as part of Burke's 'Economical Reforms'.
1784	A new Committee for Trade and Foreign Plantations was established, but the newly created Home Office (the heir of the old Southern Department), the Admiralty and the Treasury still exercised varying degrees of control. The Committee eventually developed into the Board of Trade and relinquished responsibility for the colonies.
1794	The Secretary of State for War was given responsibility for the colonies. This made sense during the Napoleonic wars but the arrangement continued until the Crimean war made it

	essential for the Secretary of State for War to devote all his time to the war.
1854	The War Office and the Colonial Office were separated. (For Colonial Secretaries, *see* Appendix D.)

British North America

The most important part of this was the former French Canada. Britain had now to govern a colony settled by other Europeans. The only precedent was provided by New Amsterdam (New York), which had been quickly assimilated to a normal British colony of settlement. But, in Quebec, there was a large and cohesive community of French-speakers, with different traditions, political and religious, from their new rulers.

1774	Quebec Act. This was seen in the Thirteen Colonies as a hostile act and a deliberate bid for French Canadian support. In part it was, but it was also an enlightened measure for its time. French civil law was retained and the Roman Catholic church was not merely tolerated but its special position recognised. The Governor was to be assisted by a council of about 20 persons resident in the province but no elected assembly was set up, since the French Canadians distrusted the idea.
1783	The end of the American War of Independence brought a flood of Loyalist refugees into Upper Canada (the modern Ontario). They were joined by immigrants, particularly Scots and Irish Protestants. They found the French civil law, which was that of the *ancien régime*, inadequate for the conduct of business and began to petition for an assembly.
1791	Pitt's Canada Act. Tried to satisfy both communities by dividing the province into Upper and Lower Canada. Each was to be governed by a Governor, a nominated council and an elected assembly. The assemblies were to have at least 16 members in Upper, 50 in Lower Canada (representing the then population balance). There was to be a much wider franchise than in contemporary England, based on the 40 shilling freeholder in the country and the £5 tenant in the town. Special safeguards were written in for religion and for the French system of land tenure in Lower Canada.
1791–1837	Discontent became increasingly well organised in both Upper and Lower Canada. In Upper Canada it centred on the fact that the province was ruled by an oligarchy, the 'Family Compact'. In Lower Canada (as in contemporary Ireland) some of the leaders were British (Scottish) Protestants but the rank and file were (French) Catholics. The French Canadians, being steeped in the *ancien régime*, did not identify with

53

post-revolutionary France and began to look for precedents in English history, looking to control the executive by manipulating the purse strings. Their most important leader was Louis Papineau.

1806 Newspaper, *Le Canadien*, founded.

1828 Important debate in the British House of Commons led to the setting up of the Canada Committee, a Select Committee to review the situation.

1837–8 Small-scale rebellions in both Upper and Lower Canada led to the suspension of the constitution and the despatch of a leading British politician, Lord Durham, as Governor-General with powers to investigate.

1839 Publication of the Durham Report. Generally regarded as a landmark in the constitutional evolution of the British empire. Durham attributed the problems in Canada to two causes: (1) the clash of English and French nationalism ('At the root of the disorders of Lower Canada, lies the conflict of the two races, which compose its population; until this is settled, no good government is practicable'); and (2) the constant clash between the executive and the representative body. He could see no solution for the first except the assimilation of the French minority (in British North America as a whole) to the English majority. For the second he advocated what became known as 'responsible government' (although he did not himself use the phrase). He further recommended the reunion of Upper and Lower Canada and, when the Canadians themselves were ready for it, a wider federation, bringing in the Maritime Provinces.

1839–48 The struggle for 'responsible government'. Durham himself died in 1840 and those close to him disagreed as to what he had meant. His chief assistant, Charles Buller, insisted that he meant that the executive must be answerable to the assembly as, in Britain, the Cabinet was answerable to parliament. The Colonial Secretary, Lord John Russell, rejected this on the grounds that the governor and his officials must be primarily answerable to the British Crown, otherwise Canada would be an independent country. (Durham had tried to resolve this by suggesting that in local matters the executive should be answerable to the assembly, in 'imperial' matters, such as defence, to the British Crown.) Russell instructed Durham's successor, Lord Sydenham, to try to establish only 'responsive' government, i.e. to be sensitive to Canadian wishes.

1849 The then Governor-General, Lord Elgin, backed by the then Colonial Secretary, the 3rd Earl Grey, endorsed the more extensive definition of 'responsible government' by accepting the Rebellion Losses Bill, a highly controversial measure, on the grounds that it was a Canadian measure, duly passed by the assembly, and it would therefore be improper for him to withhold his consent. Within a few years this became the constitutional norm in all British colonies of settlement.

1849–67   Political deadlock continued in Canada, which operated with coalition ministries which needed to secure majorities in both Canada West (Upper Canada) and Canada East (Lower Canada). A wider federation seemed a possible solution. It was hoped it would open the way for economic development, especially the building of railways, and strengthen them in tariff negotiations with their great southern neighbour, the United States. The American Civil War (1861–5) and the possible involvement of British North America also caused great alarm.

1858   British Columbia was carved out of the territory of the Hudson Bay Company and became a Crown colony. Vancouver Island was brought in in 1866.

1859   The Canadian Finance Minister, Alexander Galt, compelled the British Colonial Secretary, the Duke of Newcastle, to concede the Canadians' right to determine their own tariff policy.

1864   The 'great coalition' was formed in Canada of habitual political opponents, including John A. Macdonald, George Brown, Alexander Galt and Georges Cartier, determined to find a solution.
Charlottetown Conference. A conference assembled in the capital of Prince Edward Island to discuss a limited federation between the Maritimes. They were joined by delegates from Canada.
The conference reconvened in Quebec City. Canada, Nova Scotia and New Brunswick agreed on a scheme for federation.

1866   Westminster Palace Hotel Conference. The plan was presented to representatives of the British government.

1867   The British parliament passed the British North America Act, establishing the Dominion of Canada. It was a 'strong' federation in that residual powers, not specifically granted to the provinces, remained with the central government. The central government consisted of the Governor-General (still nominated by London), a Senate of 72 members (24 from Quebec, 24 from Ontario and 24 from the Maritimes) nominated for life by the Governor-General, and a House of Commons of 181 members, allocated on the basis of population to be reviewed at intervals (Quebec initially had 65, Ontario, 82,

Nova Scotia, 19 and New Brunswick, 15). French and English were both official languages. No powers of constitutional amendment were written into the Act since Canada remained a colony and it was assumed that changes would be by Act of the (British) parliament. Provision was made for the accession of further provinces but not for secession. Other provinces did subsequently join.

1869   The Hudson Bay Company surrendered its vast territories to the Crown.

1869–70   Louis Riel, a *métis* (i.e. a man of mixed French Canadian and Indian blood), led an unsuccessful revolt against the entry of settlers into the Red River region.

1870   Manitoba became the first province to be carved out of the prairies.

1871   British Columbia joined on condition that the federal government would build a railway from the Atlantic to the Pacific.

1873   Prince Edward Island joined.

1885   Louis Riel led another unsuccessful rebellion in what became Saskatchewan.

1886   The Canadian-Pacific Railway was completed.

1905   Alberta and Saskatchewan became provinces.

Australia

The most pressing reason for Britain's acquisition of territory in Australia in the late eighteenth century was the need to find a new outlet for the transportation of convicts after the American War of Independence, but there were other background factors. There were rising hopes of a developing great Pacific trade, centred on China. At one time it was believed that Australia might be the *Terra Incognita Australis*, another great and populous continent, which the scientists of the day believed must exist to balance the northern continents. Explorations dashed those hopes but James Cook's voyages of 1768–71 and 1772–5 (on the first of which he visited and named New South Wales) revealed a potentially fertile land. The pre-existing population of Australia, the 'Aborigines', was sparse and regarded by the Europeans as extremely primitive. Their rights were generally disregarded and in Tasmania they disappeared altogether in what some have regarded as genocide.

1787–8   Captain Arthur Phillip sailed in command of the 'First Fleet' to Botany Bay. He was instructed to annex the whole eastern half of Australia, east of longitude 135 degrees. The expedition included 750 convicts. A week after landing he transferred his operation to Port Jackson, the site of the city of Sydney.

A French expedition, under La Perouse, arrived a few days later but was lost at sea on its return voyage. The outbreak of the French Revolution in 1789 delayed any serious challenge to the British for a generation – although the arrival of a French scientific mission precipitated the British annexation of Tasmania (Van Diemen's Land) in 1803.

1788–1823 As a predominantly convict colony, New South Wales was subject to the authority of the Governor. The military officers also enjoyed considerable power. From 1790, free settlers, mainly officials and time-expired soldiers, began to take up land grants. Convicts who had served their sentences (emancipists) also stayed on. Captain John Macarthur began his successful experiments with sheep farming and on a visit to England in 1801 secured a grant of 5000 acres and backing from substantial men. The colony, which had seemed likely to fail, began to prosper.

1823 The government of New South Wales began to approximate to that of an ordinary Crown colony by an Act (extended in 1828) which limited the powers of the Governor and created a nominated Council with financial and legislative powers.

1826 The foundation of a convict settlement at Brisbane marked the beginning of what became Queensland.

1829 Foundation of Western Australia by Captain James Stirling and others. But the enterprise was badly planned and many emigrants went on to New South Wales.
Gibbon Wakefield's *Letter from Sydney*. Purporting to be written by a settler in Sydney, this put foward Wakefield's ideas for 'systematic colonisation'.

1830 Colonization Society founded by Wakefield and later joined by Charles Buller, George Grote, Sir William Molesworth and other leading radicals.

1834 Wakefield formed the South Australia Association to found a colony which would avoid the mistakes of Western Australia. The new colony was established (after Wakefield's own resignation). It experienced similar difficulties to those of Western Australia but became prosperous under its second Governor, Sir George Grey, in the 1840s.

1834–7 Individual settlers opened up the region and Melbourne was founded in 1837. It was then still under the authority of New South Wales.

1840 Transportation to New South Wales was stopped at the request of the free settlers, although it continued to Van Diemen's Land until 1853 and convicts were also sent to Western

57

	Australia between 1849 and 1868. (In all, 137,161 persons were transported to Australia.)
1842	Representative government was introduced into New South Wales. A Legislative Council of 12 nominated and 24 elected members was created with legislative and financial powers, although some matters were reserved for the Governor and his Executive Council.
1850	An Act of parliament extended representative government to Tasmania, South Australia and Victoria.
1851	Gold discovered in New South Wales and Victoria.
	Victoria was formally separated from New South Wales.
1855	Following the Canadian precedent, New South Wales, Victoria, South Australia and Tasmania gained 'responsible government'. (The still undeveloped Western Australia only gained representative government in 1870 and responsible government in 1890.)
1859	Queensland separated from New South Wales.
1855–88	Australia became increasingly racially exclusive. Having ended the transportation of convicts, the authorities became alarmed by Asian immigration, particularly during the gold rushes of the 1850s. Such immigration was restricted and finally prohibited.
1856–94	Although racially exclusive, Australia was far in advance of Britain in the development of parliamentary democracy. Victoria instituted the secret ballot in 1856. Property qualifications for the franchise were gradually reduced until manhood suffrage was achieved. Payment for members was introduced and in 1894, in South Australia, the vote was extended to women.
1883–1900	The movement towards federation. The British government had considered the possibility in the 1850s but it was not popular in Australia. The colonies developed separately round the coasts of the continent and the dryness of the interior precluded much inland development. The Australian colonies pursued different tariff policies and did not even trouble to coordinate their railway development, adopting different gauges. They were shaken from their complacency by European, especially German, advances in the Pacific during the Scramble period.
1883	Queensland declared the annexation of eastern New Guinea (the western half was in Dutch hands) to anticipate the Germans. The British government repudiated the annexation, denying that there was any danger. Germany subsequently annexed the northern part of New Guinea.
	An attempt was made to set up a federal council in Australasia.

1889	Sir Henry Parkes, the premier of New South Wales, came out in favour of a federal solution to economic and other problems – previously New South Wales had been opposed to the idea.
1890	A conference met in Melbourne.
1891	A convention met in Sydney which drafted proposals that subsequently became the basis of federation.
1895–6	The various colonies passed Enabling Acts.
1897–8	Directly elected delegates met first in Adelaide, then Sydney, then Melbourne.
1898	A referendum failed to secure the necessary majority in New South Wales.
1899	A conference of the premiers met in Melbourne and agreed to hold a new referendum. This secured the necessary majorities in all the colonies (after a second attempt in Western Australia).
1900	The British parliament passed the Australian proposals into law with a few amendments – the only one of importance being the retention of the role of the Judicial Committee of the Privy Council. (For the significance of this, *see below* p. 108). The Australian federation differed in important particulars from the Canadian. It was a 'weak' federation, i.e. powers not specifically transferred to the centre remained with the states (as the colonies were now called). The House of Representatives was elected by the states on the basis of population. The Senate was also elected but each state had an equal number of Senators. Powers of constitutional amendment were written in but deliberately made difficult to achieve.
1901	(January) The Commonwealth of Australia came into being and a new capital was created at Canberra.

New Zealand

Captain James Cook charted the coasts of New Zealand in 1769 and whalers began to frequent the coast from about 1792. A few settlers arrived. There was a substantial Maori population, possibly as many as 100,000 in the North Island and a much smaller number (perhaps 5000) in the South Island. They were Polynesian in race and recognised as intelligent and warlike by the Europeans, who respected them.

| 1787 | New Zealand was included in Captain Arthur Phillip's commission (it had first been claimed by Cook) but no serious attempt was made to enforce the claim. |
| 1814 | English missionaries arrived, led by the Rev. Samuel Marsden. Both the Wesleyan Missionary Society and the Anglican |

Church Missionary Society made a good many Maori converts. They were disturbed when, in the 1830s, French Roman Catholic missions began to arrive.

1826   The New Zealand Company was formed and sent out a few settlers.

1837   The New Zealand Association was formed, inspired by the ideas of Gibbon Wakefield and including eminent men like Lord Durham and Sir William Molesworth. It applied for a charter modelled on that of the Massachusetts Bay Company. It was refused. Its main opponent was Sir James Stephen, the Permanent Secretary at the Colonial Office, who was closely connected with missionary interests and wished to protect the Maoris from exploitation. A bitter feud developed between Stephens and the Colonial Reformers.

1839   The New Zealand Association, renamed the New Zealand Company, sent out a group of settlers under Wakefield's brother. It was known that French companies were also planning settlement.

1840   Treaty of Waitangi. The British government sent out a Governor, Captain William Hobson, who concluded a treaty with the Maori chiefs, by which they accepted British sovereignty in return for guarantees of their land rights.

1843   Robert Fitzroy became Governor. Although Fitzroy was personally sympathetic to the Maori cause, war broke out over land rights.

1845   George Grey succeeded Fitzroy and restored calm.

1847   The Crown bought out Maori rights in part of the South Island and transferred it to Company administration. In 1848 Scottish Presbyterians established a settlement at Dunedin and an Anglican group established Christchurch. European settlement increased rapidly. By 1865 the white population was 172,000.

1851   The New Zealand Company dissolved.

1853   A new constitution provided for representative government. (The first experiments dated from 1846.) There were to be two chambers, one nominated by the Governor, the other, the House of Representatives, directly elected. The franchise was wide but based on a property qualification which excluded most Maoris, who did not hold land on British systems of tenure.

1856   Responsible government was established, although some aspects of Maori relations were 'reserved' for London.

1860–70   Series of wars with the Maoris about land rights. (The Maoris had been further alarmed by census figures that revealed that the Europeans now outnumbered the Maoris.) The final settlement left the Europeans in possession of the South Island but with substantial Maori holdings in the North Island. The refusal of Gladstone's government to send additional troops to help the settlers led to Disraeli's charges that Gladstone wished to break up the empire.

1867   Discovery of gold led to a gold rush, which rapidly increased the white population.

Four seats were reserved for Maoris in the House of Representatives.

1907   New Zealand was recognised as having dominion status with Canada, Australia and South Africa.

South Africa

The Dutch period

By the late eighteenth century the European settlers at the Cape (Dutch, Huguenot and some German) numbered about 15,000. Cape Town had become an important entrepôt, surrounded by an area of comparatively intensive farming, including wine-growing, which serviced Cape Town. Beyond that the Boers (farmers) had staked out their claims to free land. By tradition a Boer began to feel crowded if he could see the smoke from his neighbour's chimney. The land was sparsely populated by the San (Bushmen) and the Khoikhoi (Hottentots), and the Boers genuinely believed that they were occupying empty land. But when, in the late eighteenth century, they reached the Great Fish River, they ran into another stream of colonisers coming from the north. These were the people who became known to the Boers as the 'Bantu'. (*See* Glossary.)

1717   Boers began to import slaves from West Africa, Madagascar and the East Indies. (Did not attempt to enslave the Bantu, whom the Boers always regarded as aliens from beyond a definable frontier.) By 1791 there were about 17,000 such slaves in Cape Colony.

1779–81   First war between Boers and Bantu in the Great Fish River region. Began a long series of frontier wars known to contemporaries as the 'Kaffir' wars, which lasted until the 1850s. The most notable were those of 1789–93, 1799–1803, 1811–12, 1818–19, 1834–5 and 1850–3.

The British period

1795   The British occupied Cape Colony when the Dutch became a satellite power of Revolutionary France.

1803   The Cape was returned to Holland under the terms of the Peace of Amiens.

61

1806	The British re-occupied the Cape. British administration began immediately, although Britain was not formally confirmed in possession of Cape Colony until 1814. As in Quebec, the British found themselves governing the well-established colony of another European power. The Boers were united by a common language (Afrikaans, derived from Dutch), a common religion (Calvinism) and a common outlook on life, which was basically isolationist. The British attempted to conciliate the Boers by retaining existing legal and financial systems and, as opportunity arose, liberalising commercial regulations. But conflict soon resulted.
1812	'Black circuit'. Judges went out 'on circuit' from Cape Town and shocked Boer opinion by hearing 22 cases of alleged mistreatment of slaves or Hottentots.
1816	Slagter's Nek. A Boer, Bezuidenhout, refused to come to court to answer a charge of ill-treating a Hottentot servant on the grounds that he could not leave his family unprotected on a dangerous frontier. Bezuidenhout was shot in a skirmish by a posse sent to arrest him. A small rebellion followed and five of the ring leaders were hanged at Slagter's Nek. The incident made an indelible impression on Boer opinion.
1818	Dr John Philip of the London Missionary Society arrived in Cape Colony. The Boers had avoided missionary activities among non-whites (possibly because of a lingering belief that civil rights could not be denied to Christians of any colour). The missionaries, and particularly Philip, constituted themselves the champions of the non-whites, especially the slaves and the Khoikhoi. They believed that tribal units should be held together wherever possible, but their desire to protect the Africans from European exploitation sometimes led them into separatist views that seem to pre-figure twentieth-century apartheid.
1820	The renewal of the East India Company's charter in 1813 had made it possible for the British government to curtail its monopoly privileges. Cape Town was opened to foreign vessels. The colony became increasingly prosperous. Foundation of Albany Colony. Some British immigration had been encouraged since 1815. The Governor, Lord Charles Somerset, now attempted to estabilish an organised colony on the Cape's eastern borders to help to stabilise the area. Only partially successful. An English population was established in the eastern Cape but many drifted to Cape Town, confirming the tendency for the English to be town-dwellers, the Boers country-dwellers.

1828	The Cape government (i.e. Governor and Executive Council) issued the 50th Ordinance. This confirmed that the Khoikhoi were free men, not slaves, guaranteed their right to move about freely and dealt with abuses in labour contracts, the apprenticing of children, etc. Resented by Boers, who found the nomadic Khoikhoi a nuisance.
1833	Act emancipating slaves throughout the British empire. Boers were angered because they felt that, unlike the West Indian planters, they had treated their slaves humanely and because, not having agents in London, they found it very difficult to claim the statutory compensation.
1835	Beginning of the Great Trek. Many Boers 'trekked' out of Cape Colony. Moving on, 'trekking', was already deeply engrained in the colony's traditions. Where British colonists might have organised political protests, the Boers simply left. The emancipation of the slaves was only one factor. Although the Boers did feel that, influenced by the missionaries, the British were supporting the slaves and Khoi against them, they also resented the increasing anglicisation of the colony in legal and other matters and the proposal (in 1832) that in future land would be auctioned and not simply registered on the presentation of a claim.
	Governor D'Urban annexed area between Kei and Keiskamma rivers (later British Kaffraria) in an effort to stabilise the eastern border. Repudiated by London, which was determined not to extend its area of commitment.
1838	(16 December) Dingaan's Day. Boers, led by Andreis Pretorius, defeated the Zulus under Dingaan, the successor of the great Zulu general, Shaka, in a battle at Blood River. Earlier in year the most important Voortrekker leader, Pieter Retief, had been killed by Dingaan in treacherous circumstances and the victory subsequently assumed almost mythic status in Boer historiography. The Boers spread out into what became the Orange Free State, the Transvaal and Natal, believing that the territory into which they were now advancing was, like the Cape, sparsely populated. In this they were misled by their almost total ignorance of African politics and the disruptive effects of the Zulu advance (the *Mfekane*).
	The Boers established an embryonic republic at Pietermaritzburg. The small number of British settlers already in Natal had no official recognition, but the British government was reluctant to see the Boers established in Natal, where they could open communications with rival European powers. Although the British too had little understanding of the African situation, they were also alarmed at the repercussions

63

	of the Boer advance and the ways in which the displacement of populations was putting pressure on the colonial frontiers elsewhere.
1842	British troops arrived at Durban (Port Natal) to establish that Natal was British territory and the Boers British subjects. The Boers saw it as an invasion and a small war ensued. The Boers trekked out again to the Orange Free State and the Transvaal, leaving Natal to become the most British of the South African provinces.
1843	Natal was formally declared to be a British colony.
1845	Natal was organised as a dependency of the Cape.
1846–7	British attempts to keep the peace by treaty relations with African tribes broke down in the so-called 'War of the Axe'. Britain annexed British Kaffraria.
1848	Cape colonists strongly resisted a proposal to send convicts (after New South Wales refused to receive more). Became more vocal politically. Sir Harry Smith, the Governor, annexed Transorangia as the Orange River Sovereignty and defeated Pretorius at the battle of Boomplaats.
1852	Sand River Convention granted autonomy to the Boers of the Transvaal.
1853	Representative government (elected House of Representatives) established in the Cape, which had previously been governed by Governor and nominated councils. Franchise: like almost all British colonial constitutions, this was 'colour-blind'. No distinction was made on the grounds of race. The existence of a property qualification ensured that most voters would be Europeans but in the Cape a significant number of non-white voters emerged.
1854	Bloemfontein Convention granted autonomy to the Boers of the Orange Free State.
1856	Natal was separated from the Cape and given a similar constitution.
1857	(18 February) So-called 'suicide of the Xhosas' (*see* Xhosas on p. 204).
1858–9	Sir George Grey, Governor. Famously expressed views in favour of federation of whole of South Africa but then premature.
1866	British Kaffraria was transferred to the jurisdiction of the Cape.
1868	Basutos (Basothos) taken under British protection, jurisdiction being exercised by the British High Commissioner in South Africa. (Basutos had felt pressurised by the Boers since the 1830s but previous requests for protection had been refused.)

1871	Jurisdiction over Basutos transferred to Cape government.

1872	Cape Colony given responsible government by William Gladstone's administration. Had been no vocal demand for it. Some saw it as part of Gladstone's indifference to empire. May have been attempt to make Cape assume more responsibility for difficult developments in southern Africa.

India

Britain's hold on India did not weaken as a result of the American War of Independence. Some authorities have held[2] that the loss of the American colonies only confirmed trends already present in British imperial policy, namely the 'Swing to the East', a preference for trade in Asia at the expense of colonies in the west.

1784	Pitt's India Act (*see* p. 44).

1786–93	Governor-Generalship of Lord Cornwallis. Cornwallis set out to reform revenue system of Bengal. Introduced (1793) the 'Permanent Settlement'. Without intending to do so considerably advanced westernisation of Indian administrative system by regarding the *zemindars* (tax-gatherers) of the Mughal period as European-style landowners.

1798–1803	Governor-Generalship of Marquis Wellesley. British feared that their position in India would again be challenged by the French, who would make common cause with their Indian enemies. Nizam of Hyderabad agreed to dismiss French troops and replace them by British. Tipu Sultan of Mysore refused to sever his connections with the French. Defeated and killed at battle of Seringapatam (1799) Marquess Wellesley's brother, the future Duke of Wellington, defeated the Marathas at battle of Assaye (1803).

1813	The clause forbidding missionary activity was removed from the East India Company's charter as a result of a sustained campaign, led by the evangelicals, who had emphasised human rights violations such as female infanticide and *sati*.

1818	Final defeat of Marathas, who ceased to be serious challenge to the British.

1819	James Mill, who had published his important *History of India* the previous year, entered the India Office with the clear intention of reforming India in conformity with 'utilitarian'

---

2. The most powerful advocate of this interpretation was V. Harlow, *The Founding of the Second British Empire, 1763–1793*, 2 vols (1952, 1964).

principles. (In 1830–6 held post equivalent to Permanent Under-Secretary there.)

1821   Royal Asiatic Society founded in London. (Asiatic Society of Bengal, 1784.)

1828–35   Governor-Generalship of Lord William Bentinck. Sympathised with the reformist policies of the Utilitarians and helped to further their work.

Important reformers of this period included:

1. Mountstuart Elphinstone, Governor of Bombay, 1819–27. Founded Elphinstone Institute in Bombay, a college which was the nursery of many later nationalist leaders.
2. Thomas Munro, Governor of Madras, 1820–7. Introduced *ryotwari* system, based on petty proprietors, which many later saw as an alternative to Cornwallis's *zemindari* system, but which also breached the traditional Indian land system, which had not been based on private ownership.
3. Thomas Babington Macaulay. Went to India in 1834 as the law member of the Governor-General's council. In 1835 he persuaded the government to support western (and essentially English language) education. He also set in train the great codification of the chaotic Indian legal system (1859 Code of Civil Procedure, 1861 Code of Criminal Procedure).

1828   Ram Mohan Roy founded the *Brahma Sabha* with the aim of combining what was best in Indian and western philosophy.

1833   Renewal of East India Company's Charter. Laid down that no distinctions were to be made on grounds of race or colour.

1835   Acting Governor-General Charles Metcalf conceded principle of freedom of the press. Although demanded by the English residents, Indians took advantage of the measure to establish a flourishing English-language and vernacular press.

1836   Macaulay's 'Black Act'. This made European residents outside Calcutta subject to the company's courts (in which Indian judges might sit) in civil cases. Caused an outcry but Macaulay (supported by, among others, John Stuart Mill, who had entered the India Office in 1832) maintained the principle.

1839–40   Beginning of system of Grand Trunk roads to connect Calcutta and Delhi, Calcutta and Bombay and Bombay and Agra.

1839–42   Unsuccessful war in Afghanistan.

1845–6, 1848–9   War with Sikhs which culminated in annexation of Punjab (1849).

1847–56   Governor-Generalship of Lord Dalhousie saw further important technological advances. First railway track built in Bombay

(1853); first telegraph line opened from Calcutta to Agra (1854); postal system reorganised (1854).

Politically Dalhousie set out to expand the frontiers of British India by the 'doctrine of lapse' (similar to feudal principle of 'escheat'). Under the Mughal empire, if a ruler had no direct heir, a dependent state reverted to the emperor, but by custom Indian rulers had been allowed to adopt heirs in such circumstances. Dalhousie refused to recognise such adoptions in strategic localities and in 1848–54 acquired Satara, Jaitpur, Udaipur, Nagpur and Jhansi. In 1856 Dalhousie annexed Oudh, which had been a protected state since 1801.

1852   Bombay Association founded to lobby British government when East India Company's charter came up for renewal the following year. Included Hindus, Parsis and Muslims and highly sophisticated in its methods.

1857   Indian 'Mutiny'. Many explanations have been advanced: a simple army mutiny, a conspiracy of those offended by Dalhousie, the first national war of independence and the last kick of the old feudal India. Probably elements of all these were present, but most historians now favour the last (supplemented by more detailed studies of particular causes in particular regions.) It affected only part of India, essentially the Bengal Presidency, and the likelihood of it being a manifestation of nationalism in the modern sense is reduced by the fact that the newly westernised classes, who led the later nationalist movement, did not support it.

(10 May) Mutiny began at Meerut. Soldiers of 23rd Light Cavalry had been court-martialled for refusing to use new cartridges which they believed to be polluted by cow and pig fat. About 50 Europeans and Eurasians were killed. The mutineers then marched to Delhi to offer their services to the pensioned Mogul Emperor.

(13 May–1 July) Outbreaks elsewhere, including Lucknow and Cawnpore. Colonel Neil despatched with force from Calcutta. His 'severity' in dealing with mutineers was denounced by W.H. Russell in *The Times*.

(15 July) Massacre of British women and children at Cawnpore.

1858   East India Company surrendered its charter to the Crown. Ended period of dual government.

Other Asian acquisitions

1819   Sir Stamford Raffles acquired the island of Singapore from the Sultan of Johore.

1824–6	War with Burma. Acquired Assam (previously conquered by the King of Burma) and some other territory.
1826	Singapore, Penang and Malacca made up the Straits Settlements, under the jurisdiction of the East India Company.
1839	Took possession of Aden. Governed for a time from Bombay.
1842	Sir James Brooks was installed as the Rajah of Sarawak.
1846	The island of Labuan was ceded to Britain by the Sultan of Brunei.
1851–2	Second Burmese war. Annexed Lower Burma (Pegu) including Rangoon.
1867	The Straits Settlements were transferred to the jurisdiction of the Colonial Office.

THE SPANISH EMPIRE

The loss of the Spanish empire in the Americas

Although there had been strains between the interests of metropolitan Spain and those of the American colonies in the eighteenth century, Spain's loss of empire was an immediate consequence of the Napoleonic wars in Europe.

1808	The Spanish King, Charles IV, was compelled to abdicate in favour of Napoleon Bonaparte's brother, Joseph. The change was resisted in Spain and led to the Peninsular war, in which Britain assisted the Spaniards against Napoleon.
1808–14	Some royal officials in the colonies held that they were obliged to obey the *de facto* king but eventually all the American provinces declared their loyalty to Charles IV's son and legitimate heir, Ferdinand Prince of Asturias (Ferdinand VII). Despite this declared loyalty, for six years the Spanish colonies functioned in practice as autonomous republics, not accepting the authority of metropolitan Spain. Leadership passed from peninsular Spaniards to the creoles (i.e. men of Spanish descent resident in the colonies). Authority was usually exercised by *juntas* (*ad hoc* bodies of officials and leading citizens).
1810	Rebellion in Venezuela led by Francisco de Miranda and Simón Bolívar.
	Rebellion of peasants and mineworkers in Guanajuato led by Hidalgo.
	Province of Rio de la Plata had split into warring factions: Buenos Aires (Argentina), Monte Video (Uruguay) and Paraguay. Buenos Aires declared its independence from Old Spain.

1814	Napoleon defeated. Ferdinand VII became King of Spain. Initially granted a liberal charter to his people from which the colonies derived some benefits, e.g. representative assemblies and municipal councils were recognised. But an attempt was made to restore the old restrictive commercial system and Ferdinand rapidly became less liberal politically.
	General Morillo arrived from Spain with a professional army. Put down most insurgency. A number of leaders were shot. Bolívar fled to Jamaica. But Spanish army suffered heavy casualties from disease.
	Buenos Aires, though professing allegiance to Ferdinand VII, continued to assert independence from Spain.
1816–21	Simón Bolívar returned and continued his campaign to free Venezuela and New Granada, relying in part on guerilla forces, composed of *mestizos* and Indians.
1817–18	José de San Martín, an Argentinian, conquered Chile with the help of local republicans and a fleet, commanded by Admiral Cochrane (a former British officer).
1819	Spain ceded its claims to Florida to the United States in the Adams–Onis Treaty.
1820–1	General Iturbide declared New Spain (Mexico) independent of Old Spain but still recognised Ferdinand VII, although later proposing an independent constitutional monarchy under a Bourbon prince.
1821	San Martín occupied Lima and declared Peru an independent state.
1822	Royalist forces re-occupied Lima.
1822	Congress of Verona. Ferdinand asked for European military assistance against his rebellious colonies. Britain firmly opposed this. British dominance at sea made intervention without British consent impracticable.
1823	French forces entered Spain to assist Ferdinand against the Spanish liberals.
	Britain invited the United States to join in a joint declaration against any European intervention in the Spanish colonies. Instead President Monroe issued a statement (the Monroe Doctrine, 2 December) declaring that the American continents were not to be considered as 'future subjects for colonization by any European Powers', and that the United States would regard as an unfriendly act any interference with those which had declared themselves independent.
	George Canning, the British Foreign Secretary, formally recognised the independence of Buenos Aires, Mexico and Colombia.

	Iturbide overthrown as dictator of Mexico. Honduras, Nicaragua, San Salvador and Costa Rica became independent states rejecting union with Mexico.
1824	Simón Bolívar conquered Peru.
1824–30	An attempt was made to create one state – Colombia – but by Bolívar's death in 1830 this had split into its component parts, roughly the old Spanish provinces: Colombia (New Granada), Venezuela, Bolivia (Upper Peru), Ecuador (Guayaquil and Quito) and Peru.

Remaining Spanish empire

Spain still retained Cuba, Puerto Rico and the Philippines and some outposts in Africa. She was to lose the first three during the Spanish–American war of 1898.

THE PORTUGUESE EMPIRE

The loss of the Portuguese empire in Brazil

This was also a direct result of the Napoleonic wars.

1807	The regent of Portugal (1816 became King John VI) took refuge in Brazil when the French army entered Lisbon.
1821	John VI returned to Portugal, leaving his son, Pedro, as regent in Brazil. Portugal attempted to reimpose its authority on Brazil, including the revival of the navigation laws. Separatist feeling grew.
1822	Pedro proclaimed himself 'constitutional emperor' of an independent Brazil.
1825	British mediation secured an agreement on the separation of Portugal and Brazil. Britain insisted that Brazil sign a convention outlawing the slave trade.
1826	John VI died. Pedro opted to remain in Brazil and passed his rights to the Portuguese throne to his daughter, Donna Maria. Pedro's younger brother, Miguel, asserted his right to the Portuguese throne and a civil war ensued. By 1834 (after both British and Brazilian intervention) the matter was resolved in Maria's favour.
1844	On the expiry of the 1825 convention against the slave trade, Britain insisted on her right to continue to enforce it unilaterally by stopping Brazilian slave ships.
1888	Brazil abolished slavery.
1889	Brazil rejected the Braganza dynasty and became a republic.

70

Remaining Portuguese empire

Portugal still retained some claims in Africa, the most important of which were Angola and Mozambique. She also retained Macao in China and (East) Timor. She was not to relinquish these until after the Second World War.

THE FRENCH EMPIRE

France's loss of San Domingo

San Domingo (ceded by Spain to France in 1697) had an unusual constitutional position within the French empire. It had two *Conseils Supérieurs*, which were consulted about taxation. From 1764 onwards assemblies, variously constituted, were also consulted.

The 'decolonisation' of San Domingo was the direct result of the Napoleonic wars.

In 1789 it had a population of approximately 32,000 whites, 24,000 mulattos and 450,000 slaves. It was France's most prosperous Caribbean colony, which traded through its three 'free ports' with the United States and with the British and Spanish islands as well as with metropolitan France.

1790	The white planters set up an autonomous republic.
1791	The mulattos and free negroes demanded political rights. Rising suppressed. (August) The slaves rose in a general revolt.
1793	French commissioner announced that all slaves were free on the island.
1794	(February) The French Republic formally abolished slavery throughout the empire. The slave leader Toussaint l'Ouverture rallied to the support of France during the war with England. Became virtual dictator.
1795	Spain ceded her part of the island to France.
1802	Peace of Amiens. Napoleon tried to reintroduce slavery in the Caribbean islands. Negro army in San Domingo (now called Haiti) revolted against France.
1803	Renewal of war with England made it impossible for French to make second attempt to re-assert authority.
1825	Bourbon government in France recognised independent negro republic in Haiti in return for compensation for dispossessed planters.

Remaining French empire

France had lost the most important parts of her empire to Britain during the Seven Years War. She regained some minor stations, mainly in Africa, in 1783. If Napoleon hoped to re-establish the French empire at the British expense, he failed, and his final loss of interest in overseas empire would seem to be demonstrated by his willingness to sell France's remaining claims in North America to the United States (the Louisiana Purchase) in 1803. In 1848 the short-lived Second Republic not only ended slavery throughout the empire but conferred citizenship on all the inhabitants of the 'ancient colonies': Martinique, Guadeloupe, Réunion and St Louis, Gorée, Dakar and Rufisque (Senegal).

Pacific and Australasia

France saw some revival of interest in empire in the 1830s. The swift British response made it impossible for her to lay effective claims to Australia or New Zealand but she had some success in the Pacific islands.

1841	French annexation of the Marquesa Islands.
1842–4	The French proclamation of a protectorate and then the annexation of Tahiti and the cavalier treatment of a British missionary, George Pritchard, precipitated a crisis with Britain, which had well-established trading and missionary interests there. War was only averted by the calmness of the two governments in the face of public excitement. France agreed to cancel the annexation and revert to a protectorate.
1847	France had occupied the whole of the Society Islands (of which Tahiti was the chief).
1853	Annexation of New Caledonia.
1880	Annexation of Society Islands.

Africa, North

1830	Government of Charles X sent an expedition to eradicate Barbary pirates from the Algerian coast. Government of Louis Philippe which followed found it impossible to withdraw and became further sucked into Algeria.
1840s	French embarked on full-scale war with Arab leader, Abd-el-Kader. French, under Marshal Bugeaud, were successful. France began 'military colonisation', i.e. settled time-expired soldiers in the country.
1863	Napoleon III adopted the policy of establishing an 'Arab kingdom' in Algeria, i.e. semi-independent under the French Emperor.

Africa, West

1849	Libreville (French Congo) founded.
1854	Louis Faidherbe became Governor of Senegal. Subdued the hinterland of Senegal in conflicts with Muslim emirates and hoped eventually to link Senegal with the Upper Niger.

Indo-China

1787	Treaty between France and ruler of Annam (which had broken away from the Chinese empire in the fifteenth century). French enjoyed trading privileges and French Catholic missionaries arrived.
1847	Emperor Tu-Duc began to persecute missionaries.
1859	French occupied Saigon
1862	Tu-Duc promised religious toleration and ceded three eastern provinces of Cochin-China, including Saigon, to the French.
1867	France acquired four more provinces of Cochin-China.

THE DUTCH EMPIRE

No part of the Dutch empire became independent as a result of the Napoleonic wars, although parts, viz. Ceylon and the Cape of Good Hope, were lost to Britain. Britain restored Java to the Dutch. The Dutch continued to control most of the East Indies very indirectly through treaties with local rulers. The exception was Java.

Java and the culture system

Sir Stamford Raffles had abolished the system by which villages paid tributes in kind to the Dutch authorities in favour of cash payments. The Dutch restored the older system (the culture system). In 1830 the Governor, Jan van den Bosch, laid down that not more than one-fifth of the land of the village was to be used for these cash crops and that any surplus revenue should be returned to the villagers, but these safeguards were breached by his successors. Financially, the system was an enormous success and, between 1831 and 1877, Java contributed nearly one-fifth of the total Dutch budget annually. But the culture system came to be denounced as scandalous exploitation by Dutch reformers. It was abolished in 1877 and, with other changes, Indonesia ceased to subsidise the Dutch economy after 1877.

THE EUROPEAN EMPIRES AT THE BEGINNING OF THE EXPANSION PERIOD, *c.*1870

(Based on *Whitaker's Almanac*, 1870–3, and Colonial Office Lists. Some population figures are estimates. Where relevant, the racial mix is indicated.)

The British Empire

	Area (in square miles)	Population
Europe		
United Kingdom[a]	121,377	31,845,379
Malta	115	(1869) 143,003[b]
Gibraltar	2	22,100[c]
Heligoland	1	*c.*2300
British India	1,983,902	148,457,654[d]
Other possessions in the East		
Aden	N/A	N/A
Ceylon	24,700	(1868) 2,128,884
Hong Kong	32	(1865) 125,504
Labuan	45	(1865) 3828
Mauritius[e]	708	(1868) 332,805[f]
Straits Settlements[g]		
Singapore	275	(1871) 97,131
Penang (Prince of Wales Island)	126	(1871) 133,064
Malacca	1000	(1871) 77,756[h]
Canada[i]		
'Canada proper' (Ontario and Quebec)	331,280	(1869) 3,318,407
New Brunswick	27,030	(1871) 311,692
Nova Scotia (inc. Cape Breton)	16,670	(1871) 375,511
Other possessions in America (exc. West Indies)		
Prince Edward Island	2173	94,021
Newfoundland	40,200	(1869) 146,536
British Guiana	76,000	(1871) 193,491
British Honduras	13,500	(1861) 25,635
West Indies		
Antigua	183	(1863) 36,412
Bahamas[j]	3021	(1861) 35,287
Barbados	166	(1861) 152,127
Bermuda[k]	N/A	(1863) 11,796
Dominica	290	25,065
Grenada	133	(1866) 36,672
Jamaica	6400	441,255
Montserrat	47	(1861) 7645
St Christopher (St Kitts) and	68	(1861) 24,440
Anguilla	35	2500[l]

The British Empire (cont'd)

	Area (in square miles)	Population	
Nevis	50	(1861)	9822
St Lucia	250	(1866)	29,519
St Vincent	131	(1861)	31,755
Tobago	97	(1861)	15,410
Trinidad	1754	(1861)	84,438
Virgin Islands (British)	57	(1861)	6051
Turks & Caicos[m]	450	(1861)	4372
Australasia			
New South Wales	323,437	(1867)	447,620
Queensland	678,600	(1869)	107,427
Tasmania	26,215	(1871)	101,785
Victoria	86,831		703,817
Western Australia	974,000	(1866)	21,065
New Zealand	99,000	(1867)	$c.258,540$[n]
British possessions in Africa			
Cape Colony[o]	200,610	(1869)	566,158[p]
Natal	16,150	(1866)	193,103
West African settlements			
Sierra Leone	468	(1867)	41,497[q]
Gold Coast[r]	6000	(1868)	252,000[s]
Lagos	N/A	(1872)	61,021
Gambia	21	(1871)	14,190
British possessions in South Atlantic			
Ascension	35		N/A
Falkland Islands	7600	(1868)	686
St Helena	47	(1861)	6444

[a] With Channel Islands and Isle of Man.

[b] Maltese, 140,124; British residents, 1640; foreign, 1239; plus 7092 British troops and families.

[c] Inc. 6328 military.

[d] India was divided into Bengal Presidency, British Burmah, North-West Provinces, Punjab, Courg, Hyderabad and Mysore, Oudh, Central Provinces, Madras Presidency, Bombay Presidency and Sind, all under British administration. British Burma had an area of 98,881 square miles and a population of 2,500,000. In addition, there were the 'Native States under British protection' with an area $c.690,697$ square miles and a population of 47,909,190.

[e] Inc. Seychelles.

[f] Inc. 209,298 Indian coolies imported to work on sugar estates.

[g] Administration transferred from government of India to Colonial Office in 1867.

[h] Colonial Office List notes that the Chinese made up about one quarter of the population of the settlements and one sixth of that of Malacca, the majority population being Malays.

[i] Consisted of Ontario (Upper Canada), Quebec (Lower Canada), Nova Scotia and New Brunswick. Plus Hudson Bay Territory (transferred to Canada, 1869), Manitoba – formerly Rupert's Land – and North West Territory.

[j] $c.3000$ islands, about 20 inhabited.

[k] $c.300$ islands, about 15 inhabited.

[l] Inc. 100 whites.
[m] Separated from the Bahamas in 1848.
[n] White, 220, 092; Maori, *c*.38,450.
[o] Inc. British Kaffraria, annexed 1866.
[p] 'Hottentot', 81,598; 'Kaffir', 164,446; European, 187, 439; other races, 132,655.
[q] Inc. 129 whites.
[r] Defined by Convention with Dutch in 1868.
[s] Estimated.

The French empire

	Area (in square miles)	Population
Algeria	259,313	(1866) 2,926,026[a]
Africa and islands		
Senegal and its dependencies		
Réunion (Île de Bourbon)		
and St Marie (Indian Ocean)		
Mayotte and its dependencies		
Portions of Madagascar		
Portions of coast of Guinea		
Total	95,700	473,500
Americas (inc. West Indies)		
Martinique		
Guadeloupe		
French Guiana, Cayenne		
St Pierre and Miquelon		
Total	80,000	302,000
India		
Pondicherry and other towns	10,800	259,000
Pacific		
Marquesas and Tahiti		
New Caledonia		
Total	9560	84,000
Cochin-China	N/A	1,204,287

[a] 218,000 Europeans of diverse nationalities; 2,439,744 Arabs; 263,602 'Natives', i.e. Berbers.

The Spanish empire

	Area (in square miles)	Population
Cuba	48,489	1,400,0000[a]
Puerto Rico	3969	620,000[b]
Philippine Islands[c]	52,647	2,700,000

[a] Including 365,000 whites; 230,000 'free blacks'; 368,550 slaves.
[b] 325,000 whites; 250,000 'free blacks'; rest slaves.
[c] About 400 islands.

The Portuguese empire

	Area (in square miles)	Population
Azores	1134	252,894
Madeira	336	115,804
Miscellaneous possessions in Africa and Asia (inc. India)	526,041	3,687,228

The Dutch empire

	Area (in square miles)	Population
East Indies (inc. Java and Madura)	N/A	N/A
West Indies (Curacao etc.)	N/A	N/A
Total	683,776	20,094,957

The Danish empire

	Area (in square miles)	Population
West Indies (St Thomas etc.)	N/A	c.13,000[a]

[a] Inc. c.10,000 'coloured'.

4 THE NEW IMPERIALISM

A revival of interest in empire and renewed competition for colonies (usually described as the 'new imperialism') occurred in the late nineteenth and early twentieth centuries. It coincided with a change in the European state system, consequent upon the unification of Germany and Italy, and an intensification of industrialisation in Europe and the United States.

A variety of explanations have been put forward for the new imperialism: economic, political and psychological. Marxist historians, following V.I. Lenin's *Imperialism: The Highest Stage of Capitalism* (1917), believed it to be an economic phenomenon and identified it with the last stage of capitalism, monopoly capitalism, which would lead to the revolution of the proletariat. Many other historians, without subscribing to Marxist views, also believed it to be economic in origin, arising from the intense competition between industrialised nations for markets and raw materials. In a reaction to Marxist interpretations, some historians after the Second World War emphasised political explanations, the strategic and diplomatic struggles of the European great powers in the generation before the First World War.

The psychological climate of the time was also important. Whereas in the past, Europeans had been interested in, even awed by, other civilisations, notably those of Asia, few now doubted the superiority of European civilisation and of the European races. The conquest of the rest of the world by Europe seemed to be the natural working out of evolutionary forces, hopefully benevolent, but in any case inevitable. The political left, as well as the political right, was seduced by the vision and few critics of empire made their voices heard.

The most spectacular manifestation of the new imperialism in action was the 'Scramble for Africa', the partition of the whole continent of Africa between a handful of European powers.

THE SCRAMBLE FOR AFRICA

In 1870 only approximately one tenth of the continent was under European political control. In 1914 only Abyssinia (Ethiopia) and Liberia (founded by American enterprise as a home for freed slaves in 1822 and recognised as a sovereign state in 1847) were independent countries.

European colonies in 1870

Portugal

The Portuguese colonies were generally moribund, but Portugal had large territorial claims dating from the sixteenth century and still exercised varying degrees of authority in:

Angola
Mozambique
Portuguese Guinea
The islands of Principe and São Tomé
Cape Verde Islands

Spain

Spain too had only remnants of an ancient empire:

Ceuta (Morocco)
Melilla (Morocco)
Rio de Oro
Spanish Guinea

Britain

Britain had established colonies of settlement in the extreme south of the continent earlier in the nineteenth century and had trading bases with some degree of political organisation scattered along the western coasts, some dating from the seventeenth century:

The Gambia
Sierra Leone
Gold Coast (Cape Coast Castle and other stations)
Lagos
Cape Colony
Natal
Basutoland (Protectorate)
The 'Boer Republics' of the Transvaal and the Orange Free State were
   autonomous in their internal affairs but had acknowledged Britain's
   suzerainty by the Sand River Convention (1852) and the Bloemfontein
   Convention (1854) respectively.

France

Algeria
Senegal
Libreville (Gabon)
Trading posts on the west coast:
Grand Bassam (Ivory Coast)
Cotonou (Dahomey)
Porto Novo (Dahomey)

Defunct European colonies in Africa

Denmark

Christiansborg (Gold Coast) c.1660–1850, when it was acquired by Britain.

Prussia

Fredericksburg (Gold Coast) (1682–1720). Acquired as a result of the personal enthusiasm of the Great Elector but relinquished thereafter.

Netherlands

The Dutch had held posts on the Gold Coast, including El Mina (taken from the Portuguese in 1637) and Fredericksburg (1720), which they sold to Britain in 1871. They also held the coast of Angola (1641–8).

The Dutch had trading interests, e.g. on the Congo, but did not participate in the territorial scramble for Africa, being content with their prosperous empire in Indonesia.

Ottoman empire

Turkey still claimed suzerainty over Egypt and the Sudan, Tripoli, Tunis and (theoretically) Algeria.

THE EXPLORATION OF AFRICA, 1769–1884

Like the earlier phase of European expansion, the partition of Africa in the nineteenth century was preceded by an Age of Exploration. It was motivated by different triggers at different times: scientific curiosity, a desire to suppress the slave trade (both Atlantic and Arab) at its source, missionary activity and, finally, a search for an African El Dorado or, at least, commercial advantage.

1769–72	James Bruce travelled in Abyssinia, searching for the source of the Nile. Established the source of the Blue Nile. Subsequently published *Travels to Discover the Source of the Nile* (5 vols, 1790).
1788	Foundation of the African Association, a dining club presided over by Sir Joseph Banks, the President of the Royal Society. Aimed to further the scientific exploration of Africa and, especially, to discover the course of the Niger.
1795–7, 1805–6	Mungo Park's two expeditions to trace the course of the Niger met with partial success. Park was killed near Bussa in 1806. Published *Travels in the Interior Districts of Africa* (1799).
1821–5	Captain W.F. Owen surveyed the coasts of Africa.
1822	A.G. Laing established the source of the Niger.
1822–7	Hugh Clapperton and others crossed the Sahara, discovered Lake Chad and visited Kano and Sokoto.
1827	René Caillié reached Timbuktu and then crossed the Sahara to Fez. His journal was published in English as *Travels through Central Africa to Timbuctoo* (2 vols, 1830).

1830–4	After Clapperton's death, his assistant, Richard Lander, was asked by Lord Bathurst, the Colonial Secretary, to continue Clapperton's work. A desire to suppress the slave trade was now a factor. Lander sailed down the Niger from Bussa to the delta. Lander, who had previously published accounts of Clapperton's travels, published *Journal of an Expedition to Explore the Course and Termination of the Niger* (3 vols, 1832).
1848–9	Two German missionaries in the service of the English Church Missionary Society, Johann Rebmann and Johann Krapf, sighted Mounts Kilimanjaro and Kenya respectively.
1849–55	Heinrich Barth crossed the Sahara and travelled extensively in the western Sudan. His account was published in English as *Travels and Discoveries in North and Central Africa* (3 vols, 1857–8).
1849–56, 1858–64	Public interest now switched from West to East Africa with David Livingstone's travels (nominally missionary journeys but far more important as explorations). After working for eight years in Bechuanaland, he explored the Zambesi so thoroughly that it became known in England as 'Livingstone's river'. His second journey took him up the Shire River to Lake Nyasa. Livingstone's writings, *Missionary Travels in South Africa* (1857) and *Narrative of an Expedition to the Zambesi and Its Tributaries* (1865), sold widely.
1857–63	The focus of attention was now the source of the (White) Nile. Richard Burton and John Hanning Speke set off from Zanzibar and reached Lake Tanganyika. Speke discovered Lake Victoria, which, he rightly guessed, formed the source of the Nile. Speke explored further with J.A. Grant.
1861	Samuel Baker and his wife sailed up the Nile from Khartoum and met Speke and Grant. Discovered Lake Albert.
1863	Famous confrontation planned between Burton and Speke (who were in dispute about the sources of the Nile) at the British Association meeting in Bath. Speke fatally injured in shooting accident on the morning of the debate. African exploration now a matter of great public interest.
1866–73	Livingstone explored extensively in East Africa, trying to unravel the mystery of the source of the Congo (which he knew as the Lualaba, reaching it in 1871) as well as the Nile. He met Henry Morton Stanley at Ujiji on Lake Tanganyika later in 1871 and died at Tabora in 1873.
1873–4	A naval officer, Commander Verney Lovett Cameron, was commissioned by the Royal Geographical Society to aid Livingstone. Although he found that Livingstone had died, he went on to cross Africa from east to west, emerging at

Benguela in Angola. His reports of mineral wealth in Katanga attracted attention but he had been unable to trace the whole course of the Congo.

1874–6 Stanley, with heavy newspaper backing from the *New York Herald* and the *Daily Telegraph*, set out to complete Livingstone's work. He explored Lakes Victoria and Tanganyika and made contact with Uganda.

1876–7 Unwisely setting out from Zanzibar in the company of Tipu Tip, the most notorious slave trader in East Africa, and so arousing the hostility of all those through whose territory he passed, Stanley nevertheless managed to follow the Congo to its mouth.

1879–84 Stanley was employed by Leopold of the Belgians to establish his state in the Congo and explored further.

1884 Karl Peters explored East Africa and concluded 'protectorate' treaties with chiefs in the Kilimanjaro area. He returned to Germany to organise propaganda in favour of colonisation and wrote numerous books, including *New Light on Dark Africa* (1891) and *The Eldorado of the Ancients* (1902).

1888–9 Enim Pasha relief expedition. Stanley was commissioned to rescue Enim Pasha, the Governor of the southern Sudan, who had been cut off by the Mahdi's forces. Stanley chose to go in via the Congo. Although he retrieved Enim, the expedition was a disaster.

Stanley's writings were enormously popular, running through many editions and translated into many languages, but they represented the Victorian image of Africa at its worst, portraying the Africans as savages or, at best, as children who needed guidance. They included *Through the Dark Continent* (2 vols, 1878) and *In Darkest Africa, or the Quest, Rescue and Retreat of Emin, Governor of Equatoria* (2 vols, 1890).

THE COURSE OF THE SCRAMBLE FOR AFRICA

The British empire in Africa

Egypt and the Sudan

1869 Opening of the Suez Canal. This altered the strategic geography of the African continent. Although the land route across Egypt had been used, particularly since the building of the railways from the 1850s, the main British route to India and Australasia had remained that round the Cape. Britain now feared that a rival European power might seize control of the Canal.

1875	Benjamin Disraeli's government bought the Khedive's shares in the Suez Canal Company.
Late 1870s	Discontent grew in Egypt. Unwise attempts to modernise the country too quickly had led to vast debts to European financiers resulting in heavy taxation and a failure to pay the army. Some Egyptians wanted to throw off Turkish suzerainty and some to establish modern constitutional government.
1878	Congress of Berlin. Met to avert the threat of a general European war, arising from the 'Eastern Question', i.e. the decline of the Ottoman empire and the question of what was to take its place. Most powers were disquieted by Russian gains under the Treaty of San Stefano at the end of the Russo-Turkish war of 1877–8.
	By a secret agreement, the Cyprus Convention, Britain agreed to withdraw her objections to France taking control of Tunis in return for French acquiescence in Britain leasing the island of Cyprus from the Sultan of Turkey. (Cyprus was intended to provide a forward base from which to protect the northern end of the Suez Canal.)
	Britain and France established the 'Dual Control' over Egyptian finances, primarily to protect the interests of the European bondholders. France had taken the initiative.
1879	(February) Egyptian army mutinied, possibly at the instigation of the Khedive Ismail to get rid of the 'European ministry', which had been imposed upon him.
	(June) Sultan deposed Ismail in favour of weaker man, Tewfik, possibly at the request of the German Chancellor, Bismarck.
1881	After the French took possession of Tunis by the Treaty of Bardo, the Egyptians suspected every Anglo-French move as a prelude to occupation. The Sultan, angered by the French action, was unwilling to co-operate in Egypt. There were two more army mutinies (in February and September) and growing disorder in which Europeans felt threatened. Colonel Arabi Pasha became the most prominent army, and therefore nationalist, leader.
1881–3	A religious leader Muhammad Ahmad ibn Abdullah (the Mahdi) led a successful revolt against Egyptian rule in the Sudan.
1882	(11 June) Alexandria massacre. About 50 Europeans were killed in a riot.
	(11 July) Bombardment of Alexandria. A British fleet bombarded the fortifications of Alexandria. The town suffered 'collateral damage'.
	The expected joint Anglo-French intervention became impossible when the French Chamber (fearing to be duped into

overseas adventures by Bismarck) refused the necessary Vote of Credit. Gladstone's government reluctantly resolved to intervene alone. The bondholders were influential in both Britain and France but British intervention was probably prompted more by fears for the Suez Canal. (Over 80 per cent of the trade passing through the Canal was British.)

(August) A British force, under Sir Garnet Wolseley, invaded Egypt, nominally to support Tewfik against his rebellious army. The campaign was a textbook success.

(13 September) The Egyptian army surrendered at the battle of Tel-el-Kebir.

The British intended to leave Egypt as soon as a satisfactory government was in power but found they had created a political vacuum. They dared not leave in case another European great power took their place, but were handicapped by having no status recognised by international law to be in Egypt.

1882–3	Lord Dufferin, the British ambassador in Constantinople, visited Egypt and recommended a new constitution to include a Legislative Council and a General Assembly. Inaugurated what Alfred Milner called the 'Veiled Protectorate'.
1883	(September) Evelyn Baring (Lord Cromer) arrived in Egypt. In practice, although not in name, the British Governor. (November) An Egptian force, led by a British officer, General William Hicks, was defeated by the Mahdists.
1884	The British government appointed General Charles Gordon to carry out an evacuation of the Sudan.
1885	(January) Gordon was killed in Khartoum. Gordon was a national hero and his death caused a political crisis in England. (March) Convention of London. The troubles in the Sudan had further crippled Egyptian finances. The European powers agreed to a new loan in return for the permanent continuation of the *Caisse de la Dette*. Britain continued to administer Egypt but with international control of the finances. A later British Foreign Secretary, Sir Edward Grey, described Egypt as 'a noose round Britain's neck', which other powers could tighten at will.
1887	Britain made a serious attempt to withdraw by the Drummond Wolfe negotiations but failed to reach final agreement with the Sultan.
1889–90	Joseph Chamberlain visited Egypt and, by his own account, was converted to imperialism by the immense improvements Cromer had made in the economy and government of Egypt.
1895–6	There had always been some fears in London that a hostile power controlling the Sudan could obstruct the Nile waters

sufficiently to cause a crisis in Egypt. The Sudan moved centre-stage when Italy tried, unsuccessfully, to conquer Abyssinia and the French began to dream of a route from French West Africa to their base at Djibouti.

(September 1895) An Egyptian force, under the Sirdar, Sir Herbert Kitchener, recovered the province of Dongola.

1897–8	Britain resolved on the reconquest of the Sudan.
1898	(September) Kitchener defeated the Khalifa (the Mahdi's successor) at the battle of Omdurman (near Khartoum). He then discovered a small French force, under Captain Marchand, at Fashoda (Kodok). The Fashoda incident, as it became known, brought Britain and France close to war but it was eventually resolved by diplomacy.
1899	(January) Claiming the Sudan 'by right of conquest', an Anglo-Egyptian condominium was proclaimed over the country. (March) Britain and France signed an agreement which left the Sudan within the British sphere of influence.
1904	Anglo-French *entente*, in reality a series of colonial bargains. The French agreed to cease to demand Britain's withdrawal from Egypt and to agree to the 'conversion' of the Egyptian debt (urgently needed for the stability of Egyptian finances); in return the British promised not to obstruct the French assumption of the dominant position in Morocco, so long as the formal independence of that country was respected.

West Africa

Background

1865	Atlantic slave trade finally came to an end. (For the history of the slave trade, *see* Appendix A.) Report of House of Commons Select Committee recommended that Britain should do nothing to extend her commitments in West Africa and, ideally, should relinquish all her possessions there except, possibly, the harbour of Freetown in Sierra Leone.
1884–5	Berlin West Africa Conference, culminating in the Berlin Act. This regulated European claims. Although strictly only applying to the coasts of West Africa, it was soon applied to the whole continent. It stressed 'effective occupation' as a criterion and consequently powers rushed to establish administrations where previously they had only claimed general influence.

Gold Coast

Britain had old-established trading relations with the Fanti people on the coast but the strongest power in the region was the Ashanti Confederation, which owed its rise in part to its participation in the slave trade.

1823	War between British and the Ashanti, in the course of which the British Governor of Sierra Leone, Sir Charles McCarthy, was killed.
1844	Britain signed treaties with some Fanti chiefs, promising them protection.
1863	Britain became involved in fighting when Ashanti invaded Fanti territory.
1873–4	Ashanti objected to transfer of Dutch interests to British. In the resulting war, Sir Garnet Wolseley fought a textbook campaign which attracted much publicity.
1874	Britain formally constituted the coastal strip as the Gold Coast colony.
1888	First two Africans nominated to Legislative Council (which had existed in informal fashion from the 1850s).
1895–6	War with Ashanti. Lands of the Ashanti Confederation constituted as British protectorate.
1897	'Aborigines Protection Society' established by a group of chiefs, who wished to protect their rights.
1898	Britain extended her sphere to the Northern Territories in course of bargaining with France.
1900–1	War with Ashanti (War of the Golden Stool). Britain established her jurisdiction over what is now (with the addition of part of Togoland mandated in 1919) Ghana.
1914–18	The Gold Coast was a Crown colony, ruled by a Governor, an Executive Council (entirely official) and a Legislative Council, which included nine 'unofficial' members, i.e. three Europeans, three paramount chiefs and three representatives of (western) educated Africans. Its constitution was relatively advanced for the time.

Nigeria

Britain had long-established trading links with the Niger. It was the scene, in the 1840s, of the so-called 'Niger Experiment' when a group of philanthropists (many, but not all, Quakers) tried to replace the now illegal slave trade with legitimate commerce. It failed when most of the pioneers succumbed to malaria, but a thriving trade in palm oil developed.

It was a particularly difficult problem both in the colonial period and after independence because what became 'Nigeria' included very diverse regions and peoples. The main divisions were between the Yoruba peoples in the west, who had long-established trading relations with the Europeans, the Ibo people in the east, who, for geographical reasons, tended to live in isolated villages and have little contact outside them, and the Fulani or Hausa people in the north, who were Muslims and had well-developed political, legal and educational systems.

1849	John Beecroft appointed British Consul for 'the Bights of Benin and Biafra'. Gained a remarkable, although entirely informal, influence in the region.
1861	Britain annexed Lagos in last stages of struggle to end the slave trade on the coast.
1879	George Taubman Goldie persuaded a number of small British companies on the Niger to join together in the United African Company (later the National African Company) and waged a vigorous war with increasing French (and later German) competition.
1884	The British consul at Fernando Po, Edward Hewett, was authorised to sign treaties with Niger chiefs, which virtually placed them under British protection. (These replaced treaties of dubious legality concluded by Company's representatives.)
1885	Following the Berlin West Africa Conference and the German seizure of the Cameroons, Britain proclaimed a protectorate over the 'Oil Rivers', i.e. the Niger delta, and reached agreement on boundaries with Germany.
1886	The National African Company received a charter as the Royal Niger Company and effectively took over the administration of the area.
1887–*c.*1890	Serious quarrels with French and German traders about navigation rights on the River Niger.
1890s	Dangerous race between Captain Lugard, representing the Royal Niger Company, and Captain Decoeur, representing rival French interests, to secure treaties with chiefs on the Upper Niger.
1898	Britain and France concluded a treaty delimiting boundaries in West Africa.
1899	Royal Niger Company surrendered its administrative rights to the British government but remained in being as a trading company. (Unlike the other British chartered companies in Africa, it was able to pay its shareholders reasonable dividends.)
1900	Britain established the protectorates of Northern and Southern Nigeria. Lugard became the British High Commissioner for Northern Nigeria and famously pursued a policy of 'indirect rule', i.e. of co-operation between the British authorities and the existing 'native' authorities.
1904	The *entente cordiale.* A treaty between Britain and France modified some of the boundary lines.
1912	Lugard became Governor of both Northern and Southern Nigeria. 'Indirect rule' worked less well in the South, where there were less well-defined chains of command.

| 1914 | Northern and Southern Nigeria, including the Colony (the old Oil Rivers Protectorate), were joined with Lagos to form what became (with the addition of part of the Cameroons) the modern state of Nigeria. The 'Nigerian Council', consisting of 36 members (24 official, 6 'unofficial' Europeans and 6 'unofficial' Africans), was set up, but never flourished because the chiefs did not support it. |

Sierra Leone

1788	Captain John Taylor established a station for freed slaves at Freetown.
1807	The peninsula of Sierra Leone (about 250 square miles) was ceded to Britain and became the 'colony'. Freetown became an increasingly important harbour and the British Governor of Sierra Leone enjoyed some (not always well-defined) jurisdiction over all the British settlements in West Africa.
1863	The Governor was assisted by an Executive and (nominated) Legislative Council.
1896	In the course of the competition with France, Britain acquired the much larger 'protectorate' (about 28,000 square miles). Relations between the 'colony' and the 'protectorate' were never easy.

The Gambia

Although usually accounted the oldest British trading base in West Africa (dating from a charter of 1588), this became almost entirely hemmed in by French territory and was regarded as scarcely viable.

1816	The British established a garrison on the island of Banjul (Bathurst) to put down the slave trade. Trade extended up the River Gambia.
1861	A possible exchange of territory was discussed with France.
1865–6	(and on subsequent occasions up to 1904) An exchange was again discussed but always failed because of the objections of British merchants and missionaries and (apparently) a simple objection to ceding territory over which the British flag had once flown.

East Africa

Zanzibar

Zanzibar was the western end of an extremely important trade route across the Indian Ocean, connecting with Arabia and India. Until 1883 the British Consul there came under the jurisdiction of the British government in India. It attracted the attention of anti-slavery campaigners in the late nineteenth century. Having finally extinguished the Atlantic slave trade, they now wished to end the ancient Arab slave trade, which still flourished in East Africa.

1872	A Glasgow ship-owner, William Mackinnon, organised a regular mail service between Britain, India and Zanzibar.
1873	Sir John Kirk became Consul-General. British influence became predominant. The Sultan, Sultan Barghash, was persuaded to sign an anti-slavery treaty. A naval officer, Lloyd William Mathews, built up an efficient army for the Sultan. But British influence was challenged on the commercial level by German firms.
1877	Mackinnon put forward an ambitious scheme to administer large areas of the East African coast in the name of the Sultan, who claimed jurisdiction there. The scheme was deliberately sabotaged by the British government, who wanted no extension of responsibilities.
1884	The German explorer Karl Peters concluded treaties with chiefs on the East African mainland who rejected the Sultan of Zanzibar's claims to jurisdiction.
1884–5	Berlin West Africa Conference. Britain became anxious about her informal arrangements all over the African continent.
1886	Britain, Germany and France delimited their spheres of influence in East Africa. Zanzibar at this time remained independent.
1890	Germany recognised a British protectorate over the territories of the Sultan of Zanzibar in return for some small concessions in West Africa; the 'Caprivi strip', connecting German South-West Africa with the Zambesi River; and, most importantly, the island of Heligoland in the North Sea, which Britain had held since the Napoleonic wars, which would command the western exit of the new Kiel Canal.

Uganda

British interest in Uganda was partly strategic, partly commercial. It had only recently been revealed that the White Nile originated from Lake Victoria. After their occupation of Egypt in 1882, the British became very nervous about the control of the headwaters of the Nile, on which the prosperity, indeed life, of Egypt depended. Reports suggested that the area was well populated and potentially a good trading area. The British knew little of the political complexities of the four African kingdoms of Buganda, Bunyoro, Toro and Ankola, which were to make up the British Protectorate of Uganda. The area also attracted violent religious conflict as rival Muslim, Catholic and Protestant missionaries tried to convert the pagan Buganda and their ruler, the Kabaka.

1860s	Traders from the coast brought the Islamic faith with them.
1875	The explorer Henry Morton Stanley argued the rival claims of Christianity with the Kabaka (King) of Buganda, Mutesa.
1877	The Anglican Church Missionary Society sent missionaries.
1879	Cardinal Lavigerie sent the Roman Catholic White Fathers.
1884	The Kabaka Mutesa I, died and his successor, Mwanga, was unsympathetic to the new religions.
1885–6	Violence was offered to the missionaries and their converts. The Anglican bishop James Hannington was killed, as were 30 of Mwanga's pages who refused to recant. Although such violence was extremely rare in nineteenth-century Africa, it made a deep impression in Europe.
1886	The Anglo-German agreement left Uganda within the British sphere.
1888	Imperial British East Africa Company (associated with William Mackinnon) chartered and entrusted with administration of the region. Always undercapitalised.
1892	Serious possibility that Britain would abandon the area. Missionary societies, among others, organised to prevent this. Instead the British government agreed to underwrite the building of a railway line from Mombasa to Lake Victoria which, it was hoped, would bring prosperity to the area and finally drive out the slave trade.
1894	Formal protectorate proclaimed over Uganda.
1895	The Imperial British East Africa Company surrendered its charter.
1900	Uganda Agreement. This gave the Buganda a privileged position and recognised the authority of the Kabaka (under British protection). African land rights were also guaranteed.
1901	Completion of the railway. The building of the railway had brought a significant Asian community into East Africa. Although the indentured labourers employed on the building of the railway had almost all returned home, the traders who came to supply them had not. Their presence was often resented by the Africans.
1902	The eastern province of Uganda was transferred to the East African Protectorate (Kenya). Although done for administrative reasons, it had the effect of placing in Kenya all the land thought suitable for European settlement. Uganda was left without a settler problem.
1905	Uganda was transferred from the jurisdiction of the Foreign Office to that of the Colonial Office.

Kenya

Kenya was initially less valued than Uganda. It seemed less important both strategically and commercially, and one of its peoples, the formidable nomadic Masai, alarmed Europeans. But by the 1880s it was being lauded as suitable for European settlement – the 'new Australia'.

1886	Anglo-German agreement left region in the British sphere.
1888	Imperial British East Africa Company entrusted with administration.
1890	As part of the 'Heligoland Agreement', Witu was transferred from the German to the British sphere.
1895	Imperial British East Africa Company, facing bankruptcy, surrendered its charter. (June) Protectorate (East African Protectorate) proclaimed over most of what was to become Kenya, including the coastal strip, which had previously been under the jurisdiction of the Sultan of Zanzibar.
1902	Eastern province of Uganda Protectorate transferred to East African Protectorate. Concentrated all the land thought suitable for European settlement in Kenya.
1900–14	Growth of European settler population. British settlement had been advocated by Frederick Lugard, Harry Johnston and others. Sir Charles Elliot (Commissioner, 1901–4) reported in favour after an inquiry. The British had doubted whether they had the right to grant lands in a protectorate but concluded (in 1899) that they had. Existing African land rights were supposed to be protected but the British believed the land to be sparsely populated. (They were unaware that the population had recently been reduced by a series of natural disasters, including smallpox and rinderpest, and failed to understand the land needs of nomadic peoples like the Masai.) The Land Department, created in 1901, allowed Europeans to buy 160 acres on advantageous terms and, when they had developed it, 480 acres more. In 1902 there were less than 12 Europeans cultivating land in Kenya but immigrants began to arrive from South Africa, Australia and Britain. Often men with capital. Established plantation-style farming, producing coffee, tea and cotton. The Kikuyu tribe, who were often unable to prove title to their lands, suffered most from the arrival of the Europeans. The white settlers had clear views on their political rights and expected ultimately to become a dominion. Lord Delamere was the most important settler leader.
1903	Colonists' Association formed to demand a voice in the government.

1906–7	The East African Protectorate was transferred from the jurisdiction of the Foreign Office to that of the Colonial Office and assimilated to the status of a Crown colony, with a Governor, Executive Council and Legislative Council. The Legislative Council included an 'unofficial', although not elected, element.
1911	The Convention of Associations (popularly nicknamed the 'Settlers' Parliament') represented a number of settler organisations, all demanding more political power.
1914	The Colonial Office admitted to having little idea of the population but estimated the total at about 4 million, including about 200 Europeans in Mombasa, 1,200 in Nairobi and about 400 farmers in the vicinity of Nairobi.

South Central Africa

This rather clumsy term is conventionally used to denote what in colonial times became Northern and Southern Rhodesia and Nyasaland.

Nyasaland

1859–63	David Livingstone explored the region and brought it to European attention.
	Missionaries, particularly Scottish Presbyterians, subsequently entered the country and established schools, which proved exceptionally successful. Young men from Nyasaland spread all over southern Africa as clerks.
1881	Appointment of a British Consul.
1889	Sir Harry Johnston reported on Arab slave raiding.
1891	British protectorate proclaimed. (Known from 1893 to 1907 as the British Central Africa Protectorate.)
	Treaty defining boundaries signed with Portugal.
1904	Transferred from Foreign Office to Colonial Office control.
1907	Government of Governor and nominated Executive and Legislative Councils established. Although there were small European and Asian communities there, the overwhelming majority of the population was African.
	(Estimated just before 1914 as 733 Europeans and 463 Asians out of a population of about one million.)

Rhodesia

(Originally known as Charterland and subsequently divided into Northern and Southern Rhodesia.)

This was to a quite exceptional extent the creation of one man, Cecil John Rhodes, already established as a South African politician and a millionaire on the basis of his interests in the Kimberley diamond fields and the Witwatersrand gold mines. Rhodes wished to see all Africa south of the Zambezi under British control. It was originally supposed that Southern Rhodesia would prove to be rich in gold, partly on the basis of ancient workings. When the gold proved illusory, settlers were encouraged to establish large-scale farming. Originally fewer hopes were entertained for Northern Rhodesia, and the great copper deposits there were not discovered until the 1920s.

When Europeans first penetrated into the area, the majority population in what became Southern Rhodesia were the Mashona but the dominant group were the Matabele (Ndebele), an offshoot of the Zulu peoples, originally led by Mzilikazi, but now ruled by Lobengula. There had been some missionary activity there, the Scotsman John Moffat being the most influential. The Portuguese and the Boers, as well as the British, were interested in the area.

1887	Two Boers, the Grobler brothers, claimed to have obtained a treaty from Lobengula giving them considerable rights. There were no independent witnesses and Lobengula subsequently repudiated it. The incident alarmed the British and they persuaded Lobengula to agree not to alienate his territories without the agreement of the British High Commissioner in South Africa.
1888	Rudd Concession. C.D. Rudd, acting on Cecil Rhodes' behalf, persuaded Lobengula to grant the concessionaires exclusive mineral rights in his country in return for money and weapons. The agreement conferred no political rights apart from an ill-defined right to defend and administer the mining concession. Lobengula, uninterested in the minerals and believing that this group had no territorial ambitions, signed in the hope of freeing himself from other quarrelling claimants.
1889	Rhodes bought out other groups such as the Bechuanaland Exploration Company and obtained a charter from the British government for his own South Africa Company. The government was suspicious of Rhodes but agreed because they felt it imperative to forestall the Germans, Portuguese and Boers in the area. (The Colonial Office concluded in 1892 that Rhodes had deceived them but retreat was now politically impossible.)
1890	Rhodes sent his 'Pioneers', led by Frank Johnson, into Mashonaland, avoiding Matabele territory. They established a base at Fort Salisbury and took possession of the territory in the name of the Queen. At first shares in the Company boomed, but it then became apparent that no gold had been found.
1891	Agreements were reached with Portugal and Germany on boundaries and the charter was extended over what became Northern Rhodesia.

1893	The Pioneers advanced into Matabele territory on the excuse of further Matabele raids on the Mashona. War ensued with the Matabele. Lobengula fled, repudiating the agreement with Rudd.
1895	Jameson Raid (*see* p. 112).
1896–7	To British surprise the Mashona also rose and were difficult to put down. Rhodes met the African leaders in the Matoppo Hills to reach a final settlement.
1891–1911	The European population in Southern Rhodesia rose rapidly from about 1500 (1891) to 23,000 (1911). They had grievances against Company rule and began to demand regular political institutions.
1898	A Legislative Council was established in Southern Rhodesia.
1907	The Legislative Council was remodelled with five nominated members and four elected. The franchise had no colour bar but was based on a property qualification which excluded poor whites and practically all Africans.
1922–4	Company rule survived the First World War in both Northern and Southern Rhodesia. In 1924 Northern Rhodesia became a protectorate with a Crown colony type of government. The situation in Southern Rhodesia was more complicated. A referendum in 1922 rejected the possibility of joining South Africa and in 1923 Southern Rhodesia became a 'self-governing colony', with responsible government in internal matters. In practice it was treated like a dominion.

High Commission Territories (South Africa)

Basutoland (see above pp. 64–5)

Bechuanaland

The so-called 'Missionaries' Road' passed through Bechuanaland but, as a trading route, it was much older than the missionaries. It was an obvious route to the north from Cape Colony and was even dubbed its 'Suez Canal' by Cecil Rhodes. Its value seemed to be enhanced by some sporadic gold discoveries.

1882	Boers from the Transvaal established small republics, Stellaland and Goschen, on land granted them by Bechuanaland chiefs.
1884	The Germans established themselves in Demaraland and Namaqualand (South-West Africa) and were believed to have ambitions in Bechuanaland.
1885	Britain annexed Bechuanaland south of the Malopo River as a colony and proclaimed a protectorate over the much larger area to the north of the river.
1891	An Order in Council placed the area under the jurisdiction of the British High Commissioner in South Africa.

Swaziland

Swaziland was and remained an African kingdom, but in the 1890s it became a joint protectorate of Britain and the Boer Republic (the Transvaal).

1894	Protectorate transferred to the Boer Republic.
1899	Outbreak of the Boer war ended this arrangement.
1906	Transferred to jurisdiction of British High Commissioner in South Africa.
1909	The Union of South Africa Act envisaged the ultimate incorporation of all the High Commission Territories in the Union, but this was never carried out.

Summary of political state of British colonies in 'Black' Africa in 1914

A sharp distinction existed between those colonies with a significant settler element (Kenya and Southern Rhodesia) and the rest. The position of Southern Rhodesia was unique in that it was still administered by a chartered company, the South Africa Company. White settlers in both Kenya and Southern Rhodesia expected progress to dominion status on the Canadian or Australian model. It was not until after the First World War that the British government made it clear that it had obligations to the majority non-white populations which might conflict with those ambitions.

Some colonies, e.g. Uganda and East Africa (Kenya), were originally protectorates and so came under the jurisdiction of the Foreign, not the Colonial, Office. But the norm, to which most territories were eventually assimilated, was 'Crown colony' government, i.e. a Governor, assisted by an Executive Council, made up of officials, and a Legislative Council, where nominated or elected members (the 'unofficials') might be added to the official membership. 'Unofficials' could and did include Africans or (in East Africa) Asians but they were few in number. Nevertheless, this provided a growth point for the establishment of representative governments later in the twentieth century.

The French empire in Africa

In 1783 France had recovered her stations on the west coast of Africa which had been lost to Britain during the Seven Years War. She had become involved in Algeria in 1830 (*see* p. 72).

North Africa

Algeria

1871	Establishment of Third French Republic. This reversed Napoleon III's policy of creating an 'Arab kingdom' in Algeria and opened the territory to French settlement, including refugees from Alsace and Lorraine. A civil Government-General was established. The Arab insurrections in Algiers and Constantine were suppressed.

1876, 1879, 1881–4	Further Arab uprisings but European settlement continued.
1887	Naturalisation Act. This extended French citizenship to all European residents.
1895	*Senatus consultus.* This allowed non-Europeans to apply for French citizenship and so escape the inferior *indigenat* (native) status. They then gained civil rights and became subject to French, instead of Islamic, law. Few applied, because they saw it as renouncing their religion.
1905	*Les Jeunes Algériens* founded among young Algerians who had received a French-style education and were looking for secular reforms, which would give them a greater say in government. But they were often at odds with other protest groups, who were intent on re-asserting their Islamic heritage.
1914	Algeria was regarded as an integral part of France, divided into three *départements*, Algiers, Oran and Constantine, under a Governor-General, assisted by a Consultative Council.

Tunis

1830s–1840s	France had developed financial interests in the area and assisted the Bey (ruler) of Tunis largely to escape from the control of the Ottoman empire, the nominally suzerain power. But Britain had successfully discouraged the French from expanding their control from Algeria to Tunis.
1878	Congress of Berlin. Britain and France concluded a secret deal by which Britain would withdraw her opposition to the French moving into Tunis if France would agree to Britain leasing Cyprus from the Sultan. The French did not take advantage of the arrangement until Italian involvement in Tunis made them fear for their predominant position there.
1881	Treaty of Bardo (Kasser-Said). The Bey was coerced into accepting a French protectorate. The Bey remained in office but was 'assisted' by a French Resident-General and Tunis was increasingly governed as if it had been a French colony. There was some French immigration, although not on the scale of Algeria. The Sultan was deeply offended by the French seizure of Tunis and this influenced his refusal to co-operate with Britain and France in Egypt.
1906	'Young Tunisians' formed. This was inspired by the Young Turk movement and generally advocated secular reforms, but it did maintain links with pan-Islamic groups.

Morocco

1844	French naval bombardment of Tangiers as a reprisal for Moroccan aid to Abd-el-Kader. This angered the British, who

saw Tangiers as the supply base of Gibraltar, and an international crisis resulted. France was effectively warned off, and British, rather then French, influence predominated during most of the nineteenth century. However, Morocco began to look more and more like the 'missing piece' of France's African empire.

1904   Anglo-French Entente. Britain withdrew her opposition to an increase of French influence in Morocco (*see below* p. 123).

West Africa

After Faidherbe finally left Senegal in 1865, his ambitious plans went into abeyance. They were to be revived in the late 1870s and received support from a number of leading French politicians, notably Admiral Jauréguiberry, a former Governor of Senegal, who became Minister of Marine in 1879, and Charles de Freycinet (Prime Minister in 1882). Freycinet had been a railway engineer and was attracted by the idea of a railway to link Senegal, Algeria and the Upper Niger. The conquest of the French Soudan, roughly the savanna belt from Senegal to Lake Chad, was the preserve of the French army, which often paid scant attention to directions from Paris. The whole area was acquired piecemeal, and only towards the end of the nineteenth century was any attempt made to rationalise the government of it.

1876   French forces began advance into region of Upper Senegal (Medine) and Upper Niger (and also into Mauritania). They encountered stiff resistance from the Muslim states of the region, led by Ahmadou and, mostly famously, by Samori (who fought the French, 1881–98).

1878   Treaty gave France rights over Cotonou.
Verdier named as 'Resident' in Ivory Coast.

1883   Bamako (Niger) fell.
Renewed old protectorate over Porto Novo, which had lapsed in 1868.

1886   Fixed boundary between Senegal and Portuguese Guinea.

1887–1904   Conquest of land between Niger and Lake Chad.

1889   Boundary with the Gambia (British) fixed.

1892   Conquest of Dahomey completed.
French Soudan organised under *commandant supérieur*.

1893   Occupation of Timbuktu. Battles with Toaregs of the Sahara began.
Governor appointed for the Ivory Coast.

1895   Senegal, French Guinea, French Soudan and Ivory Coast brought under jurisdiction of Governor-General in Dakar.

1898   Demarcation of Niger boundaries with Britain after races between Frederick Lugard and Captain Decoeur to obtain treaties with African chiefs had nearly led to war.

| 1904 | General administrative reorganisation of French West Africa, which then consisted of Senegal, Upper Senegal/Niger, Niger Military Territory, French Guinea, Ivory Coast and Dahomey, under the Governor-General in Dakar. |
| | Some further boundary adjustments on the Niger as a result of the Anglo-French *entente*. |

Equatorial Africa

1875–82	Exploration of Savorgnan de Brazza in the Congo Basin. Concluded a number of protectorate-type treaties with local chiefs. (Popularly known in France as 'Makoko' treaties.) At first the French government showed little interest.
1882	(November) After a considerable press campaign, fuelled by French resentment at British actions in Egypt, the government accepted the 'Makoko' treaties.
1884	France obtained promise of reversion of the Congo Free State to her if Leopold II relinquished it. Alarmed Britain and helped to precipitate her treaty with Portugal and its consequence, the Berlin West Africa Conference of 1884–5.
1885	France ceded some territory, including Kinshasa, to the Congo Free State.
1885–91	France made advances in Gabon, Middle Congo, Ubanghi-Shari and Chad.
1910	French Equatorial Africa, then consisting of Gabon, Middle Congo and Ubanghi-Shari, was constituted into an administrative unit, with a Governor-General in Brazzaville.
1913	Finally conquered Chad region.

East Africa

| 1862 | Formally annexed Obok and Djibuti on Somali Coast. |

Madagascar

Although lying off the coast of Africa, Madagascar had a very mixed population of Africans, Arabs and Asians, but it had achieved a good degree of unity under the Hova dynasty. Both France and Britain had old-established trading interests there, as well as some missionary interests.

1840s	French established limited protectorate in the north-west and treaty rights protecting their nationals.
1885	France gained control of Malagasy foreign relations and established a virtual protectorate over the island, although still working through the Hova dynasty. The French position was resented and caused unrest.
1890	Britain recognised the French protectorate.

1895	France despatched an expedition to Madagascar.
1896	Annexed the island.
1898	Conquest complete.

The German empire in Africa

The Prussian colonies founded by the Great Elector had long ago been lost and Germany had no colonies in Africa prior to unification in 1871, although German missionaries and traders had been active there and some of the most important explorers, such as Heinrich Barth, had been German.

German South-West Africa

| 1883 | The German government enquired whether Britain claimed jurisdiction there. The British government, suspecting that the Germans really wanted Britain to protect German missionaries and, punctiliously, consulting the Cape government, delayed a reply. |
| 1884 | (May) Germany declared a protectorate over Angra Pequena. The Cape government protested and, for a time, Anglo-German relations were strained. |

Cameroons (Kamerun)

| 1884 | The British, who already had some interests in the area (although they had previously turned down a request from the chiefs for a protectorate), facilitated the visit of the explorer Gustav Nachtigal, at the German government's request. They were correspondingly annoyed when Nachtigal proclaimed a German protectorate over the area in July. |

Togoland

| 1884 | Nachtigal also proclaimed a protectorate over this region, where Germany already had some missionary interests. |

German East Africa (Tanganyika)

1884	The German explorer Karl Peters concluded treaties with a number of chiefs in the general area of Kilimanjaro, already noted as an area for possible European settlement, although he had been warned by the German government before he set out that he had no authority to do so.
1885	(February) Immediately after the conclusion of the Berlin West Africa Conference, Bismarck accepted and acted upon Peters' treaties.
1886	A boundary was agreed between British and German spheres in East Africa.
1890	Some modifications were made to the boundaries.

The Italian empire in Africa

Italy, like Germany, only became fully united in 1871.

Abyssinia and the Horn of Africa

1870s	Individual Italians got commercial concessions.
1880	The Italian government obtained rights to Assab (Eritrea) from a trading company.
1881	Annoyed by French seizure of Tunis and looked for outlet elsewhere.
1889	Concluded ambiguous treaty with claimant to the Abyssinian throne in return for military assistance.
1891	British accepted reality of Italian protectorate over Abyssinia (mainly as a safeguard against the French). The French encouraged the Abyssinians to throw out the Italians.
1896	The Italians were defeated by the Abyssinians at the battle of Adowa (one of the very few African victories over a European army in the Scramble period) and were compelled to withdraw. They retained control of the colony of Eritrea and the protectorate of Somaliland, reaching agreements with Emperor Menelek of Abyssinia (1908) and the Sultan of Zanzibar.

Libya (Tripoli and Cyrenaica)

1912	Italy took these from the Ottoman empire in a war.

The Portuguese empire in Africa

The Portuguese had ancient claims to many parts of the African coast but they had allowed most of them to lapse. Only in Angola and Mozambique were there still centres of Portuguese administration, but even here Portuguese claims were largely dormant until the Scramble began. It seemed likely, even in the early twentieth century, that the Portuguese empire would collapse completely, and Britain and Germany began to make arrangements for such an eventuality (see pp. 122–4).

Angola

1884	The northern boundaries of Angola were obscure, although the Portuguese claimed rights over the mouth of the Congo. Britain had previously rejected such claims, partly because Portugal had a bad record in suppressing the slave trade, but, nervous about French ambitions, in February she signed a treaty recognising a number of Portuguese claims in return for an agreement about the free navigation of the Congo. Other powers disputed Britain and Portugal's right to decide

the navigation of the Congo bilaterally and the treaty led to the meeting of the Berlin West Africa Conference (November 1884–February 1885), which laid down the ground rules for the Scramble.

Mozambique

The boundaries of Mozambique were also uncertain and became pawns in international diplomacy.

1875	French arbitration awarded Delagoa Bay to Portugal, as against British claims. Although this thwarted some later plans of Cecil Rhodes, it also prevented the Boer Republics from gaining an independent outlet to the sea at Lourenço Marques.
1894	Completion of the Pretoria to Lourenço Marques railway, much desired by Boers.

The Belgian empire in Africa

This was the strangest case of all. Neither the Belgian parliament nor the Belgian people felt any enthusiasm for an African empire. It came into being entirely as the result of the ambitions of one man, King Leopold II.

The Congo

1876	King Leopold II hosted a conference of geographers and explorers in Brussels, which led to the setting up of the *Association Internationale Africaine* (AIA) for the suppression of the slave trade and the opening up of Central Africa.
1876–84	Leopold employed various agents, including Henry Morton Stanley, to 'open up' the Congo region, by building roads and concluding treaties with the chiefs.
1885	The United States was the first country to recognise the Congo Free State, which Leopold had created, as a sovereign state. Rumours were already circulating of malpractices in the region.
*c.*1890	In order to increase immediate profits, the Congolese were compelled to deliver large quotas of rubber to various concessionary companies in which Leopold had a controlling interest. Failure to do so led to executions and mutilations.
1906	The publication of E.D. Morel's *Red Rubber* and the investigations of Roger Casement meant that the scandal (the worst of the whole colonial era) could no longer be hidden.
1908	The Congo ceased to be a kind of personal fief of Leopold II and became an ordinary colony under the control of the Belgian parliament.

European empires in Africa in 1914

Portugal

Portuguese Guinea
Cape Verde Islands
Islands of Principe and São Tomé
Angola (considerably enlarged)
Mozambique (considerably enlarged)

Spain

Part of Morocco
Rio de Oro
Spanish Guinea

Britain

The Gambia
Sierra Leone
Gold Coast
Nigeria (Oil Rivers Protectorate, 1885; Chartered Company, 1886–99)
Uganda
British Somaliland
East African Protectorate (Kenya) (Chartered Company, 1888, Protectorate, 1895)
Zanzibar
Northern Rhodesia
Southern Rhodesia
Nyasaland
Union of South Africa
Walvis Bay
Basutoland
Bechuanaland
Swaziland

In addition Britain governed:

Egypt (occupied 1882, Protectorate, 1914)
Sudan (occupied 1898; condominium with Egypt, 1899)

France

Algeria
Tunis
Morocco
French West Africa included:
  Senegal
  French Guinea
  Ivory Coast
  Upper Volta

Dahomey
Niger
French Equatorial Africa included:
  Gabon
  French Congo
  Ubangi-Shari
  Chad
Madagascar

Germany

Togoland
Cameroons
German South-West Africa
German East Africa (Tanganyika)

Italy

Eritrea (1889)
Italian Somaliland (1899)
Libya (Tripolitania and Cyrenaica) (1912)

Belgium

Congo Free State (in effect personal fief of king, Leopold II, 1885; colony under control of Belgian parliament, 1908)

THE SCRAMBLE FOR THE PACIFIC

Although Africa saw the most spectacular impact of the new imperialism in action, the Pacific Islands were also partitioned. This gave an opening to two powers which came late to the race for empire, Germany and the United States. The Dutch were already well established in what is now Indonesia.

Trade and supposed strategic advantages were obviously important but missionaries played an unusually active role in international rivalry here. The London Missionary Society began its work here in 1795 and Catholic missions arrived in some strength in the 1830s. (For Tahiti and the Society Islands, *see above* p. 72).

1874	British annexation of Fiji.
1877	Sultan of Brunei granted territories in North Borneo to a London syndicate, Dent Brothers. They were challenged by both Spain and the Dutch. Appealed to the British government. In 1881 they were granted a charter as the North Borneo Company to administer the territory. Revived a form of chartered company, which it had been assumed had ended with the East India Company in 1858 but which was to be the model for the creation of the British chartered companies in Africa.

1877–99	Disputes between Britain, Germany and the United States about the Samoan Islands, which were eventually partitioned between Germany and the United States. (Britain accepting Tonga as compensation.)
1883	The Australian colony of Queensland announced the annexation of eastern New Guinea but its action was repudiated by the British government.
1884–5	Germany annexed north-eastern New Guinea and the adjacent islands (the Bismarck archipelago). Britain proclaimed a protectorate over south-eastern New Guinea.
1886	A treaty assigned the Marianne, Marshall, Caroline and northern Solomon Islands to Germany and the Gilbert, Ellice and southern Solomon Islands to Britain.
1888	North Borneo became a protectorate. British New Guinea became a Crown colony. (It was made a territory of the Commonwealth of Australia in 1906.)
1898	American annexation of Hawaii and the Sandwich Islands.

THE ABORTIVE SCRAMBLE FOR CHINA

The partition of the Pacific represented in part a jockeying for position for a share of the spoils in China. China was recognised as an enormous prize in economic and trading terms but its political weakness in the late nineteenth century was such that it was expected that it too would soon be partitioned among the western powers, including the United States.

In the eighteenth and early nineteenth centuries the Chinese had annoyed the European powers by refusing to open what the latter regarded as normal diplomatic and trading relations. The matter was complicated by the opium question. The English East India Company had found that it could pay for luxury goods from China by the export of opium from India. Chinese government objections to this led to the first military clash.

1792	A mission led by Lord Macartney tried to open diplomatic relations with the Chinese Emperor but were humiliatingly rebuffed.
1839–41	So-called 'Opium War' between Britain and China. In fact the issues were much wider than the import of opium.
1842	Treaty of Nanking. China ceded the island of Hong Kong to Britain and opened five 'treaty ports' to British trade. France and the United States secured similar concessions.
1850s	Taiping rebellion (mainly a movement of agrarian discontent) revealed the weakness of the Manchu government. Put down with help of British general, Charles Gordon.

1856	*Arrow* war arising from the Chinese arrest of a ship flying the British flag (probably illegally). Other European powers and the United States joined in.
1857	Anglo-French forces occupied Canton.
1858	Allied forces, which now included Russians and Americans, took Tientsin and concluded treaty by which Chinese agreed to open more treaty ports, establish normal diplomatic relations and protect Europeans, including missionaries.
1859–60	Hostilities resumed. The Chinese held hostages in the Summer Palace in Peking, which the British force burned in retaliation. Tientsin treaties confirmed in the Convention of Peking. Further destabilised the Manchu empire.
1895	Japan defeated China in Sino-Japanese war. A European alliance of Russia, Germany and France intervened to limit Japanese gains. But Japan retained Formosa (Taiwan) and a sphere of influence in Korea. The loans China had to raise to pay the Japanese war indemnity further mortgaged her finances to the European powers.
1898	Russia leased Port Arthur; Germany, Kiao-Chow; Britain, Wei-hai-wei; and France, Kwang-Chow-Wan. But more important than these ports (not all of them very valuable) were the maps which were being drawn up of railway and other concessions, which began to look increasingly like a full-scale partition of China. Russia predominated in Manchuria and northern China, as far south as the capital, Peking; Britain in the Yangtze basin; Germany in Shantung; and France in the extreme south.
1898–1900	The Boxer rebellion brought the direct intervention of European, American and Japanese forces. But, by now, a kind of equilibrium of competing ambitions prevented further advance in the immediate future.

THE FRENCH IN INDO-CHINA

The French were already well established in Cochin-China by 1870. Apart from hoping that Saigon might become an entrepôt to rival Singapore, they also hoped that Indo-China would provide a route into the southern provinces of China proper. But, as in West Africa, pressure for expansion often came from the military men (in this case the navy) and ran ahead of intentions in Paris.

1873	Lieutenant François Garnier published his *Voyage d'Exploration*, enthusiastically recommending the Red River route into southern China.
	French extended their influence into Tonkin. (Garnier himself was killed in a skirmish with the 'Black Flags', irregular troops supported by China, outside Hanoi on 21 December.)

1874	An ambiguous treaty (Treaty of Hue) arguably made Annam a protectorate and Cochin-China a colony.
1884–5	Campaigns in Tonkin brought down Jules Ferry's government, although they were ultimately successful.
1884–6	Occupation of Cambodia.
1887	French created Indo-Chinese Union of Cochin-China, Annam, Tonkin and Cambodia.
1893	Sent forces into Laos and Siam. Britain objected to the latter action.
1896	Treaty by which Britain recognised French position in Laos and in Siam east of the Mekong River but guaranteed the independence of the rest of Siam.
1904	Anglo-French *entente* divided Siam into spheres of influence: French in the east, British in the west (bordering Burma) and neutral between.

FURTHER EXPANSION OF THE BRITISH EMPIRE IN ASIA

1874–96	The Federated Malay States (Perak, Selangor, Negri Sembilan and Pahang), although remaining legally 'Princely States', came under British rule.
1885–6	Third Burmese war. Upper Burma annexed. Burma was governed as part of India.
1906	Brunei became a British protectorate.
1909	Five more Malay states (Kedah, Kelantan, Trengganu, Johore and Perlis), sometimes called the 'Unfederated States', passed from the jurisdiction of Siam to that of Britain.

(Afghanistan. Britain fought wars in Afghanistan in 1839–42 and 1878–80. Both were marked by spectacular disasters for Britain, although in 1880 she had scored some military success before the Gladstone government decided to withdraw and trust the new Amir, Abdur Rhaman, to maintain his independence against the Russians. However, Britain did retain the Khyber Pass, the Kurram Valley and Quetta.)

THE GOVERNMENT OF THE EUROPEAN EMPIRES IN THE NINETEENTH CENTURY

The British empire

Interest in empire began to revive about 1870. Interest in the existing empire of settlement preceded any thought of further expanding the empire. The 'Great Depression', which lasted from the early 1870s to the late 1890s and was marked by low prices, low interest rates and unemployment, and affected both industry and agriculture, although a complex and often contradictory phenomenon, alarmed people and gave rise to a number of parliamentary inquiries, of which the Royal Commission appointed in 1885 to inquire into the Depression of Trade and Industry was the most important.

Britain was peculiarly reluctant to return to protectionism, attributing her prosperity after 1846 to the repeal of the Corn Laws and the triumph of free trade, but pleas for 'fair trade' (i.e. defence against the discriminatory practices of other powers) were heard and it seemed worth acquiring colonies to keep them out of the hands of protectionist rivals.

The depression in both industry and agriculture led to an increase in emigration from the British Isles. From 1880 to 1913 the annual figure rarely dropped below 200,000. There was also a significant change of destination. In 1880, 166,570 of the 227,542 emigrants went to the United States. In 1912 only 117,310 of the 476,666 emigrants went to the States; of the rest, 186,147 went to British North America, 96,800 to Australia and New Zealand, and 28,216 to South Africa. As a result many families, including working-class families, had close relatives in the colonies and were therefore interested in them.

Disraeli and Gladstone

The Conservative Benjamin Disraeli was the first to take political advantage of the growing interest in empire, in speeches in Manchester and at the Crystal Palace (London) in 1872. He tried to discredit his liberal rival, William Gladstone, with charges of wishing to break up the empire. In fact Gladstone (who had started his long ministerial career in a junior post at the Colonial Office) probably understood the colonies of settlement better than Disraeli did. Neither man was in favour of the indiscriminate expansion of the empire. Disraeli was fascinated by India and much concerned about the safety of the route to India, but neither man cared much about Africa. In the 1870s and 1880s more new territory was acquired under Liberal than under Conservative administrations. Both were reactive, rather than proactive, in the new competition for empire. Their successors, Lord Salisbury and Lord Rosebery, were regarded as more committed and articulate imperialists, but they were acting in a world which had been almost entirely carved up by the western powers and imperial questions merged with more general diplomatic ones. A late convert to imperialism was Joseph Chamberlain, who, though never becoming Prime Minister, was recognised as one of the dominant politicians of his age, but he was more committed to the good organisation of the empire than to its expansion.

Imperial policy was generally bi-partisan. Growing interest in empire was shown by a number of developments – the foundation of the Colonial Society (later the Royal Colonial Institute) in 1868 and of the small but influential Co-efficients in 1902, the increasing number of mentions of empire in the serious press and periodicals and the pro-empire policy of the popular press, the *Daily Mail* (founded 1896) and the *Daily Express* (1900). The first two bodies cut entirely across party lines, while the left-wing Fabian Society, although not always uncritical, emphasised the possibilities of empire.

107

Only after the shattering experience of the Boer war did the critics become vocal, led by J.A. Hobson's popular treatise *Imperialism: A Study* (1902).

The constitutional development of the British empire, *c.*1870–1914

Paradoxically, while the empire expanded and the 'new' empire was generally governed in an authoritarian manner, the trend towards devolution continued.

Development of dominion status

By 1914 the older and larger colonies of settlement, Canada, Australia and New Zealand (South Africa is a special case dealt with in more detail below), had already become virtually independent nation states in their control of their internal affairs. In law they were not quite independent, being subject to the Colonial Laws Validity Act of 1844, which invalidated any colonial legislation which conflicted with any British legislation applying to that colony, but this had fallen into disuse. (A major constitutional crisis was detonated in the 1920s when it was invoked to invalidate Canadian legislation, abolishing criminal appeals to the Judicial Committee of the Privy Council in London, and resulted in the passage of the Statute of Westminster of 1931, which removed all restraints on dominion legislation.) These colonies had also (since 1859) been in a position to control their own tariffs and trade. But their rights in foreign affairs were much less secure. In international law, the British empire was one state, and when, in 1914, Britain declared war on Germany, the dominions (as they by then were) were also automatically at war.

Attempts to achieve closer co-operation

There was no longer a general belief that empire was a transient state and would disintegrate – at least not in the foreseeable future. Closer co-operation seemed desirable in three (possibly four) fields: (a) foreign policy, where the dominions hoped to gain a voice; (b) defence, where Britain hoped that the dominions would share responsibility, and cost, for the defence of a world-wide empire; (c) tariff policies; and (d) law. The last was less important than the others, but some, notably Joseph Chamberlain, hoped that they would all keep in step. The obvious mechanism for this was the Judicial Committee of the Privy Council, which had provided an ultimate appeal court for the whole empire.

Establishment of Colonial (Imperial) Conferences

1887	Informal meetings between British ministers and politicians from the colonies in London for Queen Victoria's golden jubilee.
1897	Rather more structured meetings at the time of the diamond jubilee. The 11 self-governing colonies (the Australian colonies were still separate) were represented by their prime ministers. The conference discussed both imperial defence and imperial preference (tariff) policy.

1902	Met after the South African war. Britain had been pleased (and a little surprised) when both Australia and Canada volunteered troops to fight the Boers.
	But attempts to persuade the self-governing colonies to pool their naval and military resources failed. They preferred to command their own forces. The conference voted in favour of imperial preference.
1907	(The first to be called an Imperial Conference.) Defence and tariffs were again discussed, but, more importantly, membership was more closely defined and the British Colonial Secretary announced the creation of a separate 'Dominions Department'. Although it had to wait for its classic definition until the Balfour Report in 1926, dominion status was now an accepted and defined reality.
1911	This met under the shadow of the Agadir crisis and defence was felt to be a major issue, but all substantive discussions were transferred to the greater privacy of the Committee of Imperial Defence. The Committee also discussed the possibility of imperial federation, but only New Zealand showed any marked enthusiasm for it.

Imperial Federation Movement

This was an attempt to bind the empire closer together. In particular it might be a way of giving the dominions a voice in foreign affairs, without breaking up the unity of the empire. But it proved to be a blind alley.

1884	Imperial Federation League founded. Various schemes were put forward for a parliament for the whole empire, or at least some kind of 'Great Council', which would control defence, trade and foreign policy. It attracted some support in Britain and also in New Zealand, but the larger self-governing colonies feared it would rob them of their recently acquired powers.
1893	League disintegrated, although some continued to advocate its ideals.

Imperial Zollverein (customs union)

This was especially associated with the name of Joseph Chamberlain. It originated from the belief that the future lay with big states like Germany and the United States. Britain could only continue to compete economically with them if she was herself the centre of a great empire working as one. Most of the world was increasingly protectionist. Britain remained committed to free trade but her self-governing colonies had very diverse tariff policies by about 1900. Chamberlain advocated imperial preference; the empire was to become an internal free trade zone or, at least, preference was to be accorded to goods from other parts of the empire. This gained some support in the colonies but never won over the British electorate. It split the Conservative Party.

Committee of Imperial Defence

This had ill-defined roots in informal meetings at the time of the Penjdeh crisis with Russia. It became a formal body in 1902. It was chaired by the British Prime Minister and attended by the Secretaries of State for India and the Colonies, as well as by the ministers responsible for the armed services and by senior military officers. Its significance for commonwealth history was that representatives of the dominions were also invited to attend in an effort to co-ordinate policy.

Special cases

South Africa

South Africa was ultimately to follow the same course as Canada, Australia and New Zealand, but here there was an extra dimension, which contemporaries would have called 'racial'. By this they did not mean relations between the white settlers and the much larger African population (to which were to be added a small but important Asian population). They meant relations between the British and the Boers.

In the 1850s the two Boer republics had become autonomous. The Boers hoped to pursue a pastoral life, little disturbed by the outside world. The British hoped to avoid further involvement in the interior. The hopes of both sides were to be destroyed by the international Scramble for Africa and by the discovery of immense mineral wealth in southern Africa.

1870–1	Rich diamond field (to be named Kimberley after the British Colonial Secretary) discovered in sensitive area in angle of Orange and Vaal rivers. The Transvaal, the Orange Free State and Cape Colony all had claims to the area – which they had not pressed when it seemed valueless. It was currently occupied by the Griquas, a community of mixed race descended mainly from the Khoikhoi and the Cape Dutch (whose very existence was an embarrassment to the Boers). Robert Keate, the Governor of Natal, was called in to arbitrate on the boundaries. His Award was not regarded as impartial by the Boers. He judged that the diamond field lay within the boundaries of Griqualand West, which the Cape government now formally annexed.
1875–7	Disraeli's Colonial Secretary, Lord Carnarvon, impressed by the success of Canadian federation, urged a similar solution on the South Africans, but made no progress.
1877	Annexation of the Transvaal. The Transvaal was virtually bankrupt and facing a serious threat from a resurgent Zulu power under Cetewayo. Theophilus Shepstone, the Commissioner for Native Affairs in the Transvaal, was sent with authority to annex the country if the Boers requested it. Boer and British sources have never agreed as to whether there was genuine consent to the annexation.

1879	Battle of Isandhlwana. Sir Bartle Frere settled the disputed boundary between the Boers and the Zulus largely in the Zulu favour but then demanded Zulu demobilisation. What would have been a normal request in a European situation was impossible in a military monarchy like the Zulus. War ensued. Zulu *impis* surprised a British force at Isandhlwana. Casualties were heavy on both sides but the Zulus were victorious – one of the very rare occasions when an African army defeated a European army in this period. The British felt that honour had been restored by their successful defence of Rorke's Drift a few days later. But from a military point of view the important engagement was at Ulundi (4 July), when the Zulus were heavily defeated. Zululand became a protectorate (annexed 1887).
1880s	Great growth in Boer national feeling, not only in the Transvaal but in the Cape too. (Afrikaaner Bond founded 1879.) Transvaal itself became expansionist. Boers set out to secure rights in Mashonaland and Bechuanaland (*see* pp. 93, 94). They also hoped for an outlet to the sea at Delagoa Bay, which would not go through British territory. (The railway between Pretoria and Delagoa Bay was opened in 1895.)
1880	With the defeat of the Zulus, Boers, like Paul Kruger, who had never accepted the legality of the annexation of the Transvaal, became free to demand the restoration of their independence. The Liberals under Gladstone had condemned the action of the Conservatives in 1877, and, when Gladstone won the general election of 1880, the Boers expected a speedy restoration of independence. But the Liberals too thought that the long-term solution in South Africa must be federation and were in no hurry to act.
1880–1	First Boer war. In December 1880 the Boers rose against the British, and defeated them at Majuba Hill in February 1881. Gladstone declined to continue the war and preferred to negotiate.
1881	Convention of Pretoria. The Transvaal was granted self-government 'subject to the suzerainty of Her Majesty'. There was to be no commercial discrimination against the other British colonies in South Africa and Britain was to control the Transvaal's relations with other powers.
1884	Convention of London replaced the Convention of Pretoria and the Preamble, clearly spelling out British suzerainty, was dropped but, by Article IV, Britain continued to control the Transvaal's treaty-making powers. Two views could therefore be held as to whether the Transvaal was genuinely independent.

111

1886	Huge gold deposits were found in the Transvaal on the Witwatersrand but the gold was difficult to extract, requiring a heavy capital outlay to sink deep mines and also a large labour force.
1886–99	The Transvaal was transformed in ways totally uncongenial to Boers like Paul Kruger, now President. They refused to grant citizenship to the many Europeans who had come in (the Uitlanders). This in turn was unacceptable to men like Cecil Rhodes, who saw the whole of southern Africa as British.
1895	Jameson Raid. Rhodes' close associate, Dr Jameson, led an armed force into the Transvaal on the pretext of restoring order after a Uitlander rising in Johannesburg in a territory where Britain had ultimate responsibility. The raid became a fiasco when the rising failed to materialise, but it destroyed any remaining confidence between British and Boers, especially as the British Colonial Secretary, Joseph Chamberlain, was widely believed to have known of the plot in advance. An international dimension was added when the German Kaiser sent a telegram to Paul Kruger congratulating him on surmounting the crisis without having to call on the help of 'friendly powers'.
1897	Alfred Milner was sent out to South Africa as British High Commissioner. Both he and Paul Kruger were intransigent men.
1898–9	Tom Edgar case. Edgar was a Uitlander shot by a Transvaal policeman, who was subsequently tried for murder but acquitted. Angry English workers on the Rand petitioned the British government and Milner wrote his famous 'helots despatch', saying it was intolerable that British subjects should be 'kept permanently in the position of helots', i.e. denied civil rights.
1899	(May–October) Milner and Kruger negotiated fruitlessly. (September) Transvaal secured an alliance with the Orange Free State. (9 October) Kruger presented an ultimatum to Britain. War ensued.
1899–1902	South African war (second Boer war). Bitterly divided British opinion. Jingoism on one side – symbolised by the excitement when siege of Mafeking was lifted. Disapproval of 'bullying small nations', i.e. the Boers, on the other. No discussion of rights or position of non-European majority in South Africa (although they participated in the fighting). Ironically, though, the attack on the 'Rand capitalists' triggered a debate on the morality of the whole 'new imperialism', e.g. in J.A. Hobson's *Imperialism: A Study* (1902). In Britain the Liberal party was split down the middle and, arguably, never recovered.

The war did not go well for Britain, but the Boers made fundamental mistakes. At the beginning of the war their forces were three times as large as the British, but instead of striking straight for Cape Town, and perhaps enlisting the sympathy of the Cape Boers, they attacked Natal (the most English province) to try to secure a port and wasted time investing Kimberley, Ladysmith and Mafeking. The British had time to get their army to South Africa.

1900 (May) Orange Free State annexed. By October the Boers had been completely defeated in the field. (25 October) The Transvaal was annexed.

1901–2 Boers resorted to guerilla warfare. At first had remarkable success. Women and children were 'concentrated' in camps to prevent them aiding the guerillas. Typhoid and other diseases broke out in the camps and caused many deaths.

1902 (31 May) Peace of Vereeniging signed. British government deliberately offered generous terms to the Boers, partly because they were shaken by public anger at the treatment of the women and children but more because they hoped that the ultimate outcome would be the amicable federation of the whole of South Africa. Some terms were unexceptionable, such as the re-stocking of Boer farms; so, in principle, was the promise of a return to representative government, but, to conciliate Boer opinion, it was provided that the franchise would be agreed with them at a later date.

1902–9 Much discussion of future political organisation of South Africa. In the Cape the British organised the Progressive Party as a reply to the Afrikaner Bond. Won a narrow victory in the 1904 election, led by Dr Jameson. New constitutions were introduced into the two former Boer republics in 1905–7 and several Boer war generals emerged as the leading politicians. Louis Botha and Jan Smuts won power in the Transvaal; James Hertzog and Abraham Fischer in the Orange River Colony. Group of civil servants associated with Milner (of whom Lionel Curtis was the most prominent) began to work for federation.

1906 Zulu rebellion alarmed whites and helped federation movement – which also had economic objectives.

1908 (October) National Convention met in Durban with 12 delegates from the Cape, 8 from the Transvaal and 5 each from Natal and Orange River Colony. Transvaal group, led by Smuts, took the lead. Adjourned sessions to Cape Town and Bloemfontein.

1909 (February) Produced draft constitution, submitted to four provincial assemblies and to a referendum in Natal. When approved, taken to London for action by British parliament. (September) South Africa Act. A 'stronger' form of federation than the Canadian, because they feared centrifugal forces, with most power at the centre. There was to be a Senate with eight members from each province, plus eight nominated by the Governor-General in Council, of whom four must be 'especially knowledgeable' about African affairs. There was no direct African representation in the Senate. Membership of the lower house was distributed roughly on the basis of the white population: 51 members for the Cape; 36 for the Transvaal; and 17 each for Natal and the Orange River Colony. Each province was to retain its own franchise, i.e. in the Transvaal and the Orange River Colony only whites could vote; in Natal a property qualification confined the vote in practice to Europeans; Cape Colony had a combination of property and educational qualifications which some Coloureds (i.e. those of mixed race), Africans and Asians did meet. The parliament did have powers of amendment, but some clauses were 'entrenched', i.e. could only be changed if two-thirds of Senate and Assembly sitting together agreed. These included the status of both Dutch and English as official languages and the Cape franchise. The last became a major battlefield during the apartheid era after the Second World War.

India

While it might be expected that the British colonies of settlement would continue to evolve towards greater independence, it was perhaps more surprising that India should be embarked upon the same course (albeit slowly and hesitantly) from the Government of India Act of 1858.

1853	Last renewal of East India Company's charter created a Legislative Council. Although this was an entirely official, unelected body, Dalhousie allowed it to act like a miniature parliament.
1858	(August) Government of India Act substituted the Crown for the dual government of Crown and Company. A Secretary of State for India was appointed in London and the Governor-General in Calcutta became the Viceroy.
	(November) Queen Victoria's Proclamation. The inhabitants of 'British' India were now subjects of the Queen and, while promising to respect their ancient rights and customs, the sovereign also promised that all her subjects 'of whatever race or creed, be freely and impartially admitted to offices in our service'.[1] The promise was not always kept but it remained the ideal.

---

1. C.H. Philips, *Select Documents of the History of India and Pakistan*, vol. IV (1962), p. 11.

1861   Indian Councils Act empowered the Governor-General to summon between 6 and 12 additional members to his Legislative Council. It was intended that some of these should be Indians. Similar legislative councils were set up in Madras and Bombay and subsequently in other provinces.

1864–9   A small number of Indians entered the Indian Civil Service (ICS), the élite British service which effectively governed India. The two most famous were Surendranath Banerjea (later Sir Surendranath), who was expelled from the service for alleged irregularities but became a prominent, and moderate, nationalist, and R.C. Dutt, who later became Commissioner (in effect Governor) of Orissa province but left to further the nationalist cause from the outside.

1866   Dadabhai Naoroji, an Indian resident in London, founded the East India Association to influence British opinion. Its members included John Bright and Henry Fawcett and it had some success in influencing parliamentary opinion. Some Indians also formed links with Irish nationalists.

1883   Ilbert Bill. Ilbert was the legal member of the Governor-General's Executive Council and he introduced a bill to extend the jurisdiction of Indian magistrates over Europeans in criminal cases (which they already had in civil cases). He regarded it as a mere tidying up measure, but it caused a great outcry to which the government partly yielded. Indian indignation at the success of this campaign contributed to their determination to become politically organised themselves.

1885   First meeting of Indian National Congress in Bombay. This was initiated by a Scotsman, Alan Octavian Hume, and for a time it had the blessing of the Viceroy, Lord Dufferin, who saw it as a useful sounding board of Indian opinion. But it also had Indian antecedents. In 1876 Banerjea had founded the Indian Association of Calcutta to work for a united India and begun a very successful campaign, reaching into the Punjab and the United Provinces. An Indian National Conference with delegates from all over India met in Calcutta in 1883. Its second session met in 1885 and accounted for the absence of some prominent Indians from the Bombay meeting, but Banerjea and others saw the advantages of an organisation with the ear of the government and thereafter attended meetings of the Congress.

The first meeting of the Indian National Congress (INC) consisted of 70 highly respectable men, mostly lawyers, teachers and journalists, representing essentially the forward-looking western educated class. It was thus drawn from a narrow class base and, more disturbing, there were only two Muslim

115

delegates, reflecting the differential uptake of western education by Muslims and Hindus.

1885–1905 For 20 years or so the Congress continued as an extremely
moderate body, although sometimes hard-hitting in its criticisms of British rule. Although it asked for an expansion of
representative government, it was generally more concerned
with changes in the rules (particularly the age limits of the
entrance examinations) which would allow more Indians to
enter the ICS. It deplored the 'drain' of Indian wealth to
Britain, which aggravated the perennial problem of Indian
poverty.

1892 Indian Councils Act enlarged the membership and powers
of both the Governor-Generals' and the provincial councils.
Although this was modest, it opened the way for some degree
of indirect elections.

Dadabhai Naoroji was elected to the Westminster parliament
as MP for Central Finsbury.

1899–1905 Viceroyalty of Lord Curzon brought matters to a head.
Curzon's intentions were good. He had always desired the
Viceroyalty and performed important services for India in
setting up the Agricultural and Archaeological Departments,
but he was intensely authoritarian (an Indian critic called
him 'the last of the Mughal emperors'). Indian opinion was
no longer prepared to tolerate this. Two measures in particular
offended Indian opinion.

1904 Universities Act. Although this was intended as a rationalisa-
tion measure to concentrate resources on major institutions
such as the University of Calcutta, it was seen as an attempt to
bring education under closer government control.

1905 The partition of Bengal. This too was intended to rationalise
the sprawling administration of the province but was seen as
an attack upon the development of Indian politics.

Two parties emerged in Congress – the 'moderate' constitutional party, associated with G.K. Gokhale, and the 'extrem-
ist' traditionalist (or Hindu) party, led by B.G. Tilak. Tilak
saw little advantage in negotiating with the British or appeal-
ing to British public opinion and was prepared to resort
to violence. Both wings had learnt lessons from Irish nationalism and the American War of Independence. A favoured
tactic was the *swadeshi* movement, which advocated buying
Indian goods and boycotting western goods (and sometimes
ideas).

Curzon resigned after a major quarrel with the Commander-
in-Chief, Lord Kitchener.

Japan defeated Russia. This victory by an Asian power impressed young Indians, including the future Prime Minister, Jawaharlal Nehru.

1906 Election of Liberal government in Britain with a landslide majority and a determination to bring in reforms.

(December) Formation of All-India Muslim League. Muslims made up between a fifth and a quarter of the population, scattered throughout India, although strongest in the north-west and north-east. They had never entirely trusted the Congress to represent them and feared that in any future elections they would always be overwhelmed by the Hindu majority. They therefore campaigned for, among other things, separate electorates.

1907 Surat split. The Indian National Congress split so violently between 'Moderates' and 'Extremists' at its annual conference that many thought that its influence was at an end.

1909 Indian Councils Act (commonly called the Morley–Minto Reforms, from the Secretary of State, John Morley, and the Viceroy, Lord Minto). This provided for the (generally indirect) election of 'unofficial' members to the Viceroy's and the provincial legislative councils. The Viceroy's council was to retain an official majority, but this provision did not apply to the provincial councils. Morley reluctantly agreed to the creation of separate Muslim electorates, under the euphemism of 'special groups'. Indian opinion was initially pleased by these reforms.

1911 Great Durbar held to mark the coronation of George V and Queen Mary, who attended in person. The Indian Princes were deliberately flattered. The seat of government was moved from Calcutta to the old Mughal capital of Delhi. (New Delhi, designed by Lutyens, was built, 1912–32.) A deliberate gesture of conciliation was made in the partial reversal of the partition of Bengal.

1914 Outbreak of First World War. As part of the British empire, India was automatically at war with Germany. This coincided with public opinion as the Indians generally sided with Britain and played an important part in the struggle (*see below* p. 132).

The French empire

After France's defeat by Prussia in 1870–1, French opinion was deeply divided about the value of colonies. Some saw them as a means of regaining great power status, but many others saw them as a dangerous distraction from France's European role and perhaps even as a Bismarckian plot to lure the French army overseas and prevent a war of revenge to regain Alsace and

Lorraine. Anti-colonial feeling reached its height in 1885 when mobs in the streets of Paris demanded the blood of Jules Ferry (himself a Lorrainer but a strong advocate of a colonial policy) after reverses in Indo-China.

The colonial movement gradually gathered strength in France. The year 1891 saw the foundation of the *Comité de l'Afrique Française*. This gave rise directly to the *Comité du Maroc* (1904), formed to work for the incorporation of Morocco in the French empire, and less directly to the *Comité de l'Asie Française* (1901) and similar committees (in fact pressure groups) for the Pacific Islands and Madagascar. There was also an association of businessmen, the *Union Coloniale Française*, founded in 1893.

A number of politicians became converts to the colonial cause, among them Félix Faure, Gabriel Hanotaux, Eugène Étienne and Théophile Delcassé. Although they belonged to different parties, in the confused politics of the Third Republic they could sometimes muster a considerable 'squadron' (estimated at its peak at 200 deputies) to vote on colonial issues.

Philosophy of empire

French colonial policy differed radically from that of Britain. Where the British tended towards devolution and 'indirect rule', the French tended towards centralisation and had many fewer inhibitions about interfering with other peoples' civilisations than did the British. This was not, in itself, either illiberal or racialist. It went back to the ideals of the eighteenth-century philosophers, who believed that it was possible to discover the laws which governed society, just as scientists were discovering the laws that governed the natural world. Once discerned, this knowledge should be employed to remodel and improve society. The French had tried to remake their own society during the French Revolution and had spread their ideas throughout Europe during the revolutionary and Napoleonic wars. They believed that the laws of good government were universal and applied equally to Europeans and non-Europeans. Consequently, their ideal for their empire was 'assimilation' to the best French models.

It was a clearer and simpler model than the British but it broke down on the harsh facts of geographical distance and cultural diversity. As the empire expanded rapidly in the late nineteenth century, it became clear that 'assimilation' was impossible in the foreseeable future and it was replaced by the vaguer idea of 'association'. But the ideal of shared representation in Paris was not abandoned until after the Second World War.

Representation of the colonies in Paris

The French hoped that one day all their colonies would be represented in the Chamber of Deputies in Paris, which would govern the whole empire. Such representation had been allowed briefly during the First and Second French Republics but abolished under the Second Empire. It was revived under the Third Republic.

But the franchise was restricted to French citizens. This included expatriate Frenchmen, those of any race who had the good fortune to be born within the boundaries of the *anciennes colonies*, which had been granted full rights of citizenship in 1848, and some who had gained citizenship under various pieces of legislation. The majority of the population, especially in the African colonies, were not citizens but 'subjects' (*sujets*). These had inferior rights and were sometimes even liable for labour service. The status of *sujet* was not abolished until 1946.

In practice the colonies were usually represented by ex-patriate Frenchmen. The first full-blooded African elected to the Chamber of Deputies was Blaise Diagne of Senegal in 1914.

Central organisation

Until 1881 the administration of the colonies was under the Ministry of Marine. In that year Gambetta appointed Félix Faure as Under-Secretary for the Colonies. The Under-Secretaryship was variously attached to the Ministries of Marine and Commerce. The most notable Under-Secretary was Eugène Étienne (1887–8 and 1889–92), who fought for an independent jurisdiction. In 1894 a Ministry of the Colonies was at last set up.

Economic policy

France had traditionally been strongly protectionist, but in the 1860s, the *Pacte colonial* was gradually dismantled. However, France reinstated a protectionist tariff in 1882, and in 1892 a new attempt was made to assimilate colonial tariffs to those of metropolitan France.

Beginnings of resistance to French rule in Indo-China

1885–1913	*Can Vuong*, or Monarchist Movement, organised sporadic armed resistance.
1907–8	*Dong Kinh Nghin Thuc*, or Private Schools Movement. Vietnamese, who had been unwilling to send children to western schools, began to see the advantages of western ideas. Led (1908) to demonstrations demanding taxation and educational reforms.
	Phan Boi Chau fled to Canton, where, with other refugees, he formed the *Viet-Nam Quang-Phuc Hoi*, or Association for the Restoration of Vietnam, with a network of cells in Vietnam. He went on to Tokyo, Bangkok, Hong Kong and Singapore, where he built up the *Dong-A-Dong Minh*, the League of East Asian Peoples.

The German empire

After France's defeat in the Franco-Prussian war in 1871, some groups urged the German government to take France's colonies rather than Alsace-Lorraine, but the German Chancellor, Otto von Bismarck, showed no interest. The German colonial lobby grew in strength after about 1879, helped by the continuing economic depression. Friedrich Fabri published his *Does Germany Need Colonies?* in 1879. Colonial societies grew rapidly. Among the most important were the *Kolonialverein*, founded in Frankfurt in 1882, which united with Karl Peters' *Gesellschaft für Deutsche Kolonialisation* in 1887 to form the *Deutsche Kolonialgesellschaft*. German advocates of colonialism believed that it would solve the pressing 'social problem' at home, the poverty which might otherwise lead to public disorder. They were also alarmed by the emigration statistics. Over a million Germans had emigrated in the 1850s (after the unsuccessful revolutions of 1848–9) and again in the 1880s in the face of economic depression. Most went to the United States (although large numbers also went to South America) and so were lost to the German Reich. In the event, Germany, coming late to the race, acquired few areas suitable for European settlement. (In 1914 there were fewer than 20,000 Germans settled in the colonies.)

Otto von Bismarck was not an enthusiast for colonies, although he saw their potential as diplomatic bargaining counters. Only for a short period in 1884–5 did he support the colonialists. He may have been genuinely annoyed by the British annexation of Fiji and British delay in recognising German claims in South-West Africa, and in 1884 he took advantage of international irritation at the Anglo-Portuguese treaty on the control of the Congo River, to summon the Berlin West Africa Conference. He apparently hoped to conciliate the French (still thirsting for revenge after 1871) at the price of a quarrel with Britain, but dropped the strategy when he found that German colonial interests were better served by co-operation with Britain. By 1889 he was regretting that he had ever ventured into the colonial field.

Germany was a colonial power for only a short time. She never developed a philosophy of empire comparable to those of France or England. A product of the late nineteenth century, the German empire never doubted the inferiority of all non-Europeans to all Europeans. It was essentially authoritarian and much occupied with 'pacifying' native resistance. The violent suppression of the Hereros rising in South-West Africa in 1904–7 and of the Maji-Maji rising in Tanganyika in 1905–6 attracted international condemnation.

The Italian empire

The Italian entry into the colonial field in the late nineteenth century has sometimes been ascribed to simple nationalist exuberance after the achievement of unification, which could not be simply switched off. A desire to prove that Italy was a great power and to revive memories of the Roman empire was a part of it. Her only important gain was Libya, which the Italians meant to open up for settlement, as the French were doing in Algeria. Elaborate plans were drawn up for official emigration schemes. Italy was suffering from a population explosion. The population grew from 18 million in 1800 to 41 million in 1900, and lack of the raw materials of the first industrial revolution (iron and coal), which Italy also sought, unsuccessfully, in Africa, made it difficult to develop an economy which would support the burgeoning population.

5 IMPERIALISM AND THE FIRST WORLD WAR

Marxist writers, following Lenin's lead in *Imperialism: The Highest Stage of Capitalism* (1917), described the First World War as the imperialist war, which would provoke the revolution of the proletariat and bring the capitalist era to an end. Rosa Luxemburg believed that so long as the European powers could resolve the contradictions of capitalism by expansion into the rest of the world, the system could endure, but once the world was completely divided, the crash must come. Later writers, however, have concluded that Lenin was using the word 'imperialism' in a very special sense to mean the monopoly stage of capitalism, which was not synonymous with its common usage to describe the partition of the rest of the world among the European powers (and the United States).

Leaving aside the specialist Marxist usage of the term, the relationship between imperialism and the First World War is a complex one. On the one hand, the great powers had always avoided a war among themselves arising from colonial disputes, however sharp, in the decades before 1914. Some historians (e.g. D.K. Fieldhouse) have even suggested that colonial disputes provided a comparatively safe outlet for the tensions in Europe. On the other hand, colonial rivalries certainly contributed to the arms race before the war, most notoriously to the naval rivalry between Britain and Germany. They also contributed to the noisy nationalism of the period.

SUMMARY OF THE EUROPEAN SITUATION, 1870–1914

1870–1	Franco-Prussian war
1870	Completion of unification of Italy with the acquisition of Venetia and Rome.
1871	Proclamation of the German empire.
1877–8	War between Russia and Turkey
1878	Treaty of San Stefano.
	Congress of Berlin, called to modify the treaty of San Stefano. A number of private deals, e.g. the Cyprus Convention, had implications for colonial questions.
1879	Austro-German alliance. The open, self-balancing system established at Vienna in 1815 was increasingly replaced by a system of tight alliances which culminated, in 1914, in the Triple Alliance of Germany, Austria and Italy, confronting the Dual Alliance of France and Russia.

1882	Triple Alliance of Germany, Austria and Italy formed; Italy partly motivated by irritation at French action in Tunis.
1884–5	Berlin West Africa Conference established the ground rules for the Scramble for Africa.
1890	Kaiser dismissed Otto von Bismarck as the German Chancellor. Germany became increasingly interested in *Weltpolitik* and (in 1898) the Anglo-German arms race began.
1894	Dual Alliance of Russia and France.
1895	Sino-Japanese war. Germany, France and Russia intervened in the peace settlement.
1900	European intervention in the Boxer rebellion in China.
1902	Anglo-Japanese alliance.
1904	*Entente* between France and Britain.
1904–5	Russo-Japanese war. Russia defeated.
1912–13	Balkan wars.
1914	Outbreak of First World War.

COLONIAL DISPUTES AND AGREEMENTS

The colonial disputes (and in some cases their resolution) which have traditionally been seen as, in one sense or another, forerunners of 1914 are as follows:

1884	The Anglo-German dispute over Angra Pequena (German South-West Africa) (*see* p. 99).
1898	The Anglo-French clash at Fashoda (*see* p. 85). Britain and Germany guaranteed a loan to Portugal, with the Portuguese colonies as collateral. They reached a private agreement as to which power should have which colonies in the event of Portugal defaulting.
1900	Britain renewed old guarantees of Portuguese integrity. This was believed in Berlin, but not in London, to be incompatible with the 1898 agreement. In the midst of the Boxer rebellion and with the entry of foreign troops into China, Britain and Germany signed an agreement to uphold the integrity of China (the China Agreement).
1901	Britain tried to activate the China Agreement to put pressure on Russia to withdraw from Manchuria. The Germans refused, maintaining that the Agreement had never applied to Manchuria.
1903	Germany secured a concession for a railway from Berlin to Baghdad. Britain opposed the project for both commercial and security reasons.
1904	Britain and France reached what was essentially a series of bargains to resolve outstanding colonial disputes. They agreed on

spheres of influence in Siam; some modification of boundaries in West Africa; and a compromise about the rights of French fishermen in Newfoundland. Most importantly, in secret agreements, France promised to aid Britain in resolving the financial problems of Egypt in return for the British withdrawing their longstanding objections to French expansion into Morocco (the 'missing piece' of France's African empire).

1905–6   First Moroccan crisis. The Germans attempted to break the Anglo-French *entente* by challenging France in Morocco, believing that Britain did not really wish to see the French there. A French mission arrived in Fez in January 1905 to negotiate with the Sultan of Morocco. Two months later the Kaiser visited Tangiers and proclaimed his support for the Sultan's total independence.

1906   The result was the Algeciras Conference, attended by almost all the European powers and the United States. Although the Germans won some concessions on the internationalisation of the Moroccan question, they found themselves for the first time since Bismarck's triumphs diplomatically isolated with only Austria-Hungary as a reliable ally.

1907   Sir Eyre Crowe, a British Foreign Office official, wrote a memorandum arguing that Germany had been hostile to Britain since the Angra Pequena crisis in 1884. Although Crowe was then comparatively junior, this accorded with a changing Foreign Office view, shared by the new Foreign Secretary, Sir Edward Grey, that France, not Germany, was now Britain's friend.

Anglo-Russian convention settling disputes in Persia, Afghanistan and Tibet opened the way for more diplomatic co-operation. Conversations had begun in 1901 on the Straits (the Dardanelles), Persia, Central Asia and the Far East but had been interrupted by the Russo-Japanese war. In 1907 Agreement was reached on Persia, Afghanistan and Tibet. Persia was divided into a Russian sphere (including Teheran, the capital) and a British sphere (which included the coast of the Persian Gulf and a large neutral zone between). Both powers agreed not to intervene in Afghanistan and to deal with Tibet only through China.

1911   Agadir crisis. Germany again chose to challenge the growing French role in Morocco by sending a German gun-boat, the *Panther*, to the port of Agadir. It is possible that it was an over-strong opening gambit intended to secure a *quid pro quo* from France rather than prevent the French advance, but again it misfired. Germany did secure some concessions from France elsewhere in Africa but at the price of cementing the Anglo-French connection. The 1904 *entente* never became a formal

123

alliance but Britain and France began to concert their military policy, notably in the 'naval conversations', which resulted in the French fleet concentrating on the Mediterranean and leaving the British to defend the North Sea and the Channel. This, arguably, imposed a moral obligation on Britain to defend the French Channel ports.

1914 Anglo-German relations improved early in 1914 when Britain withdrew her objections to the Berlin–Baghdad railway and a new agreement about the Portuguese colonies seemed possible.

There were few major colonial issues outstanding in 1914 and the fact that Britain fought in the First World War with her two great colonial rivals, France and Russia, and against her traditional allies, Germany and Austria, with whom she had had comparatively minor (or in the case of Austria, no) colonial quarrels suggests that colonial questions did not determine the alignments of the First World War.

THE OTTOMAN EMPIRE

There is, however, one possible link. Africa had been partitioned by the European powers. It had been expected that China would be. There was another 'dying empire', the inheritance of which was likely to be strongly contested by the powers, that of Turkey.

1877–8 Russo-Turkish war culminated in Treaty of San Stefano.

1878 Congress of Berlin modified terms of San Stefano but created an independent Bulgaria, placed Bosnia and Herzegovina under Austrian protection and opened the way for France to take Tunis (1881) and Britain to lease Cyprus.

1908 The reformist Young Turks compelled the Sultan to grant a constitution.
Austria annexed Bosnia-Herzegovina.

1911–12 Italy went to war with Turkey and seized Tripoli and the Dodecanese Islands.

1912–13 First Balkan war. Bulgaria, Serbia, Greece and Montenegro allied against Turkey in the hope of expelling the Turks from the Balkans altogether and won considerable success. The Treaty of London was concluded under international mediation in May 1913.

1913 Second Balkan war. Bulgaria fought Serbia, Greece, Romania and Montenegro. Ended in Peace of Bucharest (August).

1914 (28 June) Assassination of Franz Ferdinand, the heir to the Austro-Hungarian throne, in the Bosnian capital, Sarajevo.
(6 July) Germany promised Austria unconditional support.

(23 July) Austria sent an ultimatum to Serbia, whom she regarded as responsible for the assassination.

(28 July) Austria declared war on Serbia.

(30 July) Russia, Serbia's ally, mobilised.

(31 July) Austria mobilised.

(1 August) Germany mobilised and declared war on Russia.

(3 August) Germany declared war on France, Russia's ally.

(2–3 August) Germany breached Belgian neutrality, which was guaranteed by international treaty.

(4 August) Britain declared war on Germany, technically on the Belgian question.

THE EUROPEAN EMPIRES ON THE OUTBREAK OF THE FIRST WORLD WAR

Based on *Whitaker's Almanac*, 1914. Many of the statistics are approximations. Census figures are the most recent available, usually 1911, some are clearly estimates. Racial mix is indicated where possible.

The British Empire

	Area (in square miles)	Population
Europe		
United Kingdom[a]	121,390	45,647,000
Malta and Gozo	120	211,000
Gibraltar	2	20,000
Cyprus	3600	275,000
Asia		
Indian Empire[b]	1,900,000	315,132,537
Ceylon	25,500	4,100,000
Straits Settlements	1660	700,000
Federated Malay States	27,700	1,000,000
Other Malay states	14,200	800,000
Hong Kong	390	440,000
Weihaiwei	300	160,000
North Borneo	31,100	204,000
Brunei	4000	30,000
Sarawak	50,000	650,000
Africa		
South Africa, Union of	373,200	5,973,394[c]
Basutoland	10,300	403,111[d]
Bechuanaland	275,000	125,350[e]
Rhodesia	12,593,747	1,596,000
Southern	148,575	770,000[f]
Northern	290,000	826,000[g]
Gambia	4000	146,000

The British Empire (cont'd)

	Area (in square miles)	Population
Gold Coast	120,000	1,400,000
Sierra Leone	34,000	1,100,000
Northern Nigeria	255,700	10,000,000
Southern Nigeria	78,000	7,000,000
Somaliland	68,000	300,000
East African Protectorate	182,000	4,000,000[h]
Uganda	223,500	2,893,494[i]
Zanzibar	1020	200,000
Nyasaland	300,000	1,000,000
Egypt[j]	400,000	12,000,000
Sudan	1,000,000	2,000,000
Islands in Indian and Atlantic Oceans		
Mauritius	720	370,000
Seychelles	150	23,000
Ascension	40	150
St Helena	47	3500
Falkland Islands	6500	3240
South Georgia	1000	N/A
Americas		
Canada	3,530,600	7,200,000[k]
Newfoundland	40,000	240,000
Jamaica	4200	850,000
Bahamas	4400	56,000
Leeward Islands[l]	750	127,189
Windward Islands[m]	508	157,264
	170	196,000
Trinidad and Tobago	1860	330,000
British Guiana	90,300	310,000
British Honduras	8600	40,500
Bermuda	20	19,000
Australasia		
Australia	2,974,220	7,800,000[n]
New Zealand	105,000	1,070,910[o]
Fiji	7500	130,000
Papua	90,540	360,000
Pacific Islands	12,500	200,000
Total[p]	*c.*13,032,322	*c.*434,500,000

[a] With Channel Islands and Isle of Man.

[b] Inc. Burma.

[c] 1,276,242 whites; 4,019,006 Africans; 678,146 'other coloured races'.

[d] 1396 whites.

[e] 1692 whites.

[f] 23,606 whites.

[g] 1497 whites.

[h] c.1600 Europeans.
[i] 823 Europeans; 3110 Asians.
[j] Egypt was not strictly part of the empire until it was made a protectorate when Turkey entered the war on the German side in 1914.
[k] 105,492 Amerindians; 4600 Eskimos.
[l] Antigua, St Kitts, Nevis and Anguilla, Dominica, Montserrat, British Virgin Islands.
[m] St Lucia, St Vincent, Grenada, Barbados.
[n] c.180,000 Aborigines; 25,772 Chinese; 7682 other Asians.
[o] 45,663 Maoris.
[p] Inc. India.

The French empire

	Area (in square miles)	Population
Europe		
France	207,076	36,601,509
Asia		
India	200	277,700
Indo-China	309,979	16,000,000
Africa		
Algeria	1,119,416	5,563,828[a]
Tunis	46,300	1,800,000
Morocco	193,000	7,000,000
French West Africa	c.2,091,860	c.11,568,850
Senegal	74,000	1,250,500
Niger	837,000	6,036,200
Guinea	92,600	1,737,350
Ivory Coast	126,100	1,216,300
Dahomey	38,000	878,500
Sahara	924,160	450,000
French Equatorial Africa		
French Congo	513,000	9,000,000
Somali Coast	46,300	208,000
Madagascar[b]	226,000	3,153,500
America[c]	35,320	428,850
Australasia		
New Caledonia	7200	50,500
Society Islands etc.[d]	8378	81,100
Colonial total[e]		
	c.4,014,826	c.54,907,554

[a] 752,043 Europeans.
[b] Inc Réunion etc.
[c] Inc. French Guiana, Martinique, Guadeloupe and smaller West Indian islands; St Pierre and Miquelon.
[d] New Hebrides jointly administered with Britain.
[e] Inc. Algeria, which was administered as part of France.

The German empire

	Area (in square miles)	Population
Europe		
Germany	208,780	64,925,993
Africa		
Togoland	33,659	1,000,000
Cameroon	205,000	3,500,000
South-West Africa	322,348	120,000
East Africa	384,079	7,645,000
Pacific		
New Guinea	90,000	463,300
Solomon and other Islands	5160	122,000
Samoa	1050	35,000
Asia		
Kiao-Chow	193	84,000
Colonial total	*c.*1,134,239	*c.*14,890,000[a]

[a] Inc. 24,170 'whites', of whom 18,500 were reckoned permanent settlers.

The Italian empire

	Area (in square miles)	Population
Europe		
Italy	110,623	34,686,683
Africa		
Eritrea	60,000	280,000
Somaliland	131,000	300,000
Tripoli and Cyrenaica	922,000	1,000,000
Asia		
Tientsin Concession	20	17,000
Colonial total	1,113,020	*c.*1,600,000

The Dutch empire

	Area (in square miles)	Population
Europe		
Netherlands	12,761	6,102,399
Asia		
East Indies	738,000	37,717,377
Sumatra	162,000	
Java and Madura	51,000	
Borneo	115,000	
Celebes	50,000	
Moluccas	44,000	
Timor	18,000	
Western New Guinea	N/A	
America		
Surinam (Dutch Guiana)	49,845	86,233
Curaçao (and other West Indian islands)	32,585	
Colonial total	*c.*787,845	*c.*37,836,195

The Belgian empire

	Area (in square miles)	Population
Europe		
Belgium	11,373	7,516,730
Africa		
Congo	802,000	*c.*15,000,000[a]

[a] Inc. 5465 Europeans.

The Portuguese empire

	Area (in square miles)	Population
Europe		
Portugal[a]	35,500	5,960,056
Asia		
India[b]	1470	605,000
Macao	3	80,000
Timor (East)	7450	300,000
Africa		
Cape Verde Islands	1475	150,000
Guinea	14,000	400,000
São Tomé & Principe	442	45,000
Angola and Kabinda	480,000	5,000,000
Mozambique, Delagoa Bay etc.	300,000	3,200,000
Colonial total	*c.*804,840	*c.*9,675,000

[a] Inc. Azores and Madeira
[b] Goa etc.

The Spanish empire

	Area (in square miles)	Population
Europe		
Spain	196,700	19,588,688
Balearic Islands	1935	325,703
Metropolitan Spain also included as provinces:		
Ceuta	5	13,000
Canary Islands	2807	419,809
Africa		
Fernando Po and dependencies	N/A	N/A
Rio de Oro (Spanish Sahara)	N/A	N/A
Rio Muni (Spanish Guinea)	N/A	N/A
Outposts in Morocco (e.g. Melilla, Ifni)	N/A	N/A

The Danish empire

	Area (in square miles)	Population
Europe		
Denmark	15,042	2,757,076
Faroe Islands	515	12,955
Iceland	40,497	78,479
Greenland	830,000	12,968
America		
West Indian islands of St Croix, St Thomas and St John	142	32,786
Colonial total	871,154	137,188

IMPACT OF THE FIRST WORLD WAR

The First World War was a European war but, because all the leading states had colonial empires, it inevitably became a global war.

The British empire

In international law the British empire was still one state. Therefore, when London declared war, the whole empire, including the dominions and India, was automatically at war.

The dominions

Three of the dominions, Canada, Australia and New Zealand, immediately rallied to the British side, offering troops and placing their embryonic navies under the Admiralty.

The position of South Africa was more complicated. The government, under the former Boer general, Louis Botha, expressed its willingness to defend South Africa but not to send troops to Europe. A British request that they should attack South-West Africa to capture German radio stations there resulted in a small Afrikaner rebellion, but South-West Africa was taken in 1915. A call for volunteers led to South Africans serving in France, Palestine and, especially, East Africa. In British eyes, by 1918 South Africa had played much the same role as the other dominions in the war effort.

The presence of dominion Prime Ministers in the British War Cabinet, which they not infrequently attended, briefly raised hopes of some kind of imperial federation after the war.

An Imperial Conference (termed the Imperial War Conference) met in 1917 and again in 1918, taking advantage of the presence in London of dominion

131

Prime Ministers attending the War Cabinet, but it was agreed that all decisions must be left until after the war.

In 1921 the post-war Imperial Conference finally laid such hopes to rest. Smuts had already summed up the difficulties in 1917. 'Here we are,' he said 'a group of nations spread over the whole world, speaking different languages, belonging to different races with entirely different economic circumstances, and to attempt to run even the common concerns of that group of nations by means of a Central Parliament and a Central Executive is . . . absolutely to court disaster.'[1] The way of the future, as of the past, was the evolution towards completely independent nations.

India

Like the dominions, India had joined the British war effort with apparent enthusiasm. The good will created in the 1909–11 period was still manifest. Indian troops served in many theatres, including on the western front.[2]

The Indians expected recompense at the end of the war and thought that they had been promised it when the Secretary of State for India, Lord Montagu, declared in 1917 that there should be an 'increasing association of Indians in every branch of the administration and the gradual development of self-governing institutions'.[3] They had not realised how much the timing was to be left to purely British decisions, and conflict and bitterness soon resulted.

In international terms India was, however, recognised as a nation in the settlements after the First World War (albeit a nation still ruled by the British). There had been Indian representation at the Imperial Conferences of 1917 and 1918. India was also represented at the Paris Peace Conference in 1918–19. She became a founder member of the League of Nations and of the International Labour Organisation, and, like the dominions, signed international treaties such as the Washington Treaty on arms limitation in 1921.

The French empire

The war did not advance constitutional reform in the French empire in the same way as it did in the British, but whereas, in the eyes of critics, the French had allowed their empire to drift in the period 1905–14, it was now regarded as a valuable resource, for two main reasons.

---

1. A.B. Keith, *Speeches and Documents on British Colonial Policy, 1763–1917* (1953), p. 396.

2. Numbers of imperial troops engaged in the First World War. According to the official figures of the time, 8,654,567 soldiers served with the imperial forces in various theatres, of whom 1,524,187 were described as 'coloured'. The majority of the latter were from the Indian sub-continent, but significant numbers also came from Africa and the Caribbean. The 'white' dominions – Canada, Australia, etc. – contributed 1,425,964. The remaining 5,704,416 came from the United Kingdom.

   Fatal casualties were approximately: United Kingdom – 743,000; Canada – 60,000; Australia – 59,000; India – 49,000; New Zealand – 16,000; and South Africa – 8000. (Comparable casualties for the continental powers were Germany – 1,800,000 and France –1,384,000.)

3. C.H. Philips, *Select Documents on the History of India and Pakistan*, vol. IV (1962), p. 264.

First, it was seen as a vital reservoir of manpower. Although the British made extensive use of Indian and colonial troops during the war, they never valued their overseas possessions primarily for this. But the French had been increasingly alarmed as the demographic balance swung against them and in favour of Germany after 1871. (In 1914 it was calculated that France had 6 million men of military age, compared with nearly 10 million in Germany.) They mustered nearly 2 million colonial troops during the First World War, 680,000 of whom saw combat.

Second, the empire came to seem important as a source of economic strength and particularly as a supplier of raw materials. Albert Sarraut, who had been Governor of Indo-China from 1911 and was to become Colonial Minister in 1920, put forward his theory of *mise en valeur*. The colonies were to be organised in meaningful economic units and developed.

The Italian empire

The Italians saw the war as their opportunity to win a much bigger empire. They did not enter the war in 1914 on the side of Austria and Germany on the grounds that the Triple Alliance was a purely defensive treaty and that Austria, by launching a pre-emptive war against Serbia, had breached its terms. When the Italians agreed to enter the war on the allied side in the spring of 1915, they did so in return for a considerable bribe, partly at the expense of Austria but more at the expense of the Ottoman empire. The Treaty of London of 26 April 1915 promised them control of Istria, most of Dalmatia, Libya, Eritrea and parts of Asia Minor. At the end of the war, Italy did not receive what she had expected – although the Treaty of Sèvres with Turkey in August 1920 confirmed her in possession of the Dodecanese and Rhodes. Italy was left an aggrieved and revisionist power, ready for a new adventure in Abyssinia in the 1930s.

The German empire

The Germans lost the whole of their colonial empire as a result of their defeat. All their colonies had been captured in the course of the war.

1914	In the Pacific, Australia took German New Guinea, the Bismarck Archipelago and the German Solomon Islands: New Zealand, German Samoa; and Japan, the Marshall and Caroline Islands.
	In Africa, Britain and France occupied Togoland from their adjoining territories,
1914–15	The Cameroons were taken by Britain, France and Belgium.
1915	South-West Africa was taken by troops from the Union of South Africa.
1916–18	General Smuts led a combined force of British, Indian, African and South African troops against German East Africa. This was the most difficult campaign and, in 1918, General Paul von

Lettow-Vorbeck was still holding out from Portuguese territory into which his troops had retreated.

Since the American President, Woodrow Wilson, had set his face against any annexations at the end of this war, all the German colonies were 'mandated' to various powers, through the intermediary of the new League of Nations. Togoland and the Cameroons were divided between Britain and France. Most of German East Africa (Tanganyika) went to Britain, although a small part (Ruanda-Urundi) went to Belgium. South-West Africa was mandated to the Union of South Africa. The Pacific Islands north of the Equator went to Japan; those south of the Equator, including Nauru and Eastern New Guinea, went to Australia and Western Samoa to New Zealand.

THE LEAGUE OF NATIONS AND THE MANDATE SYSTEM

The greatest effect was on world public opinion. To the disappointment of peoples under European rule, especially in India, the principles of 'self-determination' to be applied to the Austro-Hungarian and Ottoman empires at the end of the war were not considered appropriate for the European empires overseas. But the 'grabbing' of territory by European powers was no longer regarded as acceptable. By implication at least, standards of colonial rule should conform to those laid down for the mandated territories by Article 22 of the Covenant of the League of Nations.[4]

---

4. For the text of Article 22, etc. *see* M.E. Chamberlain, *Longman Companion to European Decolonisation in the Twentieth Century* (1998)

BIOGRAPHIES

(*Note.* Particularly in the case of major European statesmen, only those parts of their careers which are of direct relevance to imperialism are usually noticed.)

Abd-el-Kader (1807–83): Algerian resistance leader. Born in Oran province of a family of *marabouts* (holy men), who claimed descent from the Prophet. His father was the head of the largest Algerian branch of the Sufi brotherhood. Abd-el-Kader himself has been described as a 'warrior monk'.[1] In 1832 he was chosen to lead a holy war against the French. He concluded agreements in 1834 and 1837 which would have left him in control of Oran province, but neither agreement held. He took refuge in Morocco, where he found sympathisers, but the French defeated the Moroccans at the battle of Isly in 1844 (which, combined with the French bombardment of Tangiers, caused an international crisis with England). Abd-el-Kader was compelled to surrender in 1847 and was imprisoned in France until 1852, when he retired to Damascus. In 1865 he refused Napoleon III's offer to make him Viceroy of Algeria.

Aberdare (Henry Austin Bruce), 1st Baron (1815–95): British politician. Home Secretary, 1868–73. President of the Royal Geographical Society and first Governor of the Royal Niger Company. Acted as an intermediary with the Gladstone government in 1880–5 in establishing British authority in Africa, especially in Nigeria. The Aberdare Mountains in what became British East Africa were named after him.

Ahmadou Ibn Umar Tall (*c.*1833–98): West African leader. The son of Umar bin Said Tall, who founded the Tokolor empire in the 1850s. After his father's death in 1864 it took Ahmadou 12 years to establish his position and regain the territory which had broken away. Ahmadou now had to face the French advance. In 1887 he allied with the French against his own rebels but was at war with them by 1889. Was eventually defeated by Archinard and went into exile, dying shortly afterwards.

Akbar Jelal-ed-Din Mohammed (1542–1605): The greatest of the Mughal Emperors. Re-established the empire founded by his grandfather, Babur (1483–1530). When he died the Mughal empire ruled all the northern half of the Indian sub-continent, as far south as the Vindhya hills. A man of great intellectual curiosity, he was notable for his religious tolerance. The ruler of a Muslim empire, he freely employed Hindus in its government and encouraged religious debate, listening to Christians, Buddhists, Zoroastrians and Jains, as well as Hindus and Muslims. He received three Jesuits from Goa in his then capital, Fatehpur Sikri, in 1580.

---

1. C.A. Julien, *Histoire de l'Algérie contemporaine: La conquête et les débuts de la colonisation* (1964).

137

Albuquerque Affonso d' (1453–1515): The second Portuguese Viceroy of the Indies. He first visited India in 1503 and in 1506 he accompanied Tristao da Cunha's expedition, in the course of which he briefly seized control of Hormuz. As Viceroy from 1510 to 1515 he conquered Goa, Malacca and Hormuz but failed to take Aden. Enemies at home secured his recall and he died off Goa in December 1515, returning from the capture of Hormuz. It was Albuquerque who established Portuguese government firmly in Goa. His son published extracts from his papers, recording his exploits, under the title *Commentaries*, published in English by the Hakluyt Society in 1875–84.

Almagro Diego d' (*c.*1475–1538): Accompanied Pizarro on his reconnaissance of Peru in 1526 and rescued him in the 1531–2 campaign. Pizarro controlled the north, Almagro (who ventured as far south as Chile) the south of what had been Inca territory. After a quarrel, Pizarro and Almagro's adherents fought near Cuzco in 1538. Almagro was captured and strangled in prison on Pizarro's orders.

Almeida Francisco d' (*c.*1450–1510): The first Portuguese Viceroy of the Indies, appointed in 1505. Founded trading posts in Cochin, Ceylon and Sumatra. When his son, Lorenzo, was killed in a fight with the Egyptians, he took revenge by first burning Goa and then defeating an Egyptian and Gujerati fleet off Diu. He at first refused to accept that he had been superseded by Albuquerque, whom he imprisoned, but finally, sailing for home in 1510, he landed near the later site of Cape Town in South Africa and was killed in a skirmish with the Khoikhoi.

Arabi Pasha (Colonel Ahmed) (*c.*1839–1911): Egyptian nationalist. The son of an Egyptian peasant (*fellah*) family, he joined the army and rose to the rank of colonel. In 1882 he played a leading part in forcing the Kehdive Tewfik to reconstruct his ministry and Arabi was appointed Minister of War. When Britain intervened (ostensibly at the request of the Khedive) and the Egyptian army was defeated at Tel-el-Kebir, Arabi was put on trial and sentenced to death. Instead he was exiled to Ceylon, where he became something of a celebrity, being visited by, among others, Lord Rosebery. He was allowed to return to Egypt in 1901 and lived quietly until his death without participating further in politics.

Archinard Louis (1850–1932): French soldier. Served in the Franco-Prussian war and in North Africa before being sent, in 1880, to supervise the construction of a chain of forts in the western Sudan. Succeeded Gallieni as commandant in the western Sudan in 1888. Initiated the campaign against the Tukalor empire of Ahmadou Ibn Umar Tall, whom he eventually defeated. He conquered much of Mali and installed a puppet ruler. Archinard committed his government to a forward policy, often acting without official approval and going directly against his orders in 1891 in attacking Samori Touré, who had united the people of eastern Mali and Guinea. Although he finally defeated Samori, Archinard did not prove a good Governor and was recalled to a post in the Colonial Ministry in Paris. He was later sent to Indo-China.

Atahualpa (*c*.1502–33): The last Inca ruler of Peru. On his father's death in 1525 he received Quito as his portion, while his half-brother, Huascar, inherited the rest. In the spring of 1532 Atahualpa defeated Huascar and became sole ruler. This civil war weakened the Inca empire just before the Spanish assault. In November 1532, Pizarro tricked Atahualpa into a meeting and took him prisoner. Despite paying an immense ransom – the Spaniards melted down the Inca artefacts to produce 24 tons of gold and silver – he was killed on 29 August 1533. At the end he professed Christianity in return for death by strangulation, rather than by being burnt alive.

Aurungzabe (1618–1707): The last of the great Mughal emperors. He crowned himself Emperor in 1659 after imprisoning his father, Shah Jehan (the builder of the Taj Mahal), and killing his three brothers. The Mughal empire reached its greatest territorial extent during his reign, but he pursued uncompromising Islamic policies and alienated many of his subjects. The empire was by now over-extended and began to collapse after his death.

Averroes European name for Abdul ibn Roshd (1126–98): Arab philosopher and physician. Born in Cordoba (then under the control of the Moors); subsequently became the *cadi* (magistrate) of that town. In philosophy, best known for his commentaries on Aristotle and his neo-Platonic ideas. Sometimes accused of heresy by his co-religionists. His writings were important in re-introducing classical learning to the West.

Avicenna European name for Ibn Sina (980–1037): Arab philosopher and physician, born in Bokhara, then under Persian control. His medical treatises were in general use in European universities until the seventeenth century. His commentaries on Aristotle, like those of Averroes a century later, re-introduced classical texts to the West.

Balboa Vasco Nunez de (1475–1519): Spanish conquistador. An impoverished aristocrat, he accompanied Rodrigo de Bastidos on a reconnaissance of the north coast of Panama, before settling in Santo Domingo. Obliged to flee his creditors, he joined an expedition to Darien. He usurped the position of the official leader, de Encisco, and in 1510 was appointed Captain-General of Darien. On 25 September 1513 he became the first Spaniard to see the Pacific Ocean and claimed it for the Spanish King. Although he was able to send both gold and pearls home, his enemies gained the King's ear. He was suspended and eventually executed in January 1519.

Baltimore 1st Baron (George Calvert) (*c*.1580–1623): MP from 1609 and a Secretary of State, 1619–23. Obtained land grants to settle colonists in North America. A convert to Roman Catholicism, he settled a small colony at Ferryland in Newfoundland in the 1620s and planned a larger colony in Virginia, but died (15 April 1632) before the charter for that was sealed.

Baltimore 2nd Baron (Cecil Calvert) (1606–75): The charter promised to his father was transferred to him and he founded what became the colony of

Maryland to provide a home for Roman Catholics on the shores of Chesapeake Bay.

Banerjea Sir Surendranath (1848–1925): Indian scholar and nationalist. Born in Calcutta, the son of a doctor, he was educated in Calcutta and at University College, London. He passed the entrance examination for the élite Indian Civil Service in 1869 but left it in 1874 after allegations of irregularities about his candidature and his administration. He became Professor of English literature in Calcutta in 1875, where he founded the Indian Association of Calcutta (All-India Association) in 1876 and became the proprietor of the *Bengalee* newspaper in 1878. He seized the opportunities presented by the establishment of the Indian National Congress and was its President in 1895 and 1902. He opposed the partition of Bengal but was always studiously moderate. After the First World War he hoped to make the Montagu–Chelmsford reforms work but was side-lined by younger men.

Barghash Ibn Said (*c*.1837–88): Sultan of Zanzibar. A younger son of Seyyid Said, he failed to seize the throne on his father's death in 1856 but succeeded legitimately in 1870. Strongly resisted the British attempts to end the slave trade because the Zanzibari clove plantations depended on slave labour. But, in 1873, was compelled to prohibit the export of slaves and to close the major Zanzibari slave market. In 1876, alarmed by German activities, he acceded to British demands that he forbid the inland slaving caravans. The Germans, however, compelled him to accept their treaties with inland chiefs, over whom the Sultan claimed jurisdiction.

Baring Evelyn – *see* Cromer, Lord

Barnato Barney (Rufus Isaacs) (1852–97): Speculator and diamond merchant. Born in the East End of London and, as a young man, appeared in vaudeville with his brother. In 1873 joined his brother in South Africa, where they assumed the name Barnarto and set up a diamond brokerage. They became rich by buying up supposedly 'exhausted' claims, and in the 1880s, as the Barnarto Diamond Mining Company, were strong enough to challenge De Beers Consolidated. The two companies merged in 1888. Barnarto dabbled in politics, at first backed by Cecil Rhodes, but denounced the Jameson Raid. Barnarto committed suicide in 1897.

Barth Heinrich (1821–65): German explorer. He travelled extensively in the western and central Sudan in the 1850s and 1860s, originally as a member of an English scientific expedition. He was an accomplished linguist, knowing a number of African languages. He published a scholarly account of the region in three volumes in 1857–8 in both English and German, *Travels and Discoveries in North and Central Africa*. But the public preferred sensational accounts such as J. Smith's *Trade and Travel in the Gulph of Guinea* (1851) and, a little later, those of Henry Morton Stanley.

Beit Alfred (1853–1906): Financier. Born in Hamburg into a merchant family. Went to Amsterdam in 1874 to learn about the diamond industry and the following year went out to the Kimberley diamond fields. Quickly recognised the quality of the diamonds (which many had previously underestimated). Borrowed £2000 from his father and returned to Kimberley to set up his own business. In 1882 went into partnership with J. Porges and Julius Wernher; in 1890 became the firm of Wernher, Beit & Co. But the most important influence on him was Cecil John Rhodes, whom he met at Kimberley. Beit became a naturalised British subject. He joined the board of De Beers Diamond Company and helped Rhodes in the amalgamation of all the chief diamond interests at Kimberley which resulted in De Beers Consolidated Mines (1888). The same year he visited the Witwatersrand and quickly began to invest in the gold mines. In 1889 he became a director of Rhodes' British South Africa Company. Beit was implicated in the Jameson Raid and temporarily had to leave the board of the British South Africa Company. After Rhodes' death in March 1902, Beit briefly became the leading figure in both De Beers and the British South Africa Company, but he was himself incapacitated by a stroke later that year.

Bentham Jeremy (1748–1832): English political philosopher. He was trained as a lawyer and called to the Bar in 1767, but he had enough private means to pursue his preferred career as a writer. He founded the school of thought which became known as 'utilitarianism'. He thought colonies were of little value or 'utility'. He had French citizenship conferred upon him during the Revolution and, in 1792, addressed a pamphlet entitled 'Emancipate your Colonies' to the French National Assembly. He disapproved of transportation and, as an alternative, put forward his 'Panopticon' scheme for prison reform. He was, however, worried about population growth and could not totally disapprove of emigration. Ironically, his philosophy was adopted by English reformers, including his close disciples James and John Stuart Mill, in relation to India and several attempts were made to reform India along utilitarian lines in the 1830s.

Bismarck Otto von (1815–98): Chancellor of Germany, 1871–90. His main interests and ambitions were in Europe but he briefly became interested in colonial affairs in the mid-1880s. In 1871 he had turned down pleas that Germany should take France's colonies rather than Alsace-Lorraine after the Franco-Prussian war. He may have been genuinely irritated by what he saw as England's cavalier attitude to German claims in Fiji and in South-West Africa, but, more importantly, he saw both domestic and diplomatic advantages in espousing a colonial policy in 1884. Domestically, it would split the National Liberals, on whom he was no longer dependent, between the left-wing, who were anti-colonialists of the 'Manchester School', and the right-wing, who represented the trading interests of ports like Hamburg and Bremen, and it would create a new conservative coalition of the Rhineland industrialists and the Prussian Junkers, who were moving towards protectionism in face of economic crisis. Diplomatically, he hoped that, at the cost of a temporary estrangement from England, he could buy the good will of France and achieve a reconciliation with her, similar to the one he had achieved with Austria after the Austro-Prussian war. The Berlin West Africa Conference of 1884–5 showed that

141

German interests were closer to those of England than of France. Bismarck lost interest in a colonial policy and, by 1889, was expressing regret that he had ever embarked on it.

Blunt Wilfrid Scawen (1840–1922): Traveller and poet, supporter of Egyptian, Indian and Irish causes. He entered the diplomatic service in 1858 but was able to leave it after his marriage to Lady Anne Isabella Noel (1837–1917), the granddaughter of Lord Byron, and his inheritance of the family estates on the death of his elder brother. From 1872 he travelled widely in the Middle East and India. In 1881 he bought a house in Egypt and usually wintered there. He became an ardent advocate of the Egyptian nationalist movement and defender of Arabi Pasha. He became equally passionate in his belief that British rule was responsible for Indian poverty, publishing *Ideas about India* in 1885. He took up the cause of Irish nationalism about the same time. His personal friendship with, among others, Lord Granville, the Foreign Secretary, and Lord Lytton, the Viceroy of India, allowed him to lobby them personally but did not save him on one occasion from imprisonment for his activities in Ireland. In 1907 he published his *Secret History of the English Occupation of Egypt* and engaged in a public controversy with Lord Cromer. He was among the small number of westerners at this time who appreciated the significance of the resurgence of Islam and, in 1882, published his *The Future of Islam*. His wife, who was fluent in Arabic and an intrepid traveller, accompanied him on many of his travels and was an important figure in her own right.

Blyden Edward Wilmot (1832–1912): Writer, academic, journalist and civil servant but most important as defender of black civilisation. Born in St Thomas in the Virgin Islands of free and literate parents, probably of Ibo descent. He decided to become a Presbyterian minister but found such prejudice in the United States when he went to study theology that he went to Liberia in 1851. In 1862 he became Professor of Classics in the new Liberia College, of which he was later to be the President. From 1864 to 1866 he was also Secretary of State for Liberia. In 1871–3 he lived in Sierra Leone and edited the *Negro*, the first pan-African journal in West Africa. He later edited the *Sierra Leone News* and the *West African Reporter*. He failed to become President of Liberia in 1885 but became the Liberian ambassador to both Britain and France. He wrote a number of books, of which *Christianity, Islam and the Negro Races* (1887) was the most important. He tried to build bridges between Christianity and Islam but above all he tried to make Africans conscious of and proud of their own heritage.

Bolívar Simón, called 'The Liberator' (1783–1830): General and politician who played the leading role in gaining independence for Spain's former colonies in South America. Venezuela was liberated in 1813 and Bolívar was appointed dictator but, after much dissension, he was compelled to flee to Jamaica. He returned to Venezuela in 1816 and defeated the royalist forces at Boyaca in 1819. He set up the 'Colombian Republic' of Venezuela, Colombia and Ecuador and completed the liberation of Venezuela at the battle of Carabobo in 1821. He went on to conquer Peru in 1824 and Upper Peru adopted the name

Bolivia in his honour. But Bolivar failed in his attempt to unite all the liberated countries in a federation. He escaped assassination in 1828 but died, probably of tuberculosis, with his plans in apparent disarray in 1830.

Botha General Louis (1862–1919): Boer general and politician. He was born in Natal but of Voortrekker stock. His family moved to the Orange Free State and Botha himself subsequently went to the Transvaal. In 1884 he joined the Boer commando, which intervened in the Zulu civil war on the disputed succession on the death of Cetawayo. He was only a 'field cornet' (lieutenant) at the beginning of the Boer War in 1899 but gained rapid promotion, taking part in the battles at Dundee, Colenso and Spion Kop. He took command of all the Boer forces after the death of General Joubert in March 1900 but eventually had to agree to the peace at Vereeniging in May 1902. In 1905 he founded a Boer political party, *Het Volk* (The People), with Jan Smuts, which won the Transvaal elections in 1907. The Boer generals were now the leading politicians in South Africa and Botha became the first Prime Minister of the new Union of South Africa in 1910. In 1914 he persuaded parliament to endorse British actions in the First World War and himself led the force which expelled the Germans from South-West Africa. He had achieved reconciliation with the British, which offended some Boers, but he believed in the segregation of the black and white races. His government introduced the Natives Land Act (1913), which divided the country into 'white' and 'black' areas, with whites forbidden to buy land in black areas and vice versa. Problems with Indian indentured labourers also brought him into conflict with Gandhi, who espoused their cause in the Transvaal.

Brewster William (*c.*1566–1644): English Puritan who played a prominent role in the *Mayflower* voyage. Probably converted to Puritanism when a student at Cambridge, he became the leader of a Separatist group at Scrooby in Lincolnshire which emigrated to Leiden. Brewster himself ran a printing press to disseminate Puritan pamphlets. A marked man, he had to be smuggled aboard the *Mayflower*. He was the leading layman in the new colony at Plymouth.

Brière de l'Isle Louis-Alexandre (1827–96): French soldier. Born in Martinique. He served in China in 1860 and in Indo-China in 1861 and again in 1866–8. In 1871 he was attached to the Minister of Marine as the head of the bureau for colonial troops. He was Governor of Senegal from 1876 to 1881 and revived plans to extend French territory to the Niger, but his authoritarianism cause offence and he was recalled. In 1883 he was sent to command an expeditionary force in Tonkin but was again recalled to France in October 1885 after the failure at Lang Son.

Bright John (1811–89): British radical politician and Quaker. MP for Manchester and later for Birmingham. Led the Anti-Corn Law League with Richard Cobden. A prominent member of the so-called 'Manchester School', which favoured free trade and generally disliked colonies. Bright, however, made at least a partial exception in the case of India. He wished to see India well governed but did not envisage speedy separation. He chaired the parliamentary

143

select committee which inquired into the obstacles to cotton growing in India in 1848 and took a leading role in the India Reform Society, formed in London in 1853. He opposed the British military intervention in Egypt in 1882 and resigned from the government on the issue.

Brooks Sir James (1803–68): The first 'White Rajah' of Sarawak. He was born in India, the son of a judge of the High Court of Calcutta. In 1819 he joined the armed forces of the East India Company and was severely wounded in the first Burmese war in 1824. He subsequently travelled in Malaya and, in 1839, visited North Borneo. He became involved in the civil war there and, in 1841, accepted the governorship of Sarawak from the Sultan of Brunei. He formed good relations with both the Malays and the Dayaks and had some success in putting down the piracy which was endemic in the region. The British government turned down his pleas that the area should be taken under British protection. Instead he founded a dynasty and was succeeded by his nephew, Captain James Brooke (born Charles Johnson).

Brown George (1818–80): Canadian politician and newspaper editor; one of the architects of Canadian confederation. Born in Scotland, he emigrated with his family to the United States and then, in 1843, to Toronto. In 1844 he founded the *Globe* newspaper. He was a member of the Reform Party and campaigned strongly for an end to the system by which Canada West (mainly English) and Canada East (mainly French) had equal representation in the Canadian Assembly and in favour of 'rep by pop', representation in proportion to population, which would have given the English a majority. But he saw the long-term solution to the deadlock in Canada as a wider federation of the British North American provinces and joined the 'Great Coalition' of 1864 to secure this, despite his dislike of the Conservative leader, John A. Macdonald. He continued to support federation even after he resigned from the coalition.

Bugeaud Thomas Robert, Marshal (Duke of Isly): (1784–1849) French soldier, responsible for the conquest of Algeria. He joined the army in 1804 and became experienced in countering guerilla tactics during the Peninsular War. In 1831 he was promoted to Marshal. In 1834 he suppressed a popular protest rising in Paris. He was sent to Algeria in 1836 where he fought Abd-el-Kader over a period of 11 years. He was named Governor-General of Algeria in 1840. He defeated the Moroccan allies of Abd-el-Kader at Isly in 1844. In 1848 Louis Philippe gave him command of the troops in Paris but he failed to avert the revolution. He died of cholera in 1849.

Buller Sir Charles (1806–48): Liberal politician. He was born in Calcutta, where his father was in the revenue department of the East India Company. Thomas Carlyle was his tutor for a time. Buller was called to the Bar in 1831 and was MP for various Cornish constituencies. In the Commons he was one of a group of influential radicals who took an interest in colonial affairs and included Roebuck, John Stuart Mill, Grote and Molesworth. Buller accompanied Lord Durham to Canada in 1838 as his Chief Secretary and was responsible for part of the Durham Report, particularly that relating to land issues. Because of

Durham's premature death, Buller was left to explain what he believed to have been Durham's ideas on important issues, including responsible government – in fact, it was Buller, not Durham, who coined the phrase. Buller was briefly Secretary of the Board of Control in 1841 until Sir Robert Peel succeeded the Whigs. He sympathised with the position of the Colonial Reformers and became a bitter foe of James Stephen, the Permanent Under-Secretary at the Colonial Office, accusing the Colonial Office, especially in his pamphlet, *Mr Mother Country*, of a combination of ignorance and lack of vision. In fact the clash was an ideological one. The Colonial Reformers wished to develop what they saw as 'White Man's Country' in, for example, New Zealand, while Stephen was much influenced by the missionaries' desire to protect the non-Europeans.

Burgoyne General John (1722–92): British soldier, politician and playwright. Served in Europe during the Seven Years War. In 1777 he was sent to Canada with instructions to join forces with Howe in New York State. He took Ticonderoga but was compelled to surrender to General Gates at Saratoga. Burgoyne was MP for Preston and defended himself vigorously against criticism in parliament. He was also the author of successful plays.

Burke Edmund (1729–97): British politician and writer. Born in Dublin and educated at Trinity College. He was Private Secretary to Lord Rockingham, who was Prime Minister (1765), and himself entered parliament. After Rockingham lost office, Burke was a strong opponent of George III, publishing his *Thoughts on the Present Discontents* in 1770. He supported the cause of the American colonists, whom he believed had precedent on their side in refusing to be taxed by the British government. When Rockingham returned to power in 1782, Burke became Paymaster-General and was responsible for the policy of 'economical reform', designed to reduce government patronage. One incidental result was the abolition of the new post of Secretary of State for the Colonies. Burke was deeply involved in the drafting of Fox's India Bill and a leading opponent of Warren Hastings, becoming one of the government 'managers' who prepared the impeachment in 1787. In the course of attacking Warren Hastings, Burke proclaimed his doctrines of 'trusteeship' and argued that Britain should not have interfered with Indian civilisation. He opposed the French Revolution, notably in his *Reflections on the Revolution in France* (1790), on the same philosophical grounds: society was an organic growth that could not be made over according to theories. Burke's ideas provided a formidable criticism of the utilitarians' wish to reform India.

Burton Sir Richard Francis (1821–90): British explorer and writer. While serving with the East India Company army in the 1840s, he developed a life-long interest in Islam. He became fluent in Arabic as well as other languages, including Portuguese. In 1853 he visited Mecca and Medina, disguised as an Afghan pilgrim, publishing his account as *Pilgrimage to El Medina and Meccah* in 1855–6. He served as British Consul in Fernando Po (1861), Brazil (1865–9), Damascus (1869–71) and Trieste (1872–90) and explored widely in Africa and South America. He also attained fame as a translator of Camoens and of the

145

Thousand and One Nights (from the Arabic), although his wife, Isabella Arundel, destroyed his translation of *The Scented Garden*.

Buxton Thomas Fowell (1781–1845): Anti-slavery campaigner. A brewer by profession, he became interested in social questions in general and the fight against slavery in particular. MP for Weymouth (1813–37), he succeeded William Wilberforce as the leader of the anti-slavery party in 1824. He was closely associated with the 'Niger experiment' of 1841–2, an attempt to replace the slave trade by legitimate commerce in the Niger delta. It failed because of the prevalence of malaria, but it helped to lay the foundations for the later important British trade in palm oil.

Cabot John (Giovanni Cabotto) (*c.*1450–*c.*1498): Navigator. Born in Genoa, he moved to Venice, where he became a citizen about 1473. It is not known when he moved to England, but it must have been before 1495. In 1496 he obtained letters patent from Henry VII, authorising him to 'seek out, discover and find' all hitherto unknown lands. After an abortive voyage in 1496 he left Bristol in a small ship, the *Matthew*, with his sons and a crew of 18 on 2 May 1497. His objective was a route to China. He reached land 52 days later, probably at Bonavista in Newfoundland, although rival claims have been made for Cape Breton Island and Nova Scotia. On his return the King granted him a pension of £20 a year and further letters patent, authorising him to take possession of the newly discovered lands. He sailed from Bristol with a small fleet and 300 men in May 1498. He probably reached the coast of Newfoundland and Nova Scotia and perhaps New England (discoveries there, ascribed to the English, appear in Juan de la Cosa's map of 1500), but Cabot himself died either on the voyage or immediately afterwards.

Cabot Sebastian (*c.*1474–1557): Navigator. The son of John Cabot, probably born in Venice. Probably accompanied his father on his 1497 voyage. Continued for some time in English service. May have found the entrance to Hudson's Bay on voyage in 1508–9. Drew maps for Henry VIII in 1512 but then entered Spanish service. Became Pilot General in 1518, but, after a financially unsuccessful expedition to South America in 1526–30, he was briefly imprisoned. Returned to England in 1547. In 1551 became Governor (Chairman) of Merchant Adventurers. Organised voyages to Russia of 1553, 1554 and 1556, seeking a north-east passage to China.

Cabral Pedro Álvarez (*c.*1440–1526): Portuguese navigator. In 1500 placed in command of fleet of 13 ships bound for India. Took very westerly track across the Atlantic and touched on coast of Brazil, which he claimed for Portugal. Lost four vessels off the Cape of Good Hope but secured a pilot in Mozambique and reached Calicut. Authorities refused to receive him and he bombarded the town and moved south to Cochin.

Calvert Cecil – *see* Baltimore, 1st Baron

Calvert George – *see* Baltimore, 2nd Baron

Canning Charles (1812–62): A younger son of George Canning, he succeeded Lord Dalhousie as Governor-General of India in 1855, becoming Viceroy after the Government of India Act in 1858, and remaining there until 1862. He was nicknamed 'Clemency Canning' for proclaiming an amnesty after the 'Mutiny' of 1857.

Canning George (1770–1827): British politician. He was President of the Board of Control for India, 1816–21, and had accepted the Governor-Generalship in 1822 but instead became Foreign Secretary on the death of Castlereagh. As Foreign Secretary he recognised the independence of those South American states which had thrown off Spanish rule.

Cão Diogo (*fl.* 1480s): Portuguese navigator. In 1483 reached the mouth of the Congo and sailed some distance upstream. Established first contacts between the Portuguese and the Congolese.

Carnarvon (Henry Howard Molyneux Herbert), 4th Earl of (1831–90): British politician. Colonial Secretary in Conservative administrations in 1866–7 and 1874–8. In 1867 he introduced the measure for the federation of the Canadian provinces, the British North America Act, into the British parliament. He became convinced that federation was a panacea and tried unsuccessfully to introduce it into South Africa in the 1870s.

Cartier Georges (1814–73): Canadian politician, born in Montreal. He took part in the 1837 rebellion. He became the Conservative leader in the Canadian Legislative Assembly in 1848. In 1858–62 he was joint Prime Minister with John A. Macdonald, at the time of the 'double majorities', when governments needed majorities in both Upper and Lower Canada. He was one of the 'Fathers of the Confederation', i.e. one of the architects of the 1867 constitution.

Cartier Jacques (1494–1557): French explorer. Born in St Malo. In 1534 commanded an expedition to seek the North-West Passage. Reached the Gulf of St Lawrence, although failed to find the entrance to the St Lawrence River. Traded with the Indians and took possession of the Gaspé Peninsula in the name of France. Returned with two captives. From them he learnt of the St Lawrence River. On his next expedition in 1536 he sailed up the St Lawrence to the Huron village of Stadcona (near the modern Quebec City) and then, in his ship's pinnace, to the Indian village of Hochelaga. Climbed the mountain behind it and called it the Royal Mountain (*Mont Real*). Further progress blocked by rapids which he called (apparently in disgust, not confusion) *La Chine* (China). On his third voyage in 1541 he sought minerals near River Saguenay.

Casement Roger (1864–1916): British diplomat and Irish nationalist. He served as British Consul in Lourenço Marques (1895), the Congo Free State (1898–1905) and Brazil (1908–13). He played a leading role in exposing the 'red rubber' scandal in the Congo. Came to support Irish independence, looking for German support in the First World War, and was executed by the British in 1916.

Cetewayo (Cetshwayo) (*c.*1826–84): Fourth and last independent ruler of Zululand. Succeeded his father, Mpande, in 1872. Concerned to protect his country from possible encroachment from Transvaal. After the annexation of the Transvaal by Britain in 1878, the British High Commissioner demanded the demobilisation of the Zulu forces. Cetewayo refused. Defeated a British force under Chelmsford at Isandlwana on 22 January 1879 but was crushed in battle at capital, Ulundi, on 4 July 1879. Cetewayo was arrested but released in 1882 and, the following year, allowed to return to rule a truncated Zulu kingdom. Civil war followed. Cetewayo escaped but died soon afterwards.

Chamberlain Joseph (1836–1914): British politician with a Birmingham business background. Originally a radical, he resigned from Gladstone's government in 1885 in protest at the proposed Irish Home Rule legislation, which went further than he wished. Joined Salisbury's Unionist administration in 1895, going to the Colonial Office at his own request. Was intent on 'modernising' the empire, which he saw as 'undeveloped estates'. Implicated in the Jameson Raid and blamed by some for the Boer war ('Joe's war'). He was interested in the idea of an imperial *Zollverein* (customs union). His support for imperial preference split the Unionist Party in 1903 and they subsequently lost the 1906 election. Although he lived until 1914, he never recovered from a stroke he suffered in 1906.

Champlain Samuel de (1567–1635): French soldier and seaman. The effective founder of French Canada. After serving in the wars he sailed (1601–3) to the West Indies in Spanish ships. In 1603 on a French expedition, he sailed up the St Lawrence and reached Montreal. He also planted a small colony near the mouth of the St Croix River (the settlement later moved to Port Royal in Acadia). In 1604–5 he charted the coast of what became New England as far as Cape Cod. On a new expedition in 1608 he constructed a small fort near what is now Quebec City. In 1609 he concluded an alliance with the Hurons against the Iroquois, and in an incident near the site of the later Ticonderoga he ensured a Huron victory by the use of firearms. In 1615 he began his explorations of the interior. While in France in 1619 he wrote up accounts of his voyages. In 1620 he returned to New France with his young wife, as lieutenant to the Viceroy, the duc de Montmorency and from then on made his home in Canada.

Chancellor Richard (d. 1556): English navigator. Was second in command on Sir Hugh Willoughby's expedition to find a north-east passage in 1553. When the ships were separated by a storm, Chancellor went on alone. Did not find a north-east passage but reached Moscow and was received by the Tsar. Visited Moscow again in 1556. Although Chancellor himself was drowned off Scotland in 1556, he began the trade between Britain and Russia, conducted by the Muscovy Company.

Charles V (1500–58): Holy Roman Emperor and King of Germany and Spain. Grandson of Ferdinand and Isabella, from whom he inherited the Spanish dominions, and of the Emperor Maximilian, from whom he inherited the

Habsburg lands. Crowned Holy Roman Emperor in 1520. His reign covered the early years of the Reformation, which split Europe between Catholics and Protestants and also saw the growth of the Spanish empire in South and Central America. Bullion from the New World had a serious impact on the economy of the whole of Europe. He abdicated in 1555 and Spain passed to his son, Philip II.

Charnock Job (d. 1693): The founder of Calcutta. An employee of the English East India Company, he sailed to Madras about 1655. He settled and erected a fort at what became Calcutta in 1690. Despite the unhealthiness of the site, it was to become the centre of British government in India, until superseded by Delhi in 1911.

Child John (d. 1690): Soldier and Governor of Bombay. Sent to India as a child to join an uncle. Became agent of the English East India Company at Surat in 1680. Involved in various struggles with the Mughal Emperor. Governor of Bombay in 1685 when the seat of government was transferred from Surat to Bombay. In 1686 authority extended over Bengal and Madras.

Child Sir Josiah (1630–99): London merchant and writer. An MP and a Director, later Governor, of the English East India Company. Wrote or commissioned writings in the Company's defence. Well-known for a treatise *A New Discourse of Trade* (1675), in which he compared British policy unfavourably with that of the Dutch.

Clive Robert (Lord) (1725–74): Soldier who consolidated British power in India. Went to Madras in 1744 as a clerk in the service of the East India Company but became a soldier and involved in the struggles with the French. In 1751 he took and held Arcot and secured the nawabship of the Carnatic for the English candidate. Returned to India in 1766 after three years in England to learn of the death of over 100 Englishmen in the Black Hole of Calcutta for which Siraj-ud-daula, the Nawab of Bengal, was held responsible. Clive sailed for Bengal from Madras and made common cause with Siraj-ud-daula's rival, Mir Jaffir. Won the battle of Plassey (23 June 1857) from which British domination of India is traditionally dated. Mir Jaffir replaced Siraj-ud-daula. When in England, 1760–5, became MP for Shrewsbury. Returned to India, 1765–7. The Nawab of the Carnatic was now under British control and in 1765 the Mughal Emperor granted the East India Company the *diwani* of Bengal. When Clive finally returned to England in 1767 he was fiercely attacked for his actions in India in both parliament and the press. He was cleared by an official inquiry of misconduct but, always subject to depression, he committed suicide in November 1774.

Coen Jan Pieterszoon (1587–1630): The founder of Batavia. He advocated a 'mailed fist' in opposition to colleagues who preferred a more peaceful trading policy. He seized Jakarta in 1619 in defiance of both the Sultan of Bantam and the Directors of the Dutch East India Company at home. He later claimed the surrounding land.

149

Colbert Jean-Baptiste (1619–83): French statesman. Served under Cardinal Mazarin. Appointed Finance Minister in 1661. A committed mercantilist who reorganised the whole French financial system. Developed a large fleet and founded the French East India Company. Fostered colonies in the West Indies and in Canada. The colony in Canada was highly organised. Colbert sent out balanced groups of men and women, including professional men, farmers and skilled artisans, and established a coherent community, which even today is a 'distinct society'.

Columbus Christopher (1451–1508): Sailor and explorer. Born in Genoa of a working-class family. Later joined his brother, Bartolomé, in Lisbon. Became convinced it was possible to reach Asia by a westerly route – partly because he underestimated the circumference of the globe. Unsuccessfully approached John II of Portugal to back him in 1484. Went to Spain in 1485 but only in 1492 obtained the backing of Ferdinand and Isabella. They granted him half any future profits and promised his family the hereditary governorship of all lands annexed for Castile. Set sail with three ships, the *Santa Maria* (a *não* of 100 tons), the *Pinta* and the *Nina* (both small caravels), from Palos on 3 August 1492. Voyaged by way of the Canary Islands and, either by luck or acting on prior information, picked up the trade winds. On 12 October landed in the Bahamas. Met parties of Arawaks, whom he called 'Indians' in the mistaken belief that he had reached Asia. Sailed on to Hispaniola, where the *Santa Maria* ran aground and some of the party had to be left behind. His second expedition in 1493 was much larger. He sailed from Cadiz with 17 ships. Discovered Dominica and Puerto Rico. His brother Bartolomé founded Santo Domingo on the southern side of Hispaniola. In course of third voyage in 1498 touched on South America. Had made enemies at home and new governor, Francisco de Bobadillo, sent both Christopher and Bartolomé home in chains. Rehabilitated and undertook fourth voyage in 1501 when he sailed down the coast of Central America. Although puzzled by some of his discoveries, Columbus died believing that he had reached Asia.

Cook Captain James (1728–79): British navigator. In 1783 he surveyed the coasts of Newfoundland and Labrador. In 1768 he was sent in command of the *Endeavour* to the Pacific to observe the transit of Venus on behalf of the Royal Society. After observing the transit at Tahiti, he circumnavigated and charted New Zealand. He also visited the east coast of Australia and named it New South Wales. Returned to England by way of the Cape in 1771. In 1772 he sailed in the *Resolution* to explore the great southern continent (*Terra Australis Incognita*) which scientists surmised must exist in the southern hemisphere. Found only the New Hebrides and New Caledonia. In 1773 he sailed again in the *Resolution* to explore the North Pacific and search for a western outlet to the North West Passage. In 1778 he discovered the Sandwich Islands (Hawaiian islands) and was killed on a return visit there in 1779.

Cornwallis Charles, 1st Marquess (1783–1805): British soldier and Governor-General of India. Entered the House of Lords on succeeding his father as earl in 1762. He served in the Seven Years War and (although he had opposed North's policy in parliament) in the American War of Independence, surrendering to George Washington at Yorktown in 1781. From 1786 to 1793 he was Governor-General and Commander-in-Chief in India. He was responsible for the so-called 'Permanent Settlement' of Bengal, which was supposed to rationalise the land tenure and taxation system there, and initiated what became known as the *zemindari* system, in which he tried to turn the *zemindars* or tax farmers of the Mughal empire into reforming landlords. As Lord Lieutenant of Ireland, 1798–1801, he suppressed the 1798 rising and helped to put through the Act of Union but resigned when George III refused to honour the government's pledge to remove civil disabilities from Roman Catholics. He returned briefly to India in 1805 but died in October of that year.

Cortés Hernando (1485–1547): Spanish conquistador. Conqueror of the Aztec empire. The son of a small landed gentry family, he first sailed to Hispaniola in 1504. In 1511 he joined an expedition to Cuba. In 1519 he led an expedition to Mexico of 600 Spaniards, 200 'Indian' auxiliaries and 16 horses. In August he arrived at Tenochtitlán, the capital of Montezuma II. Although he was accepted as a guest, he took Montezuma hostage. The Spanish governor, Velázquez, sent a force to recall Cortés, whom he distrusted, but Cortés persuaded them to join him and also acquired Indian allies. In May 1521 he began an attack on Tenochtitlán, supported by a small naval force which had been built elsewhere, transported to Lake Texcoco and reassembled. After 75 days of bitter fighting the city fell to Cortés. In October 1522 Charles V appointed Cortés Governor and Captain-General of New Spain. Rebuilt Tenochtitlán as Mexico City. Most of central and southern Mexico was brought under Spanish control. In 1526 he was deprived of his governorship. Successfully defended himself and allowed to return to Mexico in 1530 to run his large estate there but with a purely honorific title. Returned to Spain in 1540 but, when he died, was buried at his own request in Mexico.

Cromer Lord (Evelyn Baring, 1st Earl) (1841–1917): British pro-consul and virtual governor of Egypt, 1883–1907. A member of the Baring banking family, he was sent in 1872 to act as secretary to his cousin, Lord Northbrook, then Viceroy of India. He was in Egypt from 1877 to 1880 as the British Commissioner for the Debt and later the Controller of the Revenue. He then returned to India. In 1883 he was sent back to Egypt as British Consul-General. He saw his first task as the reconstruction of the Egyptian finances. Although some regarded him as a difficult man (the 'Great Bear'), he maintained good relations with many Egyptians and his administration was widely admired as a model. After retiring he published his *Modern Egypt* (1908), which was intended as a defence of British policy. He also became President of the Classical Association and delivered his presidential lecture on 'Imperialisms Ancient and Modern' (published 1910), in which he argued that colour consciousness was a modern phenomenon, almost unknown in the ancient world.

Cromwell Oliver (1559–1658): Lord Protector of Great Britain and Ireland, 1653–8, during the Civil War. In 1849–50 he had defeated those Irish and Scots who remained loyal to the monarchy. In his foreign policy he supported an alignment of the Protestant countries of Europe and engaged in a struggle with Spain, particularly in the Caribbean, which resulted in the capture of Jamaica in 1665.

Curzon George Nathaniel (Lord) (1859–1925): His interest in India was roused when a boy at Eton and in 1887 and 1892 he travelled widely in India and Central Asia. He became Under-Secretary for India in 1891–2 and fufilled a long-held ambition by becoming Viceroy in 1898. He established an Agricultural Department to put Indian agriculture on a scientific footing to try to combat rural poverty, and he founded the Archaeological Department, of which Sir Mortimer Wheeler was the most famous director, to study India's past. But he was intensely authoritarian – his critics called him 'the last of the Mughal Emperors' – and he had no faith in the Indians' ability to govern themselves. He mortally offended the Indian middle classes and political activists by his Universities Act and by the partition of Bengal. He resigned in 1905 after a quarrel with his Commander-in-Chief, Lord Kitchener. He served in Lloyd George's War Cabinet and became Foreign Secretary in 1919.

Dalhousie Lord (George Ramsay, 9th Earl of) (1770–1838): Became Governor of Nova Scotia in 1816 and Governor-in-Chief of all Canadian provinces from 1819 to 1828. Commander-in-Chief in the East Indies, 1829–32.

Dalhousie Lord (James, 10th Earl of) (1812–60): Governor-General of India, 1847–56. Unlike his immediate predecessors, he embarked on a policy of expanding British India. The Punjab was annexed after the second Sikh war, 1848–9, and Lower Burma after the second Burma war in 1852. He applied the 'doctrine of lapse' and thus acquired, among other states, Satara in 1849 and Jhansi and Nagpur in 1853, and also annexed Oudh in 1856. The offence he thus caused was regarded by many as an important cause of the 'Mutiny' of 1857. But his modernising of India by his support for railways, canals, roads, telegraphs and postal services was probably at least as disturbing to Indian society.

Day Francis (d. 1642): The founder of Madras. He established a factory at Armagaum on the Coramandel coast of India in 1625 but, in 1638, was instructed to find a more suitable spot, less exposed to possible Dutch attack. In 1639 he purchased five miles of land near the old Portuguese settlement of São Tomé, where he built a factory and fort which he called Fort St George. The modern city of Madras (Chennai) grew up round it.

Decoeur Henri-Alexis (1855–1900): French soldier. In 1893 he was sent to explore the hinterland of Dahomey. The French learnt of the British intention to send Lord Lugard to the Borgu region and also feared German expansion from Togoland. In August 1894 Decoeur was ordered to anticipate these moves. He arrived at Nikki, the capital of Borgu, five days after Lugard but with authority to conclude a protectorate treaty, which Lugard did not have. He went on to conclude other treaties in the region. The 'race' between Lugard and Decoeur came close to causing a war, not resolved until the Anglo-French agreement in 1898.

Delamere Lord, 3rd Baron (Hugh Cholmondeley) (1870–1931): Settler leader among European community in Kenya. President of Farmers' and Planters' Association (1903) and leading figure in Convention of Associations (popularly called the 'Settlers' Parliament') in 1911. Ultimate aim was to make Kenya a white dominion.

Delcassé Théophile (1852–1923): French politician. Elected to the Chamber of Deputies in 1899. He belonged to the group which believed that colonies would enhance French power rather than detract from France's role in Europe. He became Under-Secretary for the Colonies in 1893, Colonial Minister, 1894–5, and Foreign Minister, 1898–1905. He had to concede to the British over the Fashoda incident in 1898. He later claimed (a claim not accepted by all historians) that the Fashoda incident delayed the conclusion of an *entente* with the British which he had always desired. The 1904 Anglo-French agreements settled a number of colonial disputes and, notably, promised co-operation in Egypt and Morocco. Delcassé himself was forced to resign in 1905 because he could not carry the Cabinet with him in the Morocco crisis.

Diagne Blaise (1872–1934): Senegalese politician. His family had French citizenship by right of the 1848 grant. He became the first African elected to the National Assembly in 1914.

Dias Bartolomeu (d. 1500): Portuguese navigator. Discovered sea-route to Indian Ocean. Little is known of his early life. Left Lisbon in August 1487 with two caravels to continue exploration of the African coast. Blown out to sea by storms and on 3 February 1488 landed at what is now Mossell Bay on east coast of South Africa. Probably reached the mouth of the Keiskamma River before mutinous crew compelled him to turn back. On return voyage sighted what, according to legend, he called the Cape of Storms but which the King renamed the Cape of Good Hope. Reached the Tagus in December 1488. Employed in administration of Guinea gold trade until 1494. Accompanied Cabral's expedition to Brazil in 1500 but lost at sea.

Dingaan (Dingane) (*c.*1795–1840): Paramount chief of the Zulus, 1828–40. The half-brother of Shaka, he was spared when the latter seized the throne because he seemed weak and had not opposed him, but in 1828 Dingaan joined with others to kill him. He became involved in war with the Europeans, destroying a Portuguese garrison at Delagoa Bay in 1833. In 1837 he first agreed land grants for the Boers, then murdered a delegation of Afrikaaners led by Pieter Retief, while entertaining them. He was defeated by the Boers under Andreis Pretorius at Blood River in December 1838. In 1840 he was defeated by another half-brother, Mpande, and subsequently murdered.

Disraeli Benjamin (Earl of Beaconsfield) (1804–81): British Conservative politician. Chancellor of the Exchequer in Derby's three administrations, 1852, 1858–9 and 1866–8. Prime Minister, 1868 and 1874–80. Traditionally supposed to have held separatist views as a young politician, referring to the colonies as 'millstones', but to have become a leading advocate of imperialism from the time of his speech at the Crystal Palace in 1872. Modern research has greatly modified the picture. Except in moments of exasperation, Disraeli probably did not hold anti-empire views earlier in his career; his later interest in imperialism related almost entirely to India and the route to India. He showed little knowledge of the colonies of settlement and evinced no interest in a general expansion in Africa. But he played the empire card skilfully against his opponent, William Gladstone. He gave Britain a stake in the Suez Canal by buying the bankrupt Khedive's shares in 1875 and acquired control of Cyprus in 1878 at the time of the Congress of Berlin, in which he played a leading role. His proclamation of Queen Victoria as Empress of India received a mixed reception in Britain as well as in India. The 'forward' policy with which his government was associated in Afghanistan (the war of 1879–80) and South Africa (the annexation of the Transvaal) was partly determined by the men on the spot, but Disraeli had given hostages to fortune by appointing the expansionist Lord Lytton as Viceroy of India.

Drake Sir Francis (*c*.1540–96): English seaman and explorer. Born in Devon and related to the Hawkins family. Took part in John Hawkins' voyage to the West Indies in 1567–8. Commanded the *Judith*, which escaped the Spanish attack at San Juan de Ulua. Both Hawkins and Drake seem to have believed that their voyage was legal and sued the Spanish for compensation. In 1572 he led the expedition which captured a large treasure from the Spaniards near Nombre de Dios. Drake himself was severely wounded. Circumnavigated the globe in the *Pelican* (*Golden Hind*), 1577–80. Landed on the west coast of North America and claimed it for England under the name New Albion. Mayor of Plymouth, 1581. Sacked Vigo and attacked Spanish in the West Indies, 1585. 'Singed the King of Spain's beard' by attack on Cadiz, 1587. Served under Admiral Howard against the Spanish Armada. Failed to take Lisbon in 1598. New expedition to Isthmus of Panama in 1595–6 also unsuccessful, although briefly held Nombre de Dios. Died of fever, 28 January 1596.

Dufferin and Ava Lord (Frederick Temple Hamilton-Temple Blackwood, 1st Marquess of) (1826–1902): British diplomat and colonial administrator. He was sent as special commissioner to inquire into the massacre of the Maronites in Syria in 1860. Under-Secretary for India, 1864–6. Governor-General of Canada, 1872–8. Ambassador to Turkey, 1879–84. After Britain occupied Egypt in 1882 he was sent on a special mission to draw up a new constitution there. Viceroy of India, 1884–8. He was believed to have been sympathetic, at least at first, to the establishment of the Indian National Congress in 1885, as a 'sounding board' for Indian opinion. The 'Ava' in his title commemorated the third Burma war of 1885.

Dupleix Joseph François (1697–1763): Governor-General of French East India Company. His father was a director of the Company and Dupleix first visited India in 1715–16. He returned in 1721 as a councillor on the 'superior council' of Pondicherry. In 1730 he became the governor of French interests in

Chandernagore and, in 1742, the French Governor-General in Pondicherry. He was determined that French, not English, interests should predominate in India and at first he had some success. He supported the Nawab of Arcott against the Marathas and was awarded the honorary title of Nawab himself by the Mughal Emperor. He fought the British in the 1740s and captured Madras in 1746, only to see it returned in 1748. After 1748 he struggled and succeeded in getting control of the Deccan and the Carnatic but he had enemies among his countrymen and his government was not much interested. He was recalled in 1754.

Durham Lord (John George Lambton, 1st Earl of) (1792–1840): British radical politician. He played a major role in drafting the Great Parliamentary Reform Act of 1832 but he was a difficult Cabinet colleague and was sent as ambassador to Russia (1835–7) and as Governor-General to Canada after the rebellions of 1837, with instructions to report on the situation. He produced the famous Durham Report. He diagnosed two causes of the rebellions – the clash between the English and the French in Quebec and the fact that, although the Canadians had representative government, they could not control the executive. For the first he could propose no remedy except the absorption of the French into the English majority in Canada as a whole – which caused lasting resentment among French Canadians. He died before he could fully explain his somewhat ambiguous recommendations on the second but it came to be interpreted as 'responsible government', i.e. that colonial ministries should be responsible to elected legislatures, which guided the future constitutional development of the empire.

Dutt Romesh Chandar (1848–1909): Indian administrator, nationalist and scholar. Born in Calcutta and educated in Calcutta and at University College, London, he passed the entrance examination to the élite Indian Civil Service in 1869. He joined the Bengal service in 1871 and eventually rose to be Commissioner for Orissa in 1895, but he resigned in 1897 to have a free hand to criticise British policy. He became involved in a famous controversy with Lord Curzon, arguing that British policy was aggravating Indian poverty. He published *Famine in India* (1900), *The Economic History of India, 1757–1837* (1902) and *India in the Victorian Age* (1904). He was also a notable scholar of Sanskrit, publishing a number of translations, and was a lecturer at University College, London, 1898–1904.

Elgin Lord (James Bruce, 8th Earl of) (1811–63): British diplomat and colonial administrator. Governor of Jamaica, 1842–6. Governor-General of Canada, 1846–54 – important because he made 'responsible government' a reality by accepting the Canadian Losses Bill, of which he personally disapproved, on the grounds that it was Canadian legislation with which he could not properly interfere. In 1857 he was sent to China at the time of the *Arrow* war and negotiated the two treaties of Tientsin of 1858 and 1860. Gained some notoriety from the burning of the Summer Palace in Peking in 1860, in retaliation for the mistreatment of British and French hostages there. Viceroy of India, 1862–3.

Elphinstone Mountstuart (1779–1859): British administrator. Entered the Bengal civil service in 1796. Appointed 'resident' at Nagpur in 1804 and sent as an envoy to the Emir of Afghanistan in 1808. In 1815 he published a valuable book on his mission, *Account of the Kingdom of Cabul and Its Dependencies*. From 1811 to 1817 he was first 'resident', then commissioner, at Poona. From 1819 to 1827 he was the Governor of Bombay. He was responsible for a number of legal and educational reforms, including the foundation of the Elphinstone Institute, which later proved to be such an important nursery of Indian leaders. Although influenced by utilitarian ideas, he respected Indian civilisation and avoided precipitate intervention. In 1841 he published a *History of India*, covering the Hindu and Muslim periods. He twice turned down invitations to become Governor-General of India.

Enim Pasha – *see* Schnitzer, Edward

Eratosthenes of Cyrene (*c*.284–*c*.205 BC): Famous Greek mathematician and geographer, whose views were known during the Age of Discovery. His works included the *Geographica*, which divided the world into zones.

Étienne Eugène-Napoleon (1844–1921): Born at Oran and educated in Algiers. Became deputy for Oran, 1881. A supporter of Gambetta and Ferry. Under-Secretary for the Colonies, 1887–8 and 1889–92. Later Minister of the Interior and for War. Interested in railway development. One of the leaders of the colonial group in the Chambers, 1880–1914. Published a number of works including *Les Compagnies de colonisation* (1897).

Fabri Friedrich (1824–91): German colonial propagandist. From 1857 to 1884 he was the Director of the Barmen Rhine Missionary Society. He was an indefatigable pamphleteer on social and other questions. He advocated the acquisition of colonies as a way of solving Germany's social problems. He believed that his 1879 book *Does Germany Need Colonies?* triggered the whole German colonial movement. Although he exaggerated, it was an important catalyst.

Faidherbe Louis (1818–89): Soldier and administrator, responsible for starting French colonial advance in Sudan. Engineer officer. Served in Algiers and Guadeloupe. Sent to Senegal in 1852; Governor, 1854–61 and 1863–5. In 1854–8, subdued immediate hinterland, in conflict with Al-Hajj Omar. Established precedent of raising black troops to fight for France. Conceived idea of linking Senegal with the Niger. Founded port of Dakar, which replaced St Louis as the capital. Later held a command in Algeria and fought in the Franco-Prussian war. Elected to the Senate in 1879. A good linguist, he was interested in both archaeology and Islam.

Faure (François) Félix (1841–99): Made a fortune as a Havre ship-owner. Became deputy for Le Havre in 1881. His knowledge of commerce and of the colonies led to him being appointed Under-Secretary for the Colonies in Ferry's government in 1883. Minister of Marine, 1894. President of the Republic, 1895.

Ferdinand of Aragon (1452–1516): As a result of his marriage to Isabella, the heiress apparent to Castile, in 1469, became joint ruler when Henry IV, King of Castile, died in 1474. In 1479 also succeeded his father, John II, as King of Aragon. Reign saw Moors driven from Granada, all Jews who refused to be baptised expelled, and Inquisition reinforced. When Isabella died in 1504, lost his right to govern Castile (which was larger and much more prosperous than Aragon) but succeeded in annexing it in 1515. Ferdinand and Isabella together were known as 'the Catholic monarchs'.

Fitch Ralph (*fl.* 1583–1603): English merchant. One of the first Englishmen to visit India. Left London on 12 February 1583 with other merchants of the Levant Company. Travelled by way of Aleppo and Baghdad. Imprisoned by the Portuguese Governor in Hormuz and sent to Goa. Escaped and made their way to Akbar's court. Fitch alone of the original party returned to London after extensive travels. Arrived in London, 29 April 1591. His reports were probably influential in the setting up of the English East India Company in 1599.

Fitzroy Robert (1805–65): British sailor and colonial administrator. Commanded the *Beagle*, when it surveyed the coasts of South America (1831–6) with Charles Darwin aboard as the naturalist. Became MP for Durham in 1841. Governor of New Zealand, 1843–5. Fitzroy, who had close connections with missionary interests, was inclined to take the Maori side in disputes and was recalled after protests from the colonists that he was not supporting them.

Frere Sir Henry Bartle (1815–84): British administrator. Entered Indian Civil Service in Bombay in 1834. Governor of Bombay, 1862–67. Governor of the Cape and High Commissioner for South Africa, 1877. Arbitrated in the disputes between the recently annexed Transvaal and Zululand. Generally decided in the Zulu favour but then asked the Zulus to demobilise; an impossible request for a military monarchy to comply with and war resulted. Frere was strongly criticised at home and was recalled by Gladstone's government in 1880.

Freycinet, Charles Louis de (1828–1923): French politician. An engineer by original profession. Became the chief engineer on the Midi railway in 1856. Minister of Public Works, 1877. Reorganised railway and canal system of France. Prime Minister and Foreign Minister, 1879–80, 1882 and 1886. Foreign Minister, 1885–6. In 1878 became involved in plans for a railway linking Senegal with Algiers across the Sahara. The British regarded Freycinet as fatally indecisive during the Egyptian crisis of 1881–2.

Frobisher Martin (*c.* 1538–94): English sailor and explorer. Made three attempts to find the North-West Passage in 1576, 1577 and 1578. Discovered Frobisher Bay and Hudson Strait. Accompanied Drake to West Indies in 1585–6. Knighted for services against the Spanish Armada. Died of bullet wound received near Brest when attempting to relieve Spanish siege in 1594.

Gage General Thomas (1721–87): British soldier. Fought in the Seven Years War. Governor of Montreal 1760 and of Massachusetts, 1774. Strongly criticised by some for engagements at Lexington and Bunker Hill. Appointed Commander-in-Chief in America but resigned and returned to England.

157

Gallieni Joseph-Simon (1849–1916): French soldier. Sent by Brière de l'Isle to survey possible route of railway from Senegal to Niger in 1879. Conducted successful campaign to gain control of Upper Niger, 1886–8. Governor of Madagascar, 1896–1905, which he organised as a colony. Military governor of Paris in 1914 and Minister of War, 1915–16.

Galt Sir Alexander Tilloch (1817–93): Canadian statesman. Emigrated to Canada from Scotland in 1835. Became member of Canadian Legislature in 1849. Finance Minister, 1858–62 and 1864–7. After confederation became the new dominion's first Finance Minister. Canadian High Commissioner in London, 1880–3. In 1859 he had wrung a very important concession from the British Colonial Secretary, the Duke of Newcastle, who had tacitly conceded that the Canadians had the right to determine their own tariff policy even if it was disagreeable to London.

Gama Vasco da (*c.*1460–1524): Portuguese navigator. The son of the Governor of Sines. First Portuguese to travel by sea to India. Commissioned by Manuel I to follow up Bartolomeu Dias's discoveries, to establish direct trade with India and make contact with Prester John. Sailed July 1497 and reached Calicut, May 1498. Had tacked up east coast of Africa to Mozambique, Mombasa and Malindi. At Malindi secured services of famous Indian Ocean pilot, Ibn Majid. Returned to Lisbon, September 1499. Second expedition to India 1502. Returned as Viceroy in 1524 but died in Cochin on 24 December.

Gambetta Léon (1838–82): French politician. Generally regarded as the 'strong man' of French politics after the Franco-Prussian war, in which he had played a notable part, but he did not become Prime Minister until November 1881 and lost office in January 1882. Many thought that he would have played a more effective role in the Egyptian crisis than his successor, Charles Freycinet, but others have accused him of being too influenced by the interests of the French bondholders.

Gilbert Sir Humphrey (*c.*1539–83): English soldier and explorer. Stepbrother of Sir Walter Ralegh. MP for Plymouth. Fought against the French and in Ireland and the Netherlands. In 1583 sailed to Newfoundland with small fleet. Founded first English colony in North America at what became St John's. Died when ship foundered on return voyage.

Gladstone William Ewart (1809–98): British Liberal politician. Prime Minister, 1868–74, 1880–5, 1886, 1892–4. His first government office was as Under-Secretary for the Colonies in 1834–5 and he was Secretary for War and the Colonies, 1845–6. His understanding of Britain's relations with the colonies of settlement was good, although Benjamin Disraeli had some electoral success in the 1870s when he accused him, falsely, of wishing to break up the empire. Gladstone strongly attacked Disraeli's policy in Afghanistan and South Africa in the Midlothian campaign of 1879. He had little sympathy with the new expansionist phase of empire building in the 1880s, famously referring to Mount Kilimanjaro as the 'mountain with the unrememberable name'. But, ironically, it was under his administrations that Britain occupied Egypt in 1882 and laid claim to large parts of Africa after 1884.

Gokhale Gopal Krishna (1866–1915): Indian nationalist. A Brahmin from Bombay, he was educated at Elphinstone Institute. A moderate politician, much influenced by western liberalism, he has sometimes been called 'the Indian Gladstone'. In 1895 he was the Secretary and in 1905 the President of the Indian National Congress. In 1899 he became an elected member of the Bombay Legislative Council and, in 1902, of the Viceroy's Legislative Council. He influenced John Morley in putting through the 1909 reforms. In 1905 he founded the Servants of India Society, whose members took vows of poverty and undertook service to the poorest, including the Untouchables.

Goldie Sir George Taubman (1846–1925): Governor of Royal Niger Company. Born in the Isle of Man, he was commissioned in the Royal Engineers but had little to do with the army. Instead he travelled in Egypt and on the Niger. When, through family connections, he acquired shares in Holland, Jacques and Co., he returned to the Niger and persuaded a number of small firms trading there to amalgamate into the United Africa Company (later the National Africa Company and later still the Royal Niger Company). He was challenged by the French, notably by the *Compagnie française de l'Afrique equatoriale*. He persuaded a large number of African chiefs to sign treaties of doubtful validity transferring their territories to the Company. In 1886 he obtained a royal charter for his company. The Royal Niger Company tried to establish a virtual monopoly on the Niger, which brought them into conflict with other British merchants as well as the Germans. The Company surrendered its charter in 1899.

Gordon General Charles (1833–85): British soldier. Served in the Crimean war and in China in 1860. Assisted the Chinese government in suppressing the Taiping rebellion, 1863–4, and gained the nickname 'Chinese Gordon'. In 1873 he was seconded to serve under the Khedive of Egypt in the Sudan to suppress the slave trade. Governor of the Sudan (under the Egyptians), 1877–81. In 1884 he was sent back to the Sudan to evacuate the Egyptian forces after the Mahdi's successful revolt. Gordon's interpretation of his orders differed from that of London and he was trapped in Khartoum and killed in January 1885. His death was extremely damaging to Gladstone's government. 'Revenge Gordon' became a potent political cry.

Gorges Sir Ferdinando (*c.*1566–1647): English soldier and coloniser. Came from prosperous Somerset landowning family. Fought in France and the Netherlands. Governor of Plymouth until implicated in the Earl of Essex's rebellion. Active in promoting the Plymouth division of the Virginia Company and formed Council for New England, which replaced it in 1620. New Plymouth founded 1628 but Gorges clashed with Massachusetts Bay Company, whose grants overlapped with his own. Council for New England wound up in 1635 but in 1639 he received royal confirmation of an earlier grant for the 'Province of Maine'. His fortunes declined during the English civil wars.

159

Gosnold Capt. Bartholomew (d. 1607): English navigator. Sailed on exploring voyage, probably financed by Sir Walter Ralegh, in 1602. Charted coasts of what became New England, discovered Cape Cod and named Martha's Vineyard. Returned with sassafras (then highly valued), furs and other commodities. Associated with formation of Virginia Company in 1606. Undertook new voyage in 1606, which led to settlement at Jamestown. Died there on 22 August 1607.

Grenville George (1712–70): British politician. Prime Minister, 1763–5. Grenville was a financial expert and wished to ensure that the colonies paid a share of imperial defence. He tried strictly to enforce tariffs, which had been widely evaded, and in 1765 introduced the Stamp Act, which led ultimately to the revolt of the American colonies.

Grenville Sir Richard (c.1541–91): English sailor. Belonged to Cornish family. MP for Cornwall. Fought with Austrians against the Turks in Hungary. In 1591 was vice-admiral of squadron, commanded by Sir Thomas Howard, sent to intercept Spanish treasure fleet off the Azores. Surprised by large Spanish fleet. Most of British squadron escaped but Grenville stayed to fight. Died of wounds but action commemorated in famous poem by Tennyson, 'The *Revenge*'.

Grey (Henry George), 3rd Earl (1802–94): British politician. Son of Lord Grey of the Reform Bill. Under-Secretary for the Colonies, 1830; Secretary of State for War and the Colonies, 1846–52. Made responsible government a reality in the colonies of settlement.

Grey Sir Edward (Lord Grey of Falloden) (1862–1933): British Liberal politician. Under-Secretary for Foreign Affairs, 1892–5. Responsible for warning France that an incursion into the Egyptian Sudan would be 'an unfriendly act'. A Liberal imperialist with Herbert Asquith and others who supported the government during the Boer war. Foreign Secretary, 1905–16.

Grey Sir George (1812–98): Soldier and colonial administrator. Born in Lisbon during the Peninsular war, the son of a British officer killed at Badjoz. His first career was as a soldier. He explored parts of the coasts of Australia in 1836 and 1839. Governor of South Australia, 1841–5; of New Zealand, 1845–53 and 1861–7; and of Cape Colony, 1853–60. Prime Minister of New Zealand, 1877–84. A tough and effective governor, who pulled several colonies out of trouble, he was famous in his time, being made a Privy Councillor and buried in St Paul's Cathedral, but is now almost unknown.

Hanotaux Gabriel (1853–1944): French politician and historian. Foreign Minister, 1894–5 and 1896–8. Favoured a forward colonial policy in Africa and initiated the policy that led to Fashoda. In Europe he was a strong supporter of the Franco-Russian alliance. He was a prolific writer, mainly on historical subjects, and a member of the *Académie Française*.

Hastings Warren (1732–1818): First British Governor-General of India. In 1750 he became a writer (clerk) in the service of the East India Company. Served with Clive in Bengal, 1756–7. Member of the Council of Bengal, 1761–4. After four years in England, he returned to Madras. In 1772 he assumed the presidency of the Bengal Council and under the terms of Lord North's Regulating Act of 1773 became the Governor-General. Fought successful wars against the Marathas and Haider Ali but had a bitter enemy on his own Council in Philip Francis. The two men fought a duel in 1780. Francis returned to England and carried on a campaign against Hastings, who was recalled in 1785 and impeached in 1788 for misgovernment in India. The impeachment, in which Edmund Burke proclaimed the standards which should govern British colonial policy, was a trial of the East India Company as much as of Hastings personally. Hastings was acquitted in 1795.

Hawkins Sir John (1532–95): English sailor. Came from a prosperous Plymouth family. Mayor and MP for Plymouth. Until 1561 engaged in voyages to the Canary Islands. In 1562 shipped 300 negroes from Sierra Leone to Hispaniola. Exchanged them for merchandise he brought to England (thus inaugurating the Triangular Trade). Further voyages in 1564 and 1567. Apparently believed he was acting legally under old treaties between England and Spain but in latter year was attacked by Spanish fleet at San Juan de Ulua (near Vera Cruz in Mexico). Hawkins himself escaped. Became treasurer and comptroller of Elizabethan navy, 1572. Fought against the Armada and was knighted for his services. Sailed with Drake to the West Indies in 1595 but died of fever off Puerto Rico on 12 November.

Hawkins William (d. 1554): Plymouth merchant. Mayor of and MP for Plymouth. Father of Sir John. Traded on Guinea coast and visited Brazil, 1528. Further visit to Brazil in 1530.

Henry Prince (Henry the Navigator) (1394–1460): Son of John II, King of Portugal and grandson of John of Gaunt. Took part in the conquest of Ceuta in 1415. Became the patron and organiser of the early Portuguese voyages of discovery. Attracted scientists to Sagres in south-west Portugal, which became an important centre for navigational studies.

Hewett Edward Hyde (1830–91): British consul. Clerk to British Slave Trade Commission at Loanda in 1861. Vice Consul at Loanda, 1863 and Acting Consul, 1867–8. Consul at Fernando Po, 1880. Sent in 1885 to conclude official treaties with Niger chiefs which superseded very doubtful ones concluded by National African Company. Instructed to do the same in the Cameroons but forestalled by the German Gustav Nachtigal.

Hicks General William (Hicks Pasha) (1830–83): British soldier. Served in India and in the Abyssinian campaign of 1867–8. Left the British army in 1880 and, in 1883, appointed to command an Egyptian expedition against the Mahdi. Ambushed and defeated. Hicks was killed on 5 November 1883. Public feeling about his death increased the difficulties about a British withdrawal from Egypt.

Hidalgo y Costilla Miguel (d. 1811): Latin American revolutionary. Hidalgo was a priest who championed the down-trodden peasants and miners of New Spain. He took advantage of the political turmoil of 1810 to lead a rising in Guanajuato. He was executed in 1811.

Hobson J.A. (1858–1944): British liberal writer and propagandist. Strong supporter of free trade and critic of imperialism. Visited the Rand on behalf of the *Manchester Guardian* just before the Boer war and published *The War in South Africa* (1900) and *The Psychology of Jingoism* (1901). His most influential book was *Imperialism: A Study* (1902). Although not well structured, it was a telling attack on imperialism, claiming that it benefited only the financiers at the expense of the rest of the nation. It became very popular, and some of his arguments were taken up by Lenin.

Hudson Henry (d. 1611): English sailor. Probably the son of a London merchant. In 1607 sailed in the service of the Muscovy Company to seek the North East Passage. In 1609 and 1610 sailed in search of the North-West Passage. Explored Hudson River on the first, and Hudson's Bay on the second voyage. His crew mutinied on the second voyage and in June 1611 put Hudson and a few others adrift in small boat. Disappeared.

Ibn Rushd – *see* Averroes

Ibn Sina – *see* Avicenna

Isaacs Rufus – *see* Barnato, Barney

Isabella Queen (1451–1504): Daughter of John II of Castile and León. Married Ferdinand of Aragon in 1469. Ruled Castile jointly with Ferdinand, 1474–1504. In 1492 commissioned Columbus to sail in search of a western route to China.

Ismail (1830–95): Khedive of Egypt. He was appointed Pasha (Governor) of Egypt in 1867 in succession to his brother, Said, but persuaded the Sultan to give him the more honorific title of 'Khedive' (roughly 'Viceroy'). Ismail tried to modernise Egypt. He had some success but his plans were over-ambitious and he ran up heavy debts with European financiers. The Sultan deposed him in favour of his son, Tewfik, in 1879.

Iturbe Augustin de (1783–1824): Mexican soldier and politician. He fought for Spain against the rebels in 1810. In 1820, was given command of the Spanish army in the south of Mexico, but, in 1821, he issued a proclamation demanding independence. He forced the Spanish Viceroy to accept his proposals and was himself proclaimed Emperor of Mexico in 1822, but had to abdicate the following year and went to Europe. He returned to Mexico in 1824 but was arrested and shot.

Jameson Dr Leander Starr (1853–1917): South African politician. A medical doctor, he emigrated to Kimberley in 1878 and became a close associate of Cecil Rhodes. In 1889 he went as an envoy to King Lobengula and, after the chartering of the British South Africa Company, he became the administrator of Charterland (later Rhodesia). He organised the Jameson Raid and led it into the Transvaal, even though the expected rising in Johannesburg had not materialised. The Transvaal authorities handed him over to the British and he served a short term of imprisonment. In 1900 he became a member of the Cape Legislative Assembly and, as leader of the Progressive Party, Prime Minister, 1904–8. He returned to Britain in 1912.

Jauréguiberry Admiral Jean-Bernard (1815–87): French sailor and politician. Served on west coast of Africa, 1834–6. Took part in the expedition to the River Plate, 1837–40. Later served on Levant station and in the Indian Ocean. In Senegal and Guiana, 1852–4. Played a distinguished role in the Crimean War. Served in Indo-China and in war against China, 1858–61. Replaced Faidherbe as Governor of Senegal, 1861–3. Served in Mediterranean, 1865–70. Played a major role in Franco-Prussian war. Elected to the National Assembly, 1871. Minister of Marine and the Colonies, 1878–83. He was in favour of a forward policy in Indo-China and in West Africa but cautious about the Egyptian intervention.

Jenkins Robert (*fl.* 1730s): English sea captain. His ear was cut off by the Spaniards off Havana on 9 April 1731 as punishment for alleged illegal trading. Became *cause célèbre*. Gave evidence to a parliamentary committee in 1738. When war broke out with Spain in 1739 it was popularly known as the 'War of Jenkins' Ear'.

Johnson Sir Frank (1866–1943): British soldier and Rhodesian 'Pioneer'. Went out to South Africa as a young man to take up a position with a bank but became a soldier instead. Transferred to Bechuanaland police. Prospected for gold in Mashonaland and became the manager of the Bechuanaland Exploration Company. Tried to buy Mozambique from the Portuguese for £4 million. Over-reached by Rudd Concession in 1888 and, in 1890, volunteered to lead 'Pioneeer' column into Mashonaland. Later devoted himself to mining and other business interests and played some part in Rhodesia between the wars but eventually returned to Britain.

Johnston Sir Harry (1858–1927): British explorer and empire-builder. He travelled in North Africa in 1878–80 and in Angola and the Congo, 1882–3. In 1884 he explored the country round Mount Kilimanjaro and subsequently highly recommended it for British settlement. Served in various consular posts in the Cameroons, on the Niger coast and in Mozambique, 1885–8. In 1889 he explored Lakes Nyasa and Tanganyika and became the Commissioner for the British Central African Protectorate (Nyasaland) in 1891. He later served as the Consul-General in Tunisia, 1897–9, and as Special Commissioner in Uganda, 1899–1901. He was a strong propagandist for British expansion in Africa.

Jones Sir William (1746–94): Linguist and orientalist. Said to have been fluent in 22 languages. He was called to the Bar in 1774 but, after ill success in British politics, he opted to go to India as a judge in the High Court of Calcutta in 1783. He was drawn by his interest in Indian science and literature. He found a number of like-minded men in Calcutta, including Charles Wilkins, and established the Asiatic Society of Bengal. He learnt Sanskrit and published a number of important translations. Recognising similarities to Greek and Latin, he also began to define the idea of an Indo-European language.

Kirk Sir John (1832–1922): British Consul-General and Agent at Zanzibar. A medical doctor, he served in the Crimean war and accompanied Livingstone on his second expedition in 1858. He went to Zanzibar in 1863 and became Consul-General in 1873 and Agent in 1886–7. He played a key role in British expansion in East Africa. A strong opponent of the slave trade, he was the British plenipotentiary at the Brussels Slave Trade Conference in 1889–90.

Kitchener Herbert (Lord) (1850–1916): British soldier. He helped to survey Palestine and Cyprus in 1874–8 and was present at the bombardment of Alexandria in 1882. He served with the Egyptian forces in the Sudan in 1884–5, the Suakim operation of 1888 and the Toski campaign of 1889. He was employed to draw the boundaries between the British and German spheres in East Africa in 1886. He became Sirdar or Commander-in-Chief of the Egyptian army in 1892 and conducted the campaign for the reconquest of the Sudan of 1896–8, culminating in the battle of Omdurman. He went as Chief of Staff to Lord Roberts in South Africa in December 1899 and succeeded him in command. He was blamed for the policy of confining Boer women and children in camps during the guerilla phase of the war. He was Commander-in-Chief in India, 1902–9, and quarrelled disastrously with Lord Curzon. He became the British Agent (in effect, the Governor) in Egypt in 1911. He was Secretary of State for War in 1914 and drowned in June 1916 when a mine struck the warship on which he was travelling on a mission to Russia.

Kruger Paulus (Oom Paul) (1825–1904): Boer leader. As a boy had been one of the Voortrekkers of 1836. Fought in a number of engagements as the Boers established themselves. He was Vice-President of the South African Republic (the Transvaal) when the British annexed it in 1877 and bitterly opposed the annexation. From 1883 to 1902 he was the President of the Republic. He was a 'Dopper', a Dutch Calvinist who had no doubt that the Afrikaaners were a chosen people and believed unquestioningly in the superiority of the white man. He clashed with Cecil Rhodes, particularly over his refusal to grant rights of citizenship to those who had come into the Transvaal after the discovery of gold. He dealt cleverly with the Jameson Raid, turning the conspirators over to the British authorities. The British suspected him of conspiring with Germany, particularly after the 'Kruger telegram' episode. Kruger in fact wanted to keep his country's independence but he bought arms from the Germans, which enabled the Boers to give a good account of themselves in the war of 1899–1902. Opinions still differ as to whether Kruger wanted the war, but it led to his defeat and exile in 1901.

Lally Thomas Arthur (1702–66): French soldier. The son of an Irish father, who had supported James II, Lally took part in the Jacobite rising of 1745. He headed a French expedition to India in 1758. He failed to take Madras and had to surrender Pondicherry in 1761. He was executed for treason in France in 1766.

Lancaster James (d. 1618): British sailor and merchant. Brought up in Portugal. Served under Drake against the Armada. In 1591 commanded the *Edward Bonaventure* as part of the first British voyage to the East Indies. Reached Penang and touched on Ceylon. Returned by way of West Indies and Newfoundland.

Reached England in 1594. Most of the men who set out had died but he brought back a rich cargo. In 1600 Lancaster was appointed to command the first fleet sent out by the English East India Company. Reached Acheem and opened friendly relations with the ruler, as an enemy of the Portuguese. Established bases at Bantam and in the Moluccas. Two ships returned with good cargoes. Organised, but did not sail on, later voyages.

La Salle René-Robert Cavelier, Sieur de (1643–87): French explorer. Born in Rouen. After failing to enter the Jesuit order, went to Canada in 1667. Gained patronage of the Governor, Comte de Frontenac. In 1669 ascended St Lawrence River and in 1678–80 charted part of Great Lakes system and explored Ohio River as far as its confluence with the Mississippi. In 1682 travelled down the Mississippi to the Gulf of Mexico. Killed by his own men in 1687 trying to retrace journey from the mouth of the Mississippi.

Las Casas Fray Bartolomé (1474–1566): Spanish missionary. Born in Seville. Went to Hispaniola in 1502. About 1512 became disturbed by the Spanish treatment of the Indians and, in 1515, went to Spain to protest against their enslavement. Returned with title of Universal Protector of the Indians. But, to save the Indians, agreed to the use of negro slaves. In 1520 tried unsuccessfully to plant a colony in Venezuela. Already a priest, entered the Dominican order in 1522. Returned to Spain and was adviser to the Council of the Indies, 1539–44. In 1542 obtained a decree (New Laws) from Charles V, forbidding Indian slavery. In 1544 became bishop of Chiapa in Mexico but retired to Spain in 1547. Well known for his widely translated *Brief Account of the Destruction of the Indies* (1552) but his *Historia general de las Indas* and his *Apologética historia de las Indias* are also extremely important.

Lavigerie Charles, Cardinal (1825–92): French ecclesiastic. Became Bishop of Algiers in 1867 and Primate of Africa in 1884. Opposed slave trade and saw it as his mission to convert Africa. Founded White Fathers (1867) and White Sisters (1869). Saw conversion and advance of French influence as inextricably mixed. Once said, 'As missionaries we also work for France', and Gambetta said of him that he was worth two regiments to France.

Lenin V.I. (1870–1924): Creator of the Soviet state. In the imperial context his most important book was *Imperialism: The Highest Stage of Capitalism* (1916), originally entitled 'the last stage'. Saw imperialism as the death throes of over-ripe monopoly capitalism.

Leopold II (1835–1909): King of the Belgians. He found Belgium too small a field for his ambitions when he became King in 1865. As a young man he had travelled widely and dreamt of a colonial empire. Central Africa would not have been his first choice but he seized his opportunity. He summoned a number of distinguished geographers and explorers to a conference in Brussels in 1876 and set up an elaborate international organisation for the suppression of the slave trade and the opening up of Central Africa. This proved a mere cloak for the creation of Leopold's personal fief in the Congo. He was one of the few who made a fortune out of Africa in this period but the scandal became so great in the end that the Belgian parliament was compelled to assume responsibility for the Congo as an ordinary colony in 1908.

Livingstone David (1813–73): British missionary and explorer. Although he was compelled to work in a cotton mill from the age of 10, he offered his services to the London Missionary Society and qualified as a medical doctor. He worked as a missionary in Bechuanaland, 1840–9. He reached the Zambezi in 1851 and explored the Zambezi region, 1853–6 (seeing the Victoria Falls for the first time in November 1855). He explored the Shire River and Lake Nyasa, 1858–64. In 1866 he left Zanzibar, searching for the source of the Nile. He reached Lake Tanganyika, where Stanley found him at Ujiji in 1871. Livingstone died at Ilala in May 1873 and his followers embalmed his body and carried it to the coast. Livingstone was now a national hero and was buried in Westminster Abbey. He campaigned strenuously against the slave trade but believed that legitimate commerce was the best way to drive it out and also to raise the African standard of living. He was therefore regarded as a friend by those who wished to 'open up' Africa for commercial reasons.

Lobengula King (c.1636–1894): The last independent king of the Matabele (Ndebele). Succeeded his father, Mzilikaze, in 1868. Felt under threat from competing concession-seekers, Boers, Portuguese, German and British. Granted exclusive mineral rights to C.D. Rudd, Rhodes' emissary, in 1888 in return for money and weapons because he believed that, unlike other concession-hunters, who wanted land, Rudd wanted only minerals. When he found he was mistaken, he repudiated the concession and executed the counsellor who had advised him to agree to it. Died, probably from smallpox, although there were suspicions of poison, fleeing from Rhodes' forces in the Matabele war.

Lugard Frederick John Dealtry, 1st Baron (1858–1945): British pro-consul. Born in India and educated at Sandhurst. Served in Afghan war, 1879–80. Invalided out of the army and went to East Africa. In 1888 employed by African Lakes Company to put down slavery. In 1890 entered service of Imperial British East Africa Company. Active in Uganda and returned to Britain to persuade government and public not to withdraw from the region. In 1894 employed by Royal Niger Company. Briefly in Bechuanaland but returned to the Niger in 1897. Involved in race with French Captain Decoeur to secure treaties with chiefs, particularly at Borgu. Commanded West Africa Frontier Force, formed to protect British territory against the French. British High Commissioner in Northern Nigeria, 1900–6, where he worked out his principles of 'indirect rule'. Governor of Hong Kong, 1906–11. In 1912 returned to Nigeria as Governor of both North and South with instructions to bring about an amalgamation of the two. Found indirect rule worked less well in the South because of the more fragmented nature of the society. Retired in 1919. In 1922 published his very influential *The Dual Mandate in British Tropical Africa*, in which he argued that European and African interests were complementary, not antagonistic. Member of the League of Nations Mandate Commission, 1922–36.

MacArthur Captain John (1767–1834): British soldier who introduced sheep-farming into Australia. Sent to Australia in 1790. Quarrelled with Governor Phillip and subsequent governors. Sent home for court martial in 1801 but took a sample of wool with him and impressed both government and manufacturers with the possibilities. Resigned his commission, received a grant of 5000 acres of good land and returned in 1805. Was a leading figure in the deposition of the fourth governor, William Bligh, in the mutiny of 1808. But by 1820 was one of the wealthiest men in the colony and became a member of the Legislative Council in 1825. Died, apparently insane, in 1834.

Macartney (George), Lord (1737–1806): British diplomat and colonial governor. Well connected as a Whig politician. Governor of Grenada, 1775. Governor of Madras, 1780. Resigned in 1785 after quarrelling with Warren Hastings and the authorities in Bengal. Declined to follow Warren Hastings as Governor-General. In 1792–4 went on special mission to China to try to persuade the Chinese to open up what the West regarded as normal diplomatic and trading relations. Well received but failed to obtain main objective, a permanent envoy in the Chinese capital.

Macaulay Thomas Babbington, 1st Baron (1800–59): Perhaps best known as an historian and essayist but also an important Liberal politician. His father was Zachary Macaulay, a zealous campaigner against slavery and the slave trade. Entered parliament in 1830 and in 1833 supported successful attempts to reduce the length of time emancipated slaves would have to work as 'apprentices'. In 1832 he had become a commissioner at the Board of Control and became deeply interested in India. Went out to India as a member of the Governor-General's council, 1834–7, when William Bentinck was the Governor-General. In 1833 Macaulay produced his 'Education Minute', recommending that the government should support western education in India, in which he spoke contemptuously of Indian learning (showing a great contrast to William Jones's views 50 years earlier). But he also passed (and defended) his 'Black Act' making Europeans subject to Indian magistrates and began the enormous codification of Indian laws, not completed until 1861, which many Indians regarded as one of the most important achievements of the British period in India.

McCarthy Sir Charles (1770–1824): British soldier. Served in the West Indies and in New Brunswick. In 1812 became the Governor of Sierra Leone and also made responsible for Cape Coast Castle. In 1824 led an expedition to protect the Fanti against the Ashanti. Killed and his head taken as a trophy. According to legend it was used as a drinking cup.

Macdonald John A. (1815–91): Canadian politician. Born in Glasgow but emigrated with his family in 1820. Became a member of the Canadian Legislative Assembly, 1844. By 1851 he was the Conservative leader in Canada West (the later Ontario). He was committed to the cause of Canadian federation by 1858 and, in 1864, joined the 'Great Coalition', with Georges Cartier and others, to work for it. Led the Canadian delegation at the Charlottetown Conference in

1864 and played a leading role in the negotiations for confederation. In 1867 became the first Prime Minister of the new dominion of Canada. Lost the election of 1874 but returned to power, 1878–91.

Mackinnon Sir William (1823–93): Scottish merchant and ship-owner. His family were grocers. Went to India in 1847. In 1856 founded the Calcutta and Burmah Steam Navigation Company, which became the British India Steam Navigation Company in 1862. In 1873 he established a mail service between Aden and Zanzibar. In 1878 he negotiated with Sultan Bargharsh of Zanzibar for a large land concession, but the negotiations were sabotaged by the British government, which did not want such responsibilities. By 1886 thinking had changed under German pressure and in 1888 Mackinnon secured a royal charter for his Imperial British East Africa Company, which attempted to open up the area that became Kenya and Uganda. However, the Company was always under-capitalised and surrendered its powers to the government in 1895 after Mackinnon's death.

Magellan Ferdinand (*c*.1480–1521): Portuguese navigator. Went to India in 1505 with the first Portuguese Viceroy, d'Almeida. Visited Malacca, Java and probably Moluccas. Returned to Portugal in 1512 and was wounded in campaign in Morocco. In 1517 offered his services to the King of Spain and in 1519 was sent to find a western route to the Spice Islands. Discovered the Straits of Magellan (October 1520) and entered Pacific. Magellan himself was killed in a fight in the Philippines on 27 April 1521 but his ship, the *Victory*, and some of his expedition reached Seville, completing the first circumnavigation of the globe.

Mahdi – *see* Muhammad Ahmad ibn Abdullah

Mendoza Antonio de (1490–1552): Spanish Viceroy of Mexico and Peru. Born in Granada, he had carried out diplomatic missions for Charles V. In 1535 he became the first Viceroy of New Spain (Mexico). He had the task of consolidating royal authority over the, often disorderly, colonists and of conquering and converting the Indians. Towards the Indians he was paternalistic but opposed Bartolomé de Las Casas's defence of them, and, in particular, the law of 1542, which forbade their enslavement. He encouraged agriculture in the colony and, during his time, silver was found at Zacetecas. In 1550 he was sent as Viceroy to Peru.

Menelek II Emperor (1844–1913): The third of the 'great sovereigns' who ruled Ethiopia in the nineteenth century. From 1855 to 1865 he was imprisoned by a rival. Escaped in 1865 and proclaimed himself *Negus* or Emperor. By 1887 he had a well-equipped army and conquered Harat. He remained neutral when the Italians occupied the coast but when the rival emperor, Yohannes IV, died in battle with the Mahdists in 1889, Menelek established his authority over the whole of Ethiopia. He signed a peace treaty (the Treaty of Ucciali) with the Italians but disputed the Italian contention that it amounted to a protectorate. In 1896 he defeated the Italians at the battle of Adowa and went on to modernise his country, establishing a new capital at Addis Ababa.

Mercator Gerardus (Gerhard Kremer) (1512–94): Flemish geographer. Employed by Charles V but, as a Protestant, emigrated to the Rhineland. In 1568 produced the first map on his new system of projection, which bears his name.

Mill James (1773–1836): British political philosopher. A friend of Jeremy Bentham, he adopted his ideas of utilitarianism. From 1806 to 1817 he wrote his massive history of India and, in 1819, received an appointment at India House, the headquarters of the East India Company. He was promoted rapidly and, in 1830, became the head of the office, holding a position not unlike that of permanent under-secretary in the civil service. He gave evidence at the time of the renewal of the Company's charter in 1833 but, more importantly, he applied utilitarian ideas to the government of India. He corresponded with and influenced various officials.

Mill John Stuart (1806–73): Major British political philosopher. The son of James Mill, he was trained in the utilitarian tradition but became more liberal in its interpretation. In 1823 he became a junior clerk in India House under his father and, in turn, became head of the office in 1856. He retired in 1858.

Milner Alfred, 1st Viscount (1854–1925): British politician. Born in Germany of English parents. Had an early career as a lawyer and a journalist but, in 1884, became private secretary to G.J. Goschen. He worked under Lord Cromer in Egypt, 1889–92. He was immensely impressed, became a committed imperialist, and wrote a famous exposition of British imperial policy in *Britain in Egypt* (1894). In 1897 he was sent as British High Commissioner to South Africa. Both the Prime Minister, Lord Salisbury, and the Colonial Secretary, Joseph Chamberlain, were convinced that he was the ideal man for the job, but his critics believed that his intransigence helped to make war with the Boers inevitable. He remained in South Africa until 1905 and was associated with the early phase of plans for federation – although he would himself have preferred a different solution, which would have anglicised the country. He became a peer in 1902 and entered British politics. He joined Lloyd George's War Cabinet in 1916, becoming Secretary for War in April 1918 and Colonial Secretary in December 1918. He retired in 1921.

Minto (Gilbert Elliot), 1st Earl of (1751–1814): Governor-General of India. A friend of Edmund Burke, he assisted him in the preparation of the case against Warren Hastings. He briefly governed Corsica (1794–6) during the French wars. Became President of the Board of Control, 1806. Governor-General of India, 1807–14. He was sympathetic to Indian religions and forbade propaganda against Islam and Hinduism – attracting criticism at home for harming the progress of the Christian missions. This was the period of the Napoleonic wars and he sent missions to Persia, Lahore and Kabul (the last led by Mountstuart Elphinstone) to persuade them to support the British side – with limited success. He captured Amboyna, the Moluccas and Java.

Minto (Gilbert John Murray Elliot), 4th Earl of (1845–1910): Viceroy of India. Had an exceptionally adventurous early life, narrowly escaping being trapped during the Afghan war of 1879–80, serving in the Egyptian campaign of 1882 and helping to suppress the Riel rebellion in Canada in 1885. Governor-General of Canada, 1898–1904. Viceroy of India, 1905–19. He had to calm the situation after Lord Curzon but his most important service was his co-operation with the Secretary of State, John Morley, in securing the reforms of 1909, which set India on the path to representative government. In many particulars, Minto wished to go further than Morley.

Miranda Francisco Antonio Gabriel (1756–1816): South American nationalist. Born in Caracas, Venezuela. Went to Spain as a young man. Joined army and fought in American War of Independence. Went to France and fought with the revolutionary army in 1792–3. Fled to England during the Terror and tried to persuade the British government to liberate Venezuela from Spain. Took part in an unsuccessful rising in Venezuela in 1806 and the successful one in 1810. Became commander-in-chief and dictator but attracted dissent. Miranda was defeated and handed over to the Spaniards. Died in prison in Cadiz in 1816.

Moffat John (1835–1918): British missionary, the son of Robert Moffat. Missionary in Matabeleland, 1859–65, where he gained the confidence of the King, Mzilikaze. He left the missionary field to become the Commissioner for Native Affairs in the Transvaal, 1879–81, during the British annexation and was subsequently employed in Basutoland and Bechuanaland. In 1887 returned to Matabeleland and persuaded Lobengula, Mzilikaze's successor, to sign what became known as the Moffat Treaty, by which Lobengula agreed not to commit himself to other powers without consulting the British High Commissioner. Returned to Bechuanaland, 1892–6.

Moffat Robert (1795–1883): British missionary. Sent to Namaqualand by the London Missionary Society in 1816. Moved to Bechuanaland. His daughter married David Livingstone in 1844. In 1859 he established a mission in Matabeleland.

Molesworth Sir William (1810–55): British radical politician. Entered parliament in 1832. Impressed by colonial ideas of Edward Gibbon Wakefield and became a member of a small but influential group of MPs who frequently spoke on colonial issues in the 1830s. He became a Cabinet minister in Lord Aberdeen's coalition government in 1853 and in 1855 became Colonial Secretary, but died soon afterwards.

Monroe James (1785–1831): President of the United States, who considerably extended his country's boundaries. Fought in the American War of Independence. In 1802 negotiated Louisiana Purchase with France. President, 1817–25. In 1819 he pressurised Spain into ceding Florida in the Adam–Onis treaty. Spain was also persuaded to give up all claims to Oregon (as was Russia in 1824). In 1818 he negotiated a boundary line with British North America on the 49th parallel from the Lake of the Woods to the Rockies. Spain and other European powers were considering intervening to restore to Spanish control the Spanish colonies in South and Central America. Britain opposed this and proposed cooperation with the United States. Instead in his Annual Message of 2 December 1823, the President proclaimed what became known as the Monroe Doctrine: that the American continent was no longer open for European colonisation.

Montcalm Louis-Joseph, Marquis de (1712–59): French soldier. In 1756 he was sent to command the French forces in Canada. Initially he had considerable success, capturing Oswego, Fort William Henry and Ticonderoga, but in September 1759 he was defeated by Wolfe in the battle for Quebec, fought on the Heights of Abraham, in which both commanders were mortally wounded. Like Wolfe, he came to be regarded as a national hero.

Montezuma I (*c.*1390–1469): Aztec ruler, who began his reign in 1437. Extended his claims from the Pacific to the Gulf of Mexico and extended his capital, Tenochtitlan.

Montezuma II (1466–1520): Succeeded 1502. Further extended conquests of Montezuma I to Honduras and Nicaragua. Created disaffection among his subjects, some of whom allied with the Spanish. According to tradition, when the Spaniards arrived in 1519, he was unwilling to offend them because believed they might be emissaries of the Aztec god, Quetzalcoatl. The Spaniards took Montezuma hostage. He was subsequently killed possibly by a sling-stone aimed by his own people at the besieged Spaniards.

Morel E.D. (1873–1924): Radical campaigner. Born in France of a French father and an English (Quaker) mother, he was brought up in England and became naturalised in 1896. In 1891 he became a clerk with Elder Dempster, a trading company which had connections with the Congo. In 1900 Morel began his agitation against the brutality of European rule in the Congo, which did much to compel the Belgian government to take responsibility in 1908. He also opposed British policy in the Moroccan crisis of 1911. He campaigned for neutrality in 1914 and formed the Union of Democratic Control. In 1922, as a Labour candidate, he famously defeated Winston Churchill in Dundee.

Morgan Henry (*c.*1635–88): Welsh buccaneer. According to tradition, was kidnapped in Bristol and sold in Barbados. Escaped to Jamaica and joined the buccaneers fighting against the Spaniards. In 1672 sent to England in disgrace but found favour with Charles II, was knighted and returned to the West Indies as Lieutenant-Governor of Jamaica.

Morley John (1838–1923): British radical politician. Entered parliament in 1883. Secretary for Ireland, 1886 and 1892–4. Secretary of State for India, 1905–11. He co-operated with the Viceroy, Lord Minto, to put through the very important reforms of 1909, which cautiously started India on the path to self-government.

Muhammad Ahmad ibn Abdullah (the Mahdi) (*c.*1844–85): Born in the northern Sudan and acquired a reputation for holiness. Felt called to lead a *jihad* or holy war against the Turkish and Egyptian influences in the Sudan, which he saw as corrupting. Was supported by others who had their own grievances. In 1883 he defeated an Egyptian force under General Hicks. Britain decided on a total withdrawal from the Sudan in the course of which General Gordon was killed at Khartoum. The Mahdi made good his control of most of the Sudan but died, probably of typhus, in 1885. His theocracy continued for another 13 years under Abdullahi (the Khalif).

Munro, Sir Thomas (1761–1827): British soldier and administrator. The son of a Glasgow merchant, he entered the service of the East India Company in 1780 as an infantry cadet. He took part in a number of important actions against Haider Ali, Tipu Sultan and, later, the Marathas. He was employed in administration in Kanara and Madras, becoming Governor of Madras from 1819 until his death from cholera in 1827. He was important for his advocacy of the *ryotwari* system, that is reliance on petty proprietors, which contrasted with Cornwallis' *zemindari* system of reliance on the landlords.

Mutesa I (*c.*1838–84): Kabaka (King) of the Buganda. Became Kabaka in 1865 and did much to make his country powerful and prosperous. During his reign both Islam and Christianity were arriving. Mutesa listened to both and, to some extent, played one off against the other, as he also played the English Protestants (represented by the Church Missionary Society) off against the French Catholics (represented by the White Fathers).

Mwanga (*c.*1866–1901): Kabaka (King) of Buganda. Succeeded Mutesa I in 1884 but a very different man. Insecure and brutal. Deeply shocked European opinion by the massacre of 30 Christian pages in 1885. Was deposed by his enemies in 1888. Returned but finally fled in 1897. By then control of the country had passed to Britain.

Mzilikaze (*c.*1795–1868): Founder of the Matabele (Ndebele) kingdom during the time of the *mefcane*, the period of Zulu expansion. Originally allied with Shaka between 1818 and 1823, Mzilikaze fled after a quarrel. Led his followers north-westwards, eventually settling beyond the Limpopo River in the territory of the Shona people and establishing his capital at Bulawayo. In 1854 the missionary Robert Moffat visited him and persuaded him to open relations with the Europeans and admit traders and missionaries.

Nachtigal Gustav (1834–85): German explorer. A medical doctor, he explored parts of the Sudan between 1869 and 1874. In 1884 he was sent by the German government to the Cameroons and Togoland. The Germans sought British co-operation in his mission to the Cameroons and the British were correspondingly irritated when he concluded protectorate treaties with chiefs previously under British influence.

Naoroji Dadbhai (1825–1917): Indian political leader. Born into a Parsi family in Bombay, he was educated at the Elphinstone Institute. In 1862 he set up a commercial house in London and also founded the East Indian Association to inform the British about India. He returned to India in 1873 as chief minister for the princely state of Baroda, and his experiences led him to publish *Poverty* *and the Un-British Rule in India* (1901). In 1885 he became a member of the Legislative Council of Bombay. He played a leading role in the formation of the Indian National Congress and was its President in 1886, 1893 and 1906. In 1892 he stood for election to the British parliament as a Liberal candidate in the constituency of Central Finchley and won it, though he lost it at the next general election. In 1896 he was a member of the Royal Commission of Indian Expenditure.

Nehru Motilalal (1861–1931): Lawyer and the father of the more famous Jahawarlal Nehru. An aristocratic lawyer from Kashmir, he was a prominent member of the Indian National Congress, moving it in a secular direction and opposed to the caste system. He was a moderate and regarded as an Anglophile, but he later became more radical and was briefly imprisoned for his political activities in 1921.

Newcastle 2nd Duke of (Thomas Pelham-Holles) (1693–1768): British politician. In 1724–48 he was Secretary of State for the Southern Department, whose responsibilities included many of the colonies. In 1748 he became Secretary of State for the Northern Department and in 1754 First Lord of the Treasury, in effect Prime Minister, until succeeded by the elder Pitt in 1756. He was Lord Privy Seal, 1765–6. He tended to let sleeping dogs lie and interfered very little with the colonies. He opposed the Stamp Act.

Newcastle 5th Duke of (Henry Pelham Clinton) (1811–64): British politician. 1854 Secretary of State for War and the Colonies, but discredited by the Crimean War. Secretary of State for the Colonies, 1859–64. Accompanied the Prince of Wales to Canada in 1860. Allowed Canadians freedom to set their own tariffs in 1859 and generally sympathetic to Canadian federation.

North (Frederick), Lord (1732–92): British politician, regarded as primarily responsible for the loss of the American colonies. Became the leader of the House of Commons in 1768 and in 1770 George III made him Prime Minister. North was determined to make the Americans pay their share of the cost of colonial defence, but his vacillating policy over the next six years, lurching from severity to conciliation, brought the two sides to war. His conduct of the war was equally uncertain and in 1782 he lost power. He returned to office briefly in the North–Fox coalition of 1783.

Nzinga Nkuwu (d. 1506): Mandingo or King of the Kongo – a state which had been formed in the fourteenth century, south of the Congo River in the north of what is now Angola. King when the Portuguese explorer Diego Cao arrived in 1482. Friendly relations were established with Portugal over the next few years and Portuguese priests and technical experts came out. In 1490 Nzinga Nkuwu was baptised, taking the name João in honour of his royal brother of Portugal. He sent his son, Nzinga Mvenba, baptised as Affonso, to be educated in Portugal. His son succeeded him as Affonso I in 1506 but traditional forces had now become very hostile to Portugal, at the same time as the Portuguese were losing interest in the connection.

Ovando Frey Nicolas de (*c*.1460–1518): First effective Governor of the Spanish settlements in the Caribbean. Governor of Hispaniola, 1502–8. Arrived with 30 ships and 2500 colonists. Unlike his predecessor, Christopher Columbus, he exercised firm control over the settlers. He also exacted tribute and forced labour from the Indians. His regime was harsh and under him the Tainos, the inhabitants when Columbus arrived, died out.

Papineau Louis-Joseph (1786–1871): French Canadian leader. Elected to the Legislative Assembly of Lower Canada in 1809 and joined the *Parti Canadien* (the *Patriotes* from 1826). Speaker, 1814–37. Became the recognised leader of the French Canadians, although the party also attracted other disaffected groups. In the 1830s, angry at his inability to influence the executive government, he mounted an effective campaign of systematic obstruction by withholding supplies. In October 1837 the *Patriotes* met to consider armed rebellion. Warrants were issued for Papineau's arrest, leading to the 1837 rebellions. Papineau fled to the United States and later to France until an amnesty was declared in 1847. He again became a member of the Legislative Assembly in Canada, although he disapproved of the union of the two Canadas and, rather strangely, would have preferred annexation to the United States. He left politics in 1854.

Parkes Sir Henry (1815–96): Australian politician. Born in Britain but emigrated to Sydney in 1839. He began to sit in the New South Wales Legislature in the 1850s. He was Premier of New South Wales in 1872–5, 1877, 1878–83, 1887 and 1889–91. He was a strong advocate of confederation and convened a meeting of the colonial premiers to discuss it in 1890, which did not immediately bear fruit but put it on the agenda for 10 years later.

Philip II King of Spain (1527–98): Son of Charles V. In 1554 married Mary I, Queen of England. When his father abdicated in 1556, inherited Spain and its colonies, the Netherlands, Naples and Sicily. Regarded himself as the champion of Catholic Europe against the Protestants. Failed to subdue the Netherlands or England, against which he launched the Great Armada in 1588.

Philip Dr John (1775–1851): British missionary. Born in Scotland. Sent to South Africa by London Missionary Society in 1819. Became powerful spokesman for non-whites. Came to England to plead their cause, 1826–9. On his return to South Africa he was successfully sued for libel by his opponents. He received some support from Governor D'Urban but disapproved of D'Urban's annexation of the Transkei. Went to England to campaign against it in 1836 and helped to secure D'Urban's recall. Philip became adviser to D'Urban's successor, General Napier. Philip would have preferred to see the establishment of a buffer zone of independent 'native' states, where there would have been as little European interference as possible. But a new frontier war in 1846 ended any hope of that and Philip resigned in 1849.

Phillip Arthur (1738–1814): British naval officer and first Governor of New South Wales. He was chosen in 1786 to establish a new penal colony. The 'First Fleet' arrived in Botany Bay in 1788 but Phillip chose Sydney Cove as the site for the permanent settlement. He would have preferred to have had a good proportion of free settlers but three-quarters of the 1000 or so who landed were convicts. Tried against great difficulties to make the colony self-sufficient. Unlike some of his successors, he tried to maintain friendly relations with the Aborigines. Bad health compelled him to return to England in 1792, after which he resumed his naval career.

Pitt William (the Elder), Earl of Chatham (1708–78): British politician. Credited with the British victory in the Seven Years War. First entered the Cabinet in 1755. In 1756 became Secretary of State, and effectively Prime Minister, under the Duke of Devonshire. In 1757 formed coalition government with the Duke of Newcastle. *Dictionary of National Biography* said of him: 'During the next four years Pitt's biography is to be found in the history of the world.'[2] Forced out of office in 1761 after disagreements with Lord Bute, who had the support of the new king, George III. Briefly Prime Minister again, 1766–7. Sympathetic to American grievances. But ill-health prevented him from playing an effective role in his later years.

Pitt William (the Younger) (1759–1806): British politician. Second son of William Pitt the Elder. Became Prime Minister in December 1783 at the extraordinarily early age of 24. During his 'Peace Ministry' put through very important financial and other reforms. When war broke out with France in 1793 headed wide coalition of Tories and most Whigs. In 1800 secured Act of Union with Ireland but resigned (1801) when George III would not honour government's promises on Catholic emancipation. Prime Minister 1804 until his sudden death in 1806.

Pizarro Francisco (*c.*1475–1541): Spanish adventurer who overthrew the Inca empire in Peru. The illegitimate son of a small landowner, he went to the New World to make his fortune. Accompanied Alonso de Ojeda on unsuccessful mission to Colombia and Balboa on his crossing of the Isthmus. Became an *encomendero* in Panama. After further reconnaisances, sought permission from Charles V to establish a new province in Peru. Returned with relatives, including his brother, Gonzalo. Found Inca empire in state of civil war. Captured the ruler, Atahualpa, by trickery. Received a huge ransom but then killed Atahualpa. In 1535 he established a new capital at Lima. Struggles continued between rival conquistadors and, in 1541, Pizarro was killed by a supporter of his rival, Almagro, whom he had had executed.

Pocahontas (*c.*1595–1617): A daughter of the Indian chief Powhatan. According to tradition, she saved the life of a leading Jamestown settler, Captain John Smith, when he was captured by her father. Hostilities, however, continued and Pocahontas herself was seized and held as a hostage in 1613. She became a Christian and took the name Rebecca. In 1614 she married, with her father's

---

2. *Dictionary of National Biography*, vol. XLV, p. 358.

consent, another leading colonist, John Rolfe. The marriage alliance began eight years of peace. In 1616 she visited England but died of smallpox and was buried at Gravesend. She left one child, Thomas, who eventually returned to Virginia.

Polo, Marco (*c.*1254–1324): Venetian explorer. The son of a noble family of Venetian merchants. His father, Niccolò, and his uncle, Maffeo, had already visited Peking, where they had been well-received by Kublai Khan in 1266. In 1271 the 17-year-old Marco accompanied them on another expedition to China, where they entered the service of Kublai Khan. Marco travelled widely in the empire, preparing reports for the Emperor. He returned to Venice in 1295. He was captured during a war with Genoa in 1298 and, while awaiting release, dictated an account of his travels to a fellow prisoner, a Pisan called Rusticiano. Marco Polo's *Travels* became immensely well-known and were translated into many languages. They influenced Christopher Columbus.

Pontiac (*c.*1720–69): Ottawa Indian chief. He became involved in the Anglo-French wars on the French side. He assisted Montcalm and may have taken part in the defeat of General Braddock in 1755. He made peace with the British in 1760 but led a new coalition against them in 1763, which became known to the British as 'Pontiac's Conspiracy'. He failed to take Detroit and made peace in 1766. He was killed (by a fellow Indian) in 1769.

Powhatan (*c.*1550–1618): Indian chief. According to tradition, his father was a chief who had been forced to flee from Florida by the Spaniards. Powhatan created a powerful confederation of Algonquin tribes in what became Virginia. Suspicious of the English colonists and refused them supplies. Intermittent hostilities followed. After the marriage of his daughter, Pocahontas, to John Rolfe in 1614, the peace was kept until Powhatan's death.

Prester John: Legendary Christian king (or line of kings), who had been left behind by the advancing tide of Islam. The Portuguese hoped to establish contact with him on their early voyages. The most plausible theory is that he was based on the Emperor of Abyssinia, who was a Christian monarch, by now surrounded by Islamic states.

Pretorius Andreis (1792–1853): Boer leader. Born in Cape Colony. A prosperous farmer. In 1838 he set out with a commando of 464 men to aid the Voortrekkers in Natal after the murder of Retief. Defeated Dingaan at Blood River on 15 December 1838. Established a Boer republic centred on Pietermaritzburg but moved on to the Transvaal after the British annexed Natal. Cast off British allegiance but, after various failed attempts, negotiated the Sand River Convention with Sir Harry Smith in 1852.

Pretorius Marthinius (1819–1901): Son of Andreis. The President of the South African Republic (the Transvaal), 1856–71. Joined with Kruger and Joubert in protesting and eventually resisting the British annexation of the Transvaal in 1877.

Ptolemy (Claudius Ptolemaeus) (*fl.* 127–51): Astronomer and geographer, resident in Alexandria and variously described as Greek or as Egyptian. He realised that the earth was a sphere. His work, the *Algamest*, came back to Europe through the Arabs and was important in the Renaissance and in triggering the Age of Discovery.

Raffles Sir Stamford (1781–1826): British administrator. Born off the coast of Jamaica on a ship commanded by his father. Entered the service of the East India Company as a clerk in 1795. Sent to Penang in 1805. Governor of Java, 1811–16, while it was in British possession during the Napoleonic wars. In 1819 he advised the British government to acquire Singapore, which had the potential to become a major port. Governor of Singapore until 1824.

Ralegh Sir Walter (1552–1618): English courtier, soldier and explorer. In 1569–74, fought with the Huguenots in the French wars of religion. In 1578–9 sailed to the New World with his brother-in-law, Sir Humphrey Gilbert. Served in the Irish wars, 1579–81. After Gilbert's death in 1583, Ralegh succeeded to his patents to colonise new lands. Immediately sent an exploring expedition to the American coast and called the new territory Virginia, in honour of the Queen. Sent out his cousin, Sir Richard Grenville, to found colony of Roanoke. In 1594 led expedition to Guiana which brought back samples of gold, which roused hopes of fabled El Dorado. But, when James I succeeded to the throne in 1603, Ralegh's patents were cancelled and he was imprisoned on charges of conspiracy against the King. Released in 1616 to lead a new expedition to Guiana. Ended in failure. Spaniards asked for his execution. Was executed in 1618 but on revived 1603 charge of treason.

Retief Pieter (1780–1838): Boer leader of Huguenot descent. Served in a number of the frontier wars in the Eastern Cape. In February 1837 joined the Great Trek and, in June, elected its leader. Negotiated arrangements with a number of African chiefs, including Moshweshwe, although failed in negotiations with Mzilikaze. In April 1838 secured a grant of land for settlement from Dingaan, but Dingaan, always unstable, was suspicious, and invited Retief and his associates to a farewell feast, at which they were massacred.

Rhodes Cecil John (1853–1902): The founder of Rhodesia. He was sent to South Africa at the age of 16 to join his brother, who was growing cotton in Natal. It was hoped that the climate would be good for Rhodes, who was thought to be tubercular. He left Natal for the newly-opened Kimberley diamond field, where he laid the foundation of his fortune by 'cornering the market' in pumping equipment (urgently required because the workings were flooding). During the 1870s he commuted to the University of Oxford and began to formulate his imperial ideas from various popular theories then being canvassed. He first articulated them in a will drawn up after a heart attack in 1877. He believed British rule was benevolent and should be extended over as much of the world as possible, and hoped that the United States would rejoin the empire. In 1880 he founded the De Beers Mining Company, which became De Beers Consolidated Mines, in conjunction with Barney Barnato, in 1888, and virtually controlled world diamond supplies. He made a second fortune by investing in the Transvaal gold mines when more cautious men were still holding back. He entered the Cape Parliament in 1880 and became Prime Minister of the Cape in 1890. His relations with the Cape Boers were then amicable but he wished to see Britain in control of all Africa south of the Zambezi and was alarmed by German and Portuguese ambitions. He was instrumental in securing Bechuanaland for Britain in 1885. In 1888 his agent, C.D. Rudd, persuaded Lobengula to grant them monopoly rights over the minerals in his territories. Rhodes secured a charter for his British South Africa Company in 1889 and sent parties of 'Pioneers' into Mashonaland in 1890. War resulted with the Matabele in 1893 and with the Mashona in 1896. Rhodes personally negotiated the peace. But he quarrelled with his Boer allies when he became involved in the Jameson Raid in 1895 and had to resign as Prime Minister of the Cape. He helped to organise the defence of Kimberley during the Boer war but died of heart disease in 1902. His friend, W.T. Stead, called him 'the first of the Money Kings'. He was unusual in being a committed imperialist, who always 'thought big', whether it was Rhodesia or the Cape–Cairo railway project. A more benevolent legacy were the Rhodes scholarships which paid for places at Oxford for students from the empire, the United States and Germany.

Riel Louis (1844–85): Canadian rebel. Born near Fort Garry where Winnipeg now stands, Riel was a *métis* of mixed Indian, French-Canadian and Irish descent. When in 1869 the Hudson Bay Company sold its vast territory to the new Canadian confederation, the *métis* feared that they would be overwhelmed by new settlers. When surveyors arrived from Ontario in October 1869, Riel took the lead in opposing them. Seized Fort Garry and took 48 Canadians hostage, including Thomas Scott, who was subsequently killed. On 8 December Riel announced the setting up of a provisional government with himself as President. The British chose to negotiate and the result was the Manitoba Act of 1870, by which land was set aside for the *métis*. The *métis* subsequently complained that the agreement was not kept and retreated to the Saskatchewan Valley. In 1884 they persuaded Riel to return from the United States, where he had settled, to lead them again. In March 1885 he demanded the surrender of the North-West Mounted Police at Fort Cotton. They refused and fighting ensued. Riel was captured and hanged in Regina in November 1885. He has subsequently become something of a folk hero in Canada.

Roe Sir Thomas (*c.*1581–1644): English ambassador to the Mughal empire. The son of a wealthy London merchant family. In 1609–11 made his first voyage to explore the coast of South America between the Amazon and the Orinoco. In 1614 he was sent as ambassador to the court of Jehangir, mainly to arrange commercial treaties. Although he only obtained a general permission for the East India Company to trade in India, his mission was judged a success. He returned by way of Persia in 1619. From 1621 to 1628 he was ambassador to Constantinople and subsequently served in various European capitals. He left a full account of his mission to the Mughal empire, later published in a number of editions.

Rolfe John (1585–1622): English colonist. Shipwrecked in Bermuda on his way to Jamestown, where he arrived in 1610. Started to experiment with tobacco cultivation and founded the industry. In 1614 married Pocahontas, the daughter of Powhatan, which led to eight years of peace for the colonists.

Rosebery (Archibald Philip Primrose), Lord (1847–1929): British Liberal politician. Became converted to the imperial cause, partly as a result of his travels. In 1883–4 went on a world tour on which he visited Australia and New Zealand. While in Adelaide in January 1884 he spoke of the empire as a 'Commonwealth of Nations'. Later supported the Imperial Federation Movement. In 1886–7 he visited India. His friendship with Herbert Bismarck brought him into contact with Otto von Bismarck, while his marriage to Hannah Rothschild opened him to criticisms that he was influenced by the financiers. He was briefly Foreign Secretary in Gladstone's administration in 1886 and returned to that office in 1892. He clashed with his colleague, William Harcourt, who opposed the further expansion of the empire, on a number of issues, notably on the retention of Uganda. Rosebery triumphed and succeeded Gladstone as Prime Minister in 1894, but, having lost the 1895 election, he largely retired from politics, although he supported the Liberal imperialist cause during the Boer war.

Roy Ram Mohan (1772–1833): Indian reformer. Born in Bengal of a Brahmin family. He travelled widely as a young man and became a notable linguist. Employed by the East India Company, 1804–14. He retired with a pension and devoted himself to study and writing. He wished to restore Hinduism to its original and pure form, shorn of abuses such as caste discrimination and *sati*, and to find common ground between the Hindu scriptures and western philosophy and religion. In 1828 he founded the *Brahma Sabha* to work for reforms in India. He moved to England in 1830 and died in Bristol in 1833, while organising a conference of world religious leaders.

Rudd Charles Dunell (1844–1916): Businessman. Emigrated to South Africa in 1865. In 1870 he went to the diamond diggings, where he became closely associated with Cecil Rhodes. Went into partnership with Rhodes in 1871 to 'corner the market' in pumping equipment. Member of original De Beers Company in 1880. In 1886 accompanied Rhodes to the Witwatersrand and mainly responsible for the formation of the Gold Field of South Africa Ltd in 1887. In 1888 he went with Frank Thompson and James Rochfort Maguire to Bulawayo and persuaded Lobengula to grant the 'Rudd concession', which gave them a monopoly over the exploitation of minerals in Lobengula's land. Continued to manage various mining interests in southern Africa until retired to Scotland about the time of the Boer war.

Russell Lord John (1792–1878): British politician. Prime Minister, 1865–6. Associated with Lord Durham in drafting the Great Parliamentary Reform Act of 1832. Twice Colonial Secretary, 1839–41 and 1855. During the first, some important decisions were taken, including the annexation of New Zealand and the extension of Britain's claim to the whole of Australia. Russell, however,

179

instructed Lord Durham's successor as Governor-General of Canada, Lord Sydenham, to be extremely cautious in applying any idea of 'responsible government', which he saw as incompatible with imperial authority.

Russell William Howard (1821–1907): Journalist who usually worked for *The Times* and may reasonably be regarded as the first modern war correspondent. Best known for his exposures of the mistakes made during the Crimean war but equally frank in his coverage of the Indian Mutiny in 1857. Later covered the American Civil War and the Zulu war of 1879. He was in Egypt at the time of the Arabi Pasha rebellion and the British occupation. He accompanied the Prince of Wales to India in 1875–6.

Ruyter, Michael Adrianszoon de (1607–76): Dutch admiral. Commanded the Dutch fleet against the Spaniards in 1640–1 but best known for his exploits against England in the trade wars of the 1660s. He defeated Monk (the Duke of Albemarle) off North Foreland and entered the Thames in 1666. In 1667 he penetrated the Medway and burnt Chatham dockyard. Died at Syracuse in 1676 after being mortally wounded in a fight with the French off Messina.

Salisbury (Robert Arthur Talbot Gascoyne Cecil), 3rd Marquess of (1830–1903): British politician. Prime Minister, 1885–6, 1886–92 and 1895–1902, when the British empire was at the height of its power. In 1866 became Secretary of State for India and returned to the post in 1874. Severely criticised for his bad handling of the Bengal famine. In 1878 succeeded Lord Derby as Foreign Secretary and accompanied Disraeli to the Congress of Berlin. Secured the Cyprus Convention by which Turkey leased Cyprus to Britain in return for guarantees against Russia. In 1885, and again in 1895, became Foreign Secretary as well as Prime Minister. Relinquished Foreign Office to his nephew, A.J. Balfour, in 1900. Salisbury was not a jingoistic imperialist but was convinced of the need to defend Britain's interests in the changed world of the new imperialism. Various parts of Africa came under British control through the Chartered Companies, and in 1890–1 Salisbury negotiated various boundary arrangements, usually in Britain's favour. In 1890 he concluded the Heligoland treaty with Germany, by which Britain took Zanzibar in return for Heligoland. He was convinced of the importance of the Nile and initiated the campaign of 1896–8 to regain the Sudan. His ministry also saw the outbreak of the Boer war in 1899. Salisbury was an opponent of democracy in his own country and caused offence by his contemptuous references to other peoples, including his declaration that the Hottentots and the Hindus were unfit for self-government.

Samori Touré (*c*.1830–1900): Rival empire-builder to the French in the western Sudan. As a young man he became a trader and built up a commercial network from Guinea to Sierra Leone. By the early 1860s he was at the head of the Kamara forces and, by 1874, he had established his own state. In 1876–8 he conquered the whole of the Upper Niger. Despite his reputation for brutality, he showed considerable organising ability and carried on a flourishing trade in slaves, gold and ivory in exchange for firearms. Samori was himself a convert to Islam and in 1884 he declared his state to be Muslim and imposed

Islam on all his subjects. In the 1880s, however, he was challenged by the French advance and also resisted by other African chiefs. He gradually shifted his empire eastwards, but was eventually defeated by Archinaud in 1898 and died in exile in Gabon.

San Martin José de (1778–1850): South American nationalist. Born at Yapeyu in what became Argentina. Brought up in Spain and joined the army. Fought against the French in the early stages of the Peninsular War. In 1812 he went to Buenos Aires and joined those trying to throw off Spanish authority. Led an army across the Andes in 1817 and liberated Chile in 1818. In 1820 led expedition against Peru. Took Lima in 1821 and was chosen as Protector but in 1822 handed over authority to Bolívar. Retired to Europe and died at Boulogne.

Sarraut Albert (1872–1962): French politician. Born in Bordeaux of an old radical family. With his brother became the political masters of the South West. A lawyer by profession, Sarraut entered the French Chamber in 1902 and attached himself politically to Clemenceau. Became Governor-General of Indo-China in 1911 and successfully put down an insurrection. He entered Viviani's Cabinet just before the First World War. He served in the army at Verdun before being sent back to Indo-China. He was Minister for the Colonies, 1920–4 and 1932–3, where he became famous for his policy of *mise en valeur.*

Schnitzer Edward Carl Oscar (Enim Pasha) (1840–1892): German traveller and adventurer. Trained as a medical doctor, he went to Albania in the service of the Ottoman empire, where he took the name Mehemet Emin. In 1875 he went to the Sudan, where General Gordon appointed him as medical officer in Equatoria. When Gordon became Governor-General of the Sudan, Emin succeeded him, in 1878, as Governor of Equatoria, where he worked to eliminate the slave trade. He was cut off from Cairo by the Mahdi's forces and 'rescued' (against his will) by Henry Morton Stanley in 1889. He was killed by slave traders in the Congo in 1892.

Shaka (*c.*1787–1828): Founder of Zulu nation. His career is the subject of much legend. His parents had violated customary law by their marriage and Shaka had a disturbed childhood, virtually in exile. Served with distinction under Mtetwa chief Dingiswayo until Shaka's father, Senzangakhwana, died in 1816. Then, with Dingiswayo's help, gained control of his clan. At this time the Zulus were a small Nguni community of less than 1500. Shaka organised them into a formidable fighting force and compelled defeated enemies to integrate with the Zulus. Within a few years he commanded 60,000 men. Became paramount chief when Dingiswayo was murdered in 1818. Compelled Lesotho and Swazis to pay tribute but destabilised the whole region in what became known as the *mfcane.* Natal was largely depopulated, which opened it up for white settlement. Shaka's paranoia increased after his mother's death in 1827. He was defeated in Mozambique and stabbed to death by his half-brother, Dingaan, in 1828.

Shepstone Sir Theophilus (1817–93): Emigrated to the Cape with his family in 1820. The son of a minister, brought up on mission stations, he acquired early proficiency in the local languages. In 1835 he was employed as a translator in Cape Town. In 1838 he accompanied Major Charteris's expedition on the first, temporary, occupation of Natal. In 1845 he became the Agent, and in 1856 the Secretary, for Native Affairs in Natal. In 1872 he helped to arrange the peaceful succession of Cetewayo in Zululand. In January 1877 he was sent to the Transvaal, which was bankrupt and felt threatened by the Zulus, and in April he used the powers he had been given to annex it to Britain. He remained there as administrator until 1879, retiring from government service in 1880.

Smith Adam (1723–90): Scottish political economist. In 1751 he became a professor at the University of Glasgow but resigned in 1764 to tutor and travel with the young Duke of Buccleuch. He began to write his best-known book, *The Wealth of Nations*, published in 1776, which was to be immensely influential during the free trade era of the nineteenth century. Smith was strongly in favour of *laissez-faire* and condemned all artificial restraints on trade. He believed colonies were a burden but did not believe any nation would voluntarily get rid of them because they were thought to confer prestige and because certain influential sections of society did benefit from them. These last arguments were to be developed by many later anti-colonialists.

Smith Captain John (*c.*1580–1631): English soldier and colonist. Served in the English army in the Netherlands. In 1600 he joined the Austrians in their war against the Turks but was eventually captured and enslaved. He escaped and made his way back via Muscovy. After further travels he reached London in 1605. He was acquainted with Captain Bartholomew Gosnold and was selected as one of the Council to rule the new colony to be established in Virginia. Played an important role in the establishment of Jamestown. According to tradition, his life was saved by Pocahontas, when he was captured by her father, Powhatan. In 1608 he became the President of the Governing Council of Jamestown and the same year published his influential *A True Relation of Virginia*. He was compelled to return to England after an accident in 1609 but visited the coasts of Maine and Massachusetts in 1614. He published a number of other works, including his *A Description of New England* (the first recorded use of the name) in 1616 and his massive *The Generall History of Virginia* in 1624.

Smuts General Jan Christian (1870–1950): South African and Commonwealth soldier and politician. Born in Cape Colony, the son of a prosperous farmer and member of the Legislative Assembly. Studied law at Cambridge and practised law on his return to South Africa. At first admired Rhodes but was antagonised by the Jameson Raid. Moved to the Transvaal and, in 1898, became state attorney. Clashed with Gandhi on questions of Indian rights in the Transvaal. During the Boer war Smuts became one of the most successful guerilla leaders and took part in the peace negotiations at Vereeniging. In 1904 he joined with Louis Botha to form the *Het Volk* (The People) to work for the restitution of responsible government. Won the 1907 election in the Transvaal. Played a leading role in drafting the South Africa Act, which set up the

Union of South Africa in 1910. During the First World War suppressed the Boer rising of those who would not accept the parliament's decision to support Britain, defeated the Germans in South-West Africa and led the South African forces in East Africa. In 1917 Lloyd George invited him to become a member of his War Cabinet. Became South African Prime Minister for the first time on Botha's death in 1919. Emerged as a very important Commonwealth statesman between the wars and helped to found the United Nations in the Second World War.

Souza Martin Afonso de (*c.*1500–64): Portuguese coloniser. In 1530 he was sent out to Brazil as 'chief captain' to drive out interlopers and establish a settlement. Founded the settlement at São Vicente in 1532. He encouraged agriculture and the first sugar mill came into operation in 1533. He fought in the Portuguese cause along the coasts of India, 1534–9, and became the Portuguese Viceroy in India, 1542–5.

Stanley, Henry Morton (1841–1904): British explorer. Born John Rowlands, the illegitimate son of a Welsh farmer. After a miserable childhood, he went to the United States in 1859, where he was adopted by a cotton broker, whose name he took. Fought (on both sides) in the American Civil War. Became a journalist and covered the Indian wars in the American West and the British campaign in Abyssinia in 1868. In 1869 the *New York Herald* commissioned Stanley, among other things, to find Livingstone. Met Livingstone at Ujiji in 1871 and, after Livingstone's death, determined to finish his explorations. Crossed the African continent from Zanzibar to the Atlantic, 1874–7, but incautiously allied himself with the slave trader Tipu Tip, and encountered much hostility as a result. Worked for Leopold of the Belgians in establishing the Congo Free State, 1879–90. Conducted the Enim Pasha Relief Expedition, 1887–90. Renewed his British citizenship (he had become a naturalised American) and became an MP in 1895. Wrote copiously and his writings were very popular but presented Africa as a dark and savage place, which coloured public impressions for a generation. He attracted much criticism and was refused burial in Westminster Abbey, not because of his humble origins, but because of the disapproval of the better informed.

Stephen Sir James (1788–1859): Lawyer and civil servant. He came from an evangelical family, deeply committed to the abolition of slavery. Gave up potentially lucrative career at the Bar to work for it. Entered Colonial Office in 1825. In 1833 broke the Sabbath for the only time in his life to draft the Bill to abolish slavery throughout the British empire. Went on to become the Permanent Under-Secretary at the Colonial Office in 1836. He was the *bête-noir* of the Colonial Reformers, who accused him of ignorance and arrogance. His reputation has been considerably restored by later studies which suggest that his opposition to the plans of the Colonial Reformers, e.g. in New Zealand, arose from his understanding of the situation based on his missionary contacts and his defence of native peoples against the colonisers. He resigned from the Colonial Office in 1847 and in 1849 became Regius Professor of Modern History at Cambridge.

Tasman Abel (1602–59): Dutch navigator. Became ship's captain for the Dutch East India Company and after 1633 lived in Bataam. In 1642 he was sent on an expedition to determine whether the great southern continent hypothecated by geographers, existed. Discovered what is now Tasmania, which he called Van Diemen's Land in honour of the Dutch governor of the Company. He touched on the South Island of New Zealand, where he got into a fight with the Maoris, and sailed by the North Island, Tonga, Fiji and New Guinea. In 1644 he was sent to establish a base on Tonga but instead surveyed the north-west coast of Australia, which he called New Holland, but he reported it was barren and not worth following up.

Tewfik (1852–92): Khedive of Egypt. The eldest son of the Khedive Ismail. The Sultan deposed his father in his favour in 1879. Probably pressured into it by the great powers, who wanted a malleable ruler in Egypt. Predictably Tewfik proved very weak and unable to deal with his opponents. Theoretically, Britain intervened in Egypt in 1882 at his request. After 1883 Lord Cromer exercised the real power in Egypt.

Thomas St (*fl.* first century AD): Apostle. According to legend, the apostle of India, having landed on the Malabar coast at Cochin, possibly touched at Ceylon, and been killed in Madras. The Indian Christians, who predated the arrival of the Portuguese, claimed their traditions descended from him. In Goa they were persuaded to accept the authority of Rome at the Synod of Diamper in 1599, but many broke away again in 1653.

Tilak Bal Gangadhar (1856–1920): Indian nationalist leader. A Brahmin, born in Mahararashta. He was educated at the Elphinstone Institute but turned against western ideas. He wished to restore a Hindu golden age, supposed to have existed before the coming of Islam. He defended the caste system and child marriage and condemned education for women or health measures such as vaccination against smallpox. Unlike Gokhale, he was prepared to advocate violence and even political assassination. He was several times imprisoned by the British. Matters came to a head over the partition of Bengal when Gokhale was regarded as the leader of the 'Moderates' and Tilak of the 'Extremists'. The conflict almost destroyed the Congress.

Tipu Sultan (1750–99): Muslim ruler of southern Indian state of Mysore. He succeeded his father, Haider Ali, when the latter died during the second Anglo-Mysore war in 1782. Tipu Sultan created a prosperous state and conducted a propaganda campaign against the drunken 'Feringhees' (Europeans). He also had a remarkable automaton made showing a tiger (Tipu's emblem) devouring a British officer, with appropriate roars and groans. It was based on a real incident and is now in the Victoria and Albert Museum in London. During the French wars, the British feared that Tipu would ally with the French. He was defeated and killed in the battle of Seringapatam in 1799.

Tipu Tip (many alternative spellings, including Tippoo Tib) (1830–1905): The most powerful slave trader in East Africa. The son of a Zanzibari merchant, he established a mercantile empire stretching from Lake Tanganyika to the central Congo. At the height of his power he employed more than 4000 agents. He traded principally in slaves and ivory, which he exchanged for guns, cloth and manufactured goods. He befriended Livingstone, explored with Henry Morton Stanley and joined the Enim Pasha Relief Expedition. After about 1885 and the development of European control, his empire declined. He took service with the Belgians but retired to Zanzibar in 1890.

Toussaint L'Ouverture (François Dominique Toussaint) (1743–1803): Black Haiti leader. Born into slavery but well-educated. Took part in the slave revolt of 1791. In 1794 he joined the French Republicans, and the French Convention gave him command of the island in 1797. Proved a very effective general, drove out the French royalists, the British and the Spanish forces and, by 1801, was in control of the whole island (Spanish Santo Domingo, as well as the French Haiti). Began to work for complete Haitian independence and refused to countenance re-introduction of slavery. Napoleon sent a force against him in 1802. He was captured and died in 1803.

Townshend Charles (1725–67): British politician. Became Chancellor of the Exchequer in 1766 and, in 1767, introduced usual four shillings in the pound land tax. The opposition reduced it to three shillings. In a rash speech, Townshend promised to raise the shortfall from the Americans. He planned to establish new commissioners of customs in America and impose duties on the import of glass, lead, painters' colours, paper and tin. The announcement was met with riots and threats of embargoes. Townshend died before the policy could be implemented.

Turgot Anne Robert Jacques (1721–81): French economist associated with the Physiocrats and acquainted with Adam Smith. Believed in free trade and felt that the colonies were of little use. Supposed to have been the first writer to use the simile that colonies were like ripe fruit which would eventually drop off the tree – a phrase attributed to many later writers. In 1774 became Controller-General of Finance to Louis XVI but unable to put through the reforms which might have averted the Revolution. Dismissed 1776.

Van Diemen Anthony (1593–1645): Governor-General of Dutch East Indies, 1634–45. Went to the East Indies as a soldier after going bankrupt in Amsterdam. Attracted the attention of the Governor-General Jan Coen, who promoted him. Returned to Amsterdam as Admiral of the Fleet in 1631. Himself became Governor-General in 1636. Considerable extended Dutch empire in the East. Encouraged explorations, including those of Tasman. Expelled Portuguese from Ceylon and Malacca. Secured treaties with Acheh in northern Sumatra and with Ternate and Tidore in Moluccas. Established relations with China, Japan and Tonkin. Introduced a general legal code, Batavia Statute, in 1642.

Van Riebeeck Johan (1619–77): Dutch official. Went to the East Indies as a ship's doctor in 1640. Entered the service of the Dutch East India Company and visited Japan and Tonkin on their behalf. Returned to the Netherlands in 1648.

In 1651 the Company sent him to the Cape of Good Hope to establish a station. Arrived in April 1662. Began to organise agriculture and viniculture. As a result had to allow officials to acquire land. Left for Batavia in 1662 and remained there until his death.

Vaughan William (1577–1641): Coloniser. The son of a Welsh landed family of Golden Grove in Carmarthenshire. Well known as a poet. In 1616 he bought an interest in Newfoundland and sent out settlers in 1617–18. Visited the settlement, probably in 1622. In 1626 published *The Golden Fleece*, an allegory in praise of the colony, and, in 1630, *The Newfoundlanders Cure*, a kind of medical dictionary.

Vespucci Amerigo (1454–1512): Navigator. Born in Florence. He may have sailed to the New World from Cadiz in 1497–8 but voyage is shrouded in mystery. In 1499–1500 sailed on another Spanish expedition with Alonso de Ojeda, on which they followed the South American coast past the Amazon. In 1501–2 he sailed on behalf of Portugal on an expedition at first commanded by Goncalo Coelho, which followed the South American coast to beyond the River Plate. In 1503 sailed again to Brazil. Unlike Columbus, who, although puzzled by some of his discoveries, always supposed that he had reached Asia, Vespucci quickly realised it was a new continent and called it *Mundus Novus* (New World). In the circumstances the name 'America', suggested by others in 1507 and at first only applied to South America, does not seem unreasonable. In 1508 he became pilot major for the *Casa de Contratación* in Seville, entrusted with training pilots.

Wakefield Edward Gibbon (1796–1862): Colonial theorist. The black sheep of a highly respectable and philanthropic family, he was jailed in 1826 for abducting a wealthy heiress. While in Newgate gaol he wrote *A Letter from Sydney* (1829), supposedly from a colonist. In 1849 he published *The Art of Colonisation*. Wakefield advocated what came to be called 'systematic colonisation'. Colonies should be balanced communities including wealthy and professional men as well as artisans and farm labourers. He wished to see the surplus capital and population of the mother country made complementary to the surplus land of the colony. Land should be sold at a 'just price', not given away free. Emigrants would thus have to work for a time on arrival and would provide a labour force. Profits could be used to assist emigration or develop roads, etc. Wakefield accompanied Lord Durham to Canada in 1838 in an unofficial capacity and influenced the land section of the Durham Report. Wakefield was mainly important as a theorist. His ideas influenced a number of radical MPs in the 1830s and, in 1830, he founded the National Colonisation Society, which had a distinguished membership. But he took some practical part. In 1834 he was one of the founders of the South Australia Company, which led to the setting up of the colony. He was also associated with the New Zealand Land Association, formed in 1837, and acted as the Land Agent for the Company, 1839–46. He emigrated to New Zealand in 1853 but ill-health meant that he did not play a major role there.

Washington George (1732–99): Commander-in-Chief of the American forces during the War of Independence and first President of the United States. He fought on the British side against the French in the Seven Years War. As a member of the Virginia House of Burgesses, he opposed the Stamp Act of 1765 and later opposed the 'Intolerable Acts', meant to coerce Massachusetts. He was a delegate to the first Continental Congress in 1774 and the second Congress elected him Commander-in-Chief in 1775. After the French alliance of 1778, he commanded the French forces in America too. In 1789 he was elected the first President of the new United States.

Wellesley Richard Colley (Earl of Mornington, 1781 and Marquess Wellesley, 1799) (1760–1842): British politician. The elder brother of the future Duke of Wellington. Became member of the Board of Control, 1793. Governor-General of India, 1798–1805. He feared a challenge from the French, who were opening relations with both Hyderabad and Mysore. He made an alliance with Hyderabad (1799) and defeated Tipu Sultan, the ruler of Mysore, the same year. He also concluded alliances with Surat (1800), the Carnatic (1801) and Oudh (1801). His attempts to do the same with the Maratha confederation led to near disaster. There were five Maratha states: Poona, Indore, Gwalior, Berar and Baroda. Wellesley's alliance with the Peshwa of Poona offended the more powerful rulers of Indore and Gwalior, Holkar and Sindia. Despite the victory at Assaye in 1803, the war went badly in 1804 and Wellesley was replaced by Cornwallis in 1805. Wellesley later became Foreign Secretary (1809–12) and Lord Lieutenant of Ireland (1821–8 and 1833–4).

Wellington Duke of (Arthur Wellesley) (1769–1852): British soldier and politician. He received some of his military training in France at Angers (1786). He fought in the Netherlands in 1795 and was in India, 1797–1805, during the Governor-Generalship of his elder brother, Richard. He was involved in the campaign against Mysore which culminated in the battle of Seringapatam in 1799, although he was not in overall command. In 1803 he defeated the Marathas at the battle of Assaye. Fought successfully against Napoleon in the Iberian peninsula, 1808–13, and in France, (1813–14). He participated in the Congress of Vienna before defeating the returned Napoleon at Waterloo on 18 June 1815. After that he turned to politics. He represented Britain at the Congresses of Aix-la-Chapelle (1818) and Verona (1822). Was Master of the Ordnance (with a seat in the Cabinet), 1818–27, and Commander-in-Chief, 1827–8 and 1842–52. He was Prime Minister, 1828–30, Foreign Secretary, 1834–5, and Minister without Portfolio in Peel's administration of 1841–6.

Wilberforce William (1759–1833) British anti-slavery campaigner. The son of a well-to-do Yorkshire family and a friend of the Younger Pitt, he first entered Parliament as the member for Hull in 1780. An evangelical Christian he began his life-long campaign against slavery in 1788. In 1807 he persuaded Parliament to declare the slave trade illegal. The measure, which finally abolished slavery throughout the British empire, had been introduced into Parliament but not yet reached the Statute Book when he died in 1833.

Williams Roger (*c*.1604–83): British colonist and Puritan clergyman. Founder of Rhode Island. He sailed from Bristol to Massachusetts in 1630 but found the churches of Boston and Plymouth 'corrupt', i.e. not Puritanical enough. He did become a minister in Salem in 1634 but the following year was in trouble with the authorities and founded a new settlement in what became Rhode Island. In 1643 he went to England and, the following year, regularised his position with a charter. When a new charter was issued in 1663, he acted as assistant to the new Governor, Benedict Arnold. He several times changed his religious allegiance within the Puritan community but, believing all men to be wicked, he preached religious tolerance and democracy. He also learnt some Indian languages and published a dictionary.

Willoughby Lord Francis (*c*.1618–66): English soldier and colonist. He at first, although hesitantly, supported parliament in the English Civil War but, after being impeached in 1647, he fled to Holland and joined the royalist side. In 1647 he was made joint proprietor of Barbados with the Earl of Carlisle. He arrived in the island in 1650 and proclaimed Charles II as King. In 1651 a parliamentary fleet arrived and Willoughby was forced to leave, but by an agreement of 1652 he kept his property in Barbados, Antigua and Surinam. In 1660 he was restored to the Governorship of Barbados and made Governor of St Kitts, Nevis, Montserrat and Antigua. He also received a further land grant in Surinam. He entered on a long struggle with the Assembly of Barbados but was backed by the King and mounted a generally successful defence against French and Dutch attacks. He was lost at sea in June 1666, sailing to St Kitts to expel a French incursion.

Willoughby Hugh (d. 1554): English navigator. The original commander of the fleet sent to seek the North-East Passage in 1553 but he was lost at sea and the expedition was completed by Richard Chancellor.

Winthrop John (1588–1649): British colonist. In 1630 sailed from Britain as the Governor-Elect of the Massachusetts Bay Company with a substantial number of colonists. Settled round the Charles River (on the site of what is now Boston). He was Governor, 1630–33, 1637–9, 1642 and 1646–8, and impressed his personality on the young colony. He wished to create a godly community. The churches were organised on a congregational basis and only church members enjoyed full citizenship. He was involved in various doctrinal struggles, with Roger Williams among others.

Wolfe General James (1727–59): British soldier. Served in Europe in 1740s. Sent to North America in 1758 to serve under Amherst. Took part in the successful siege of Louisbourg. In 1759 he was sent to take Quebec (City). He famously sent a force to gain control of the Heights of Abraham by stealth. Both Wolfe and the French commander, Montcalm, were mortally wounded in the battle but Wolfe lived long enough to learn that his army was victorious. Became a national hero in Britain.

Wolff Sir Henry Drummond (1830–1908): British diplomat, politician and trouble-shooter. He made his early career in the diplomatic service and was the Secretary in the Ionian Islands, 1859–64, and concerned with preparations for their return to Greece. He resigned from the Foreign Office in 1864 and became a Conservative MP in 1874. Disraeli's government employed him in various missions to Egypt and the Balkans and he returned to the Foreign Office, 1878–80. In 1885–7 he was sent to Constantinople to regularise the British position in Egypt and facilitate Britain's ultimate withdrawal, but the agreement failed and the British government resigned itself to remaining in Egypt indefinitely.

Wolseley General Sir Garnet (1833–1913): British soldier and army reformer. Born in Ireland. Fought in Burma and the Crimea in the 1850s. Severely wounded and lost the sight of one eye. He was among the forces bound for China that were diverted to suppress the Indian Mutiny, and took part in the relief of Lucknow. He was in China in 1860 and deplored the looting of the Emperor's Summer Palace. While in Canada during the American Civil War, he visited the States. He commanded the expedition against Louis Riel's Red River rebellion in 1870 and also commanded the successful war against the Ashanti in 1873–4. He became the first administrator of Cyprus in 1878 but was sent to South Africa after the Isandhlwana disaster, arriving after Lord Chelmsford had retrieved the situation at Ulundi. He led what was widely praised as a 'textbook campaign' in Egypt in 1882. He was sent to rescue General Gordon in 1884 but failed to reach him in time. In 1890 he became Commander-in-Chief in Ireland. Throughout the latter part of his career he struggled hard to achieve reforms in the organisation of the British army.

Xavier St Francis (1506–52): Jesuit priest. The 'Apostle of the Indies'. Born at Navarre of an aristocratic Spanish–Basque family. In 1541 he sailed from Lisbon for Goa, where he made his headquarters. Visited Travancore, Malacca, Moluccas and Ceylon. Established a church in Japan, 1549–52. Died on his way to China but his body was brought back to Goa.

GLOSSARY

Amboina, massacre of (1623): The Dutch Governor executed 10 Englishmen (and several Japanese) whom he accused of trading illegally and plotting insurrection. It was long remembered and, according to tradition, was the seminal event which led to Britain abandoning the Spice Islands trade in favour of India, but more recent research suggests that the transition was less abrupt and that Britain continued to trade in the Spice Islands for some time after this.

asiento: An agreement to supply a certain quota of slaves to the Spanish colonies.

audiencias: Important bodies in the Spanish colonies in South and Central America. Although their functions were primarily judicial, they came to be advisory councils to the Viceroys and Captains-General.

Aztecs: The dominant people in Mexico when the Spaniards arrived in 1519. Their capital was at Tenochtitlan, the site of the present Mexico City. They were a sophisticated society with a remarkable system of agriculture. But they were essentially a despotism with a small ruling class. This may help to explain the extraordinary collapse of the empire before Cortés' tiny forces. Cortés may also have been helped by Aztec religion, which looked for the return of the god, Quetzalcoatl, from the east.

Bantu: In origins a linguistic classification, denoting a related family of African languages. It came to be applied to those who spoke them and has fallen into disrepute because of its (often derogatory) use during the apartheid era in South Africa to describe black Africans. The Bantu-speaking peoples moved slowly south from the Great Lakes region from about AD 400, probably driven by land hunger as the population increased.

Bojador, Cape: A headland on the coast of West Africa about 100 miles south of the Canary Islands. It gained a legendary importance in sixteenth-century explorations, being believed to be the safe limit of navigation, but, once it had been rounded (in 1434), the way seemed open, culminating in the discovery of a sea-route to India.

Boston massacre (5 March 1770): This was essentially a skirmish between British troops and a crowd. A British sentry was set upon. His comrades opened fire and five people died. It was only one of a series of brawls, but clever spin doctoring depicted it as a battle for American liberty.

Boston Tea Party (16 December 1773): An incident in the run up to the American War of Independence. The duty on tea was the only one of the Townshend Duties retained. Its price was actually reduced by allowing the East India Company to export it directly to North America, but a party of colonists, disguised as Indians, destroyed a shipment of tea in Boston harbour. In retaliation parliament passed the Intolerable Acts (*see below*), including one which closed Boston harbour until compensation had been paid for the tea.

buccaneers: British, French and Dutch seamen who established themselves in the Caribbean and harassed the Spaniards, taking advantage of the doctrine 'No peace beyond the Line', i.e. the Tordesillas line. They eventually degenerated into mere pirates. Henry Morgan (1653–88) was one of the most celebrated.

Bulls, papal: Letters and documents issued by the Pope (the name derives from his *bulla* or seal). They carried considerable weight in medieval Christendom but, like *Inter Caetera* in 1493, their authority was not recognised by Protestant powers like England and Holland and was increasingly disregarded by nominally Catholic powers.

Calcutta, Black Hole of: Incident during the struggles between the English East India Company and the Nawab of Bengal, Siraj-ud-daula. On 20 June 1756 after the Nawab's forces had taken Calcutta, 146 prisoners were confined in a small guardroom with inadequate ventilation. Only 23 survived the following morning. The tragedy made an immense impression in Britain, where it was quoted throughout the Victorian period as an example of oriental cruelty.

Canada: A potentially confusing term. In 1535 the Huron told Jacques Cartier that the name of their country (round the modern Quebec City) was 'Canada', and this was adopted for the whole of New France, stretching a thousand miles up the St Lawrence. After the British conquest this was divided into Upper Canada, later called Canada West, which became Ontario, and Lower Canada, later called Canada East, roughly the modern Quebec. Before 1867 the name was not applied to any other part of British North America, but after the British North America Act of 1867 created the 'Dominion' of Canada, it came to cover the Maritime Provinces and eventually the Prairie Provinces and British Columbia.

***capitanias*:** System used by the Portuguese in Brazil. Men of substance were granted land, mainly on the coast, with authority to govern and organise settlement. It was meant to establish a presence to keep out foreign interlopers but it had only limited success.

caravels: Fast manoeuvrable ships, with edge-to-edge planking and lateen sails, developed in the Mediterranean in the late medieval period. They were crucially important in the Age of Discovery. Columbus's ships the *Pinta* and the *Nina*, for example, were caravels.

carracks: Heavy merchants' ships, which could when necessary be used as warships, with considerable carrying capacity. If the caravels made the new discoveries possible, the carracks made the resulting trade profitable.

***Casa de Contratacion*:** The body which controlled trade in the Spanish empire. Established in Seville in 1503.

Cawnpore, massacre of: Incident in the Indian 'Mutiny' of 1857. A number of Britons were trapped in Cawnpore. The ruler, Nana Sahib, offered them safe conduct by river to Allahabad. The boats were subsequently fired upon. The women and children were imprisoned in a building, the Bibigarh. When British troops were known to be approaching, the women and children were killed. The atrocity (which was in fact only one of a number of atrocities, committed by both sides) made a profound impression in Britain.

Council of the Indies: The chief administrative body of the Spanish empire, which advised the King and also acted as the final appeal court in judicial matters. Established in Seville in 1524.

Councils, Executive: In British Crown colonies initially a group of, normally European, officials who assisted the Governor. As the colony matured politically, others, including non-Europeans, might be added to it. It provided the germ from which a Cabinet developed as a colony evolved to independence.

coureurs de bois: French explorers and traders, usually fur traders, who ventured out from French Canada to open up trade throughout North America.

Crown colonies: The most usual form of British colonial administration, normally consisting of a Governor, appointed from London; an Executive Council, largely official, which might be appointed either by the Governor or by London; and a Legislative Council. The Legislative Council could include both official and 'non-official' members and could be either nominated or elected.

Crusades: Wars waged between Christian and Islamic powers between 1096 and 1571. The First Crusade set out at the request of the Pope to recapture Jerusalem and the Holy Sepulchre from the Muslims. (Jerusalem was in Christian hands, 1099–1187.) As a result of Venetian ambition, the Fourth Crusade turned aside in 1204 to attack its supposed ally, Constantinople. The naval battle of Lepanto in 1571 relieved the pressure on Christian Europe but did not end the Ottoman Turk threat. The Ottomans took Crete in 1669 and Greece in 1715. The battle against the Muslims in the Iberian Peninsula was also regarded as a crusade; as was military action against religious dissidents in Europe.

Culture System (Kultur System): Agricultural and taxation system imposed on Java by the Dutch from 1830 to 1877. Traditionally client princes had supplied the Dutch East India Company with tribute in kind, mainly spices. During the British occupation at the time of the Napoleonic wars, this had been replaced by monetary taxation, levied directly on the people. In 1830 the Dutch Governor, Jan van den Bosch, substituted an assessment in kind. A specified proportion of land in each village was to be used to grow cash crops for the government. This proved immensely lucrative for the Dutch. Between 1831 and 1877 823,000,000 guilders were transmitted back to Holland – nearly one third of the country's budget. But the system became increasingly oppressive to the Javanese and, after humanitarian protests in Holland, it was abolished.

Diamper, Synod of (1599): Denounced all Indian Nestorian (St Thomas) Christians as heretics.

diwani: In an Islamic empire, including the Mughal empire, it was normal for the ruler to collect taxes through tax-farmers, who acquired wide powers of jurisdiction, not merely fiscal ones. In 1765 the English East India Company was granted the *diwani* of Bengal and its fortunes were made.

dominion: This term was used in the British North America Act of 1867 to avoid the shock to American susceptibilities of speaking of the 'Kingdom' of Canada, which would have been legally correct. The Canadians, who suggested it, were, however, making a sly reference to Psalm 72, which speaks of holding dominion from sea to sea (to counter American claims of their divine right to the whole of North America). It came to be applied to all Britain's colonies of settlement as they attained internal self-government. It was used as a quasi-technical term from the time of the Colonial Conference of 1907, although the classic definition is that of the Balfour Report of 1926: 'autonomous Communities within the British Empire, equal in status . . . united by a common allegiance to the Crown'.

East India Company, Dutch (*Vereenigde Ost-Indische Compagnie*, commonly abbreviated to VOC): Formed in 1602 by the amalgamation of the companies of Amsterdam, Hoorn, Enkhuizen, Rotterdam, Delft and Middelburg. It had government backing and a capital of 6.5 million guilders. It was ruled by the 17 members of the Court of Directors (the *Heeren Zeventien*). Apart from a trading monopoly between the Netherlands and Asia, it had powers to make war, conclude treaties and govern territory. In its heyday, it established an unassailable position in the Spice Islands. It was wound up in 1795.

East India Company, English: Incorporated by royal charter on 31 December 1600 under the title 'the Governor and Company of Merchants of London trading to the East Indies'. It had 125 shareholders and, initially, a capital of £70,000. It sent out 12 voyages between 1601 and 1612, all except one profitable. It held a monopoly of trade between Britain and ports east of the Cape of Good Hope but not of the 'country trade', i.e. trade within Asia. It was challenged in the east by 'interlopers', Englishmen who sometimes co-operated with foreign East India companies. It was also challenged at home by rivals such as the 'New Company' of 1698. But it maintained its powerful position. All stockholders owning £500 worth of stock were members of the Court of Proprietors, who elected the 24 members of the Court of Directors. In 1765 the Mughal Emperor granted it the *diwani* of Bengal but, after Pitt's India Act of 1784, the Company had to share its power in India with the Crown. The charter came up for renewal at intervals, notably in 1813, 1833 and 1853. In 1813 its trading monopoly began to be eroded in the face of the increasing strength of free trade views. It lost its political powers altogether to the Crown in 1858 after the 'Mutiny' and was wound up.

East India Company, French (*Compagnie des Indes Orientales*): Created by Colbert in 1664. Its main headquarters in India were at Pondicherry. It played an important role in the middle of the eighteenth century when Joseph François Dupleix was the Governor-General of the Company in India (1742–54). Dupleix made a determined effort to oust the British from Madras and gain control of the Carnatic and the Deccan. He failed to secure the support of his government and was eventually recalled. The Company was wound up in 1794.

El Dorado: Literally 'the golden one'. It came to be the symbol for the European search for fabulous wealth in South America, including Sir Walter Ralegh's expedition of 1595.

encomienda: A quasi-feudal system, previously used during the *Reconquista* in Spain itself and in the Canary Islands and applied in the early sixteenth century to the Spanish empire in America. It was first authorised by the instructions to Nicolas de Ovando, the Governor of Hispaniola, in 1503. Indian villages were 'commended' to a Spaniard, who undertook certain responsibilities, including the military protection of the villages. In return he was empowered to levy tribute, which usually took the form of labour services.

entente cordiale: Literally a 'cordial understanding' between nations, falling short of a formal alliance. It was first used of Anglo-French relations in 1843 but it is most frequently used of the series of colonial bargains struck between Britain and France in 1904, which led to their diplomatic co-operation over Egypt and Morocco, and paved the way for the Anglo-Franco-Russian alignment of 1914.

Gorée: Island in the bay where Dakar now stands. Important in the slave trade.

greased cartidges: The introduction of the Enfield with its rifled barrel meant that the cartridges had to be greased. Rumours spread in India in 1857 that the cartridges were greased with both pig and cow fat, the first unacceptable to Muslims, the second to Hindus. Some Indian soldiers (who formed the vast majority of the East India Company's army) suspected that the British wanted to make them ritually unclean to alienate them from their own people and ensure their loyalty to the British. It was the refusal of the 23rd Light Cavalry to take part in firing practice at Meerut on 24 April 1857 which triggered the 'Mutiny'.

Guanche and Canario: The aboriginal inhabitants of the Canary Islands. They became extinct as identifiable groups after the Spanish conquest in the fifteenth century. It is difficult to know to what extent they were exterminated and how far they were absorbed by inter-marriage.

Hudson's Bay Company: In 1670 Charles II granted a charter to Prince Rupert (hence the alternative name of the Hudson Bay territory as Rupert Land) and 17 others giving them a monopoly of trade on the territory watered by streams flowing into Hudson Bay as well as jurisdiction over it. From the beginning the trade in furs and skins, which they obtained from the Indians, was very lucrative, but they made little attempt to open up the area in any other way. After 1763 they were challenged by others, especially the North-West Fur Company of Montreal. The two companies amalgamated in 1821. The Company surrendered its powers of jurisdiction to the government in 1869 and the prairie provinces were carved out of its former territories, beginning with Manitoba.

Incas: When the Spaniards arrived in 1532, they were the dominant group along the Pacific coast and the Andean highlands from modern Ecuador to central Chile. Their capital was at Cuzco. They had embarked on a remarkable period of rapid conquest in the fifteenth century, which had brought 12 million people under their rule. They were a highly organised society with sophisticated architecture, irrigation and road systems. Like the Aztecs, they succumbed to tiny Spanish forces. Their weakness may have lain in a highly stratified society with a disaffected peasantry and the fact that they had just been riven by civil war.

indentured servants: Employees who had bound themselves to serve for a particular length of time in a colony, sometimes in return for a free passage there. They were often exploited and burdened by mounting debts, which made their position little better than that of slaves, although in theory they always remained free men.

indirect rule: A theory, particularly associated with the name of Lord Lugard, on which Britain ruled much of her empire in the late nineteenth and twentieth centuries. The administration was left as far as possible in the hands of the existing non-European authorities and existing laws maintained. In part it was necessitated by the fact that European administrators were always very thinly spread, but it also looked back to the Burkean idea that societies must evolve and should not be roughly changed. It worked better in areas like northern Nigeria where there was already a strong political structure.

Inter Caetera: A papal Bull or decree of 1493 which divided the newly discovered lands between Portugal and Spain by a notional line 100 leagues west of the Azores. It was superseded by the Treaty of Tordesillas between Spain and Portugal and the authority of *Inter Caetera* was never recognised by the Protestant countries.

Intolerable Acts: Five Acts of Parliament passed by the British government which led to the calling of the First Continental Congress by the American rebels in 1774. They were the closing of Boston harbour until compensation should have been paid to the East India Company for the tea destroyed during the Boston tea party; the abrogation of the Massachusetts Charter of 1691, making it into a Crown colony; the provision that British officials charged with capital offences in Massachusetts should be tried elsewhere; the provision for the billetting of British troops; and the Quebec Act (*see below*), although the last was regarded by others as an exceptionally enlightened measure.

Jamestown: The original British settlement in what became Virginia.

Kaffir: In origins an Arabic word meaning 'infidel', i.e. a non-Muslim. Ironically it came to be applied, especially in South Africa, to non-whites (some of whom may have been Muslims). An insulting word.

Kaffir wars: The long series of wars on the eastern frontiers of Cape Colony, which lasted from 1779 to 1853.

Lagos (Portugal): The site of the first African slave market in Europe (now reconstructed as an historical site). It gave its name to the better-known Nigerian Lagos.

latitude: Technically the angular distance on a meridian north or south of the equator, expressed in degrees and minutes. It was of vital importance in navigation but its use came to be understood comparatively early by sailors because it could be calculated from the position of the sun.

London Company – *see* Virginia Association.

longitude: The angular distance east or west from a standard meridian (such as Greenwich) to the meridian of any place. It was much more difficult to calculate than latitude and a satisfactory method of doing so was only established by John Harrison in 1759.

Louisiana: A vast area of North America from the 49th parallel to the Gulf of Mexico, following the line of the Mississippi River, claimed by France. Ceded to Spain in 1762 but reclaimed by France in 1800. In 1803 Napoleon sold it to the United States for $15 million.

***mamelucos*:** Portuguese term applied to those of mixed European and Amerindian descent.

Marathas: The Maratha homeland was in the Western Ghats. They first rose to prominence under Sivaji (1627–80). By the middle of the eighteenth century they formed a loose confederation of five states. Some Indian historians have seen them as the natural successors of the Mughal empire but they were defeated by the Afghans at Panipat (1761) and by the British at Assaye (1803) and finally by the British in 1818. They provided some very important later nationalist leaders, including both Tilak and Gokhale.

Massachusetts Bay Company: Founded in 1629 when John Winthrop obtained a charter from Charles II. Unusually, it did not specify that the headquarters of the company must be in England, and they were established in North America at Boston. Winthrop brought out nearly 1000 settlers in 1630 and the colony grew rapidly.

Maya: An Indian people, resident in southern Mexico and adjacent states. They had attained a high level of civilisation but it had already begun to disintegrate before the arrival of the Spaniards in the sixteenth century, and the Maya, unlike the Aztecs and Incas, were conquered piecemeal.

***mesticos*:** Portuguese term usually applied to those of mixed European and Amerindian descent, although it was also used of Eurasians. (*Mestizos* is the Spanish equivalent.)

***métis*:** People of mixed Amerindian and European blood in British North America. The *métis* were normally French-speaking and Roman Catholic in religion, although some were of Scots or Irish, rather than French Canadian, parentage. Louis Riel was the best-known *métis*.

mfecane: A Nguni word (*Difquane* describes the same phenomenon in Sotho) meaning literally 'crushing', applied to the migration of the Nguni peoples and especially the expansion and consolidation of the Zulu kingdom in southern Africa in the first half of the nineteenth century. It had immense repercussions, at least as important as the activities of the Boer trekkers, and is only just beginning to be understood.

mise en valeur: Used to describe French colonial policy, especially by Albert Sarraut. Can sometimes mean 'develop' but more exact meaning is to extract maximum value from.

Mughal empire: The Muslim empire founded in northern India by Babur (1483–1530). Akbar (1542–1605) is usually regarded as its greatest ruler, although the empire reached its greatest size under Aurungzeb (1659–1707), but by then it was over-extended. As it fell to pieces, high officials carved out hereditary principalities for themselves but then fell prey to European intervention.

mulattos: People of mixed European and African descent.

Muscovy Company: Formed in 1555 as a result of Richard Chancellor's travels in Russia. It established important trade links with Russia.

Navigation Acts: In English history a long series of Acts of parliament beginning in 1382 which regulated British overseas trade. One of the most important, which formed the basis of the 'Old Colonial System', was that of 1660. They finally came to an end in 1850 in the middle of the free trade era.

nawab: (Corrupted to nabob:) A high official under the Mughal empire. Its use was extended to denote a gentleman of high rank, and in the eighteenth century came to be applied loosely to wealthy servants of the East India Company.

Nestorians: Strictly those who followed the teachings of Nestorius, the patriarch of Constantinople (428–31), on the divine and human natures of Christ, but loosely applied to Indian Christians, who claimed to have received their Christianity from St Thomas the Apostle. They were condemned as heretics by the Portuguese.

North-East Passage: A sea-route to the East, through the Arctic seas to the north of Russia. Although attempted by some explorers who opened up trade with Russia, no practical route was ever found.

North-West Passage: A sea-route to the East, passing north of the American continent. This was eagerly sought, especially by British explorers, because it would have avoided challenging the well-entrenched Spanish position in South and Central America. The discovery of Hudson's Bay raised their hopes. Technically such a route does exist, as nineteenth-century explorers were able to demonstrate, but ice and extreme weather conditions meant that it was never of practical importance.

Orinoco project: Sir Walter Ralegh dreamt of finding immense riches (the fabled El Dorado) in the area between the Orinoco and Amazon rivers. The failure of the project (and the offence given to the Spaniards by it) led to his execution in 1617.

Plantation: The common term in English from the sixteenth to the eighteenth centuries to denote a colony of settlement.

Plymouth Company – *see* Virginia Association.

privateers: 'Letters of Marque' were issued to ships' captains, authorising them to attack and seize the ships of an enemy power. The system was widely employed by the European powers in the eighteenth century. It was abolished by international treaty only in 1856.

proprietary colonies: A system by which the British Crown allowed individuals (or groups of individuals) to found colonies at their own expense. Maryland, founded by Lord Baltimore, was one of the best-known examples.

protectorate (protected state): A term recognised in international law by which a (usually European) state extended its 'protection' to a smaller state. It assumed control of its foreign and defence policies but, theoretically, left its internal administration in place. In practice, especially in Africa in the nineteenth century, there was frequent interference and the distinction between a protectorate and a colony was often very blurred. In the British empire a protectorate came under the jurisdiction of the Foreign, not the Colonial, Office and the law officers were frequently exercised in their minds as to whether, for example, land grants could be made in a protectorate.

Quebec: A name originally applied to the whole of the French settlements along the St Lawrence River, larger than the modern province of Quebec (*see* Canada).

Quebec Act (1774): Act for the government of the former French Canada. Because it recognised extensive boundaries for the province and set out to conciliate the French Canadians by protecting French civil law and the status of the Roman Catholic church, it was regarded as one of the 'Intolerable Acts' by the American rebels.

race: English usage up to the early part of the twentieth century differed somewhat from that of today. 'Race' was often used interchangeably with 'nationality'. The conflicts between the English and the French in Canada were described by Lord Durham as a 'stuggle between the races'. Similar descriptions were applied to the conflicts between the British and the Boers in South Africa.

responsible government: A very important concept in the constitutional evolution of the British empire. It arose from the conflicts in French Canada in the 1830s and was implicit in Lord Durham's Report, although only clarified over the next decade. The executive government in a colony was to be responsible (answerable) to the locally elected assembly, rather than to London, in local matters. Foreign policy, defence and, for a time, trade remained the responsibility of the British government. The principle was accepted in the Canadian

201

colonies in the 1840s and in Australia in the 1850s. Only in the twentieth century was it extended from the colonies of settlement to all British colonies.

responsive government: An alternative to responsible government, suggested by the Colonial Secretary, Lord John Russell, to Lord Durham's successor, Lord Sydenham. Russell feared that responsible government would make a colony for all practical purposes independent, and suggested instead that the Governor should carefully 'manage' the assembly.

Royal Africa Company: A joint stock company similar to the English East India Company, it was established in 1672, replacing a number of smaller companies. It did not prosper commercially and surrendered its charter in 1750. British posts on the West African coast, such as Cape Coast Castle, were administered from 1750 to 1821 by a looser body, the Company of Merchants Trading to Africa.

Sagres: According to tradition, Prince Henry (the Navigator) founded a school of navigation at Sagres on the south-west coast of Portugal which master-minded the early Portuguese voyages of exploration. Although the facts may have become overlaid by legend, important scientific advances did take place in fifteenth-century Portugal.

sati (suttee): The practice of a Hindu widow burning herself to death on her husband's funeral pyre. Although in theory voluntary, the woman was sometimes drugged or coerced. The practice caused particular horror among Europeans and was forbidden by the East India Company in 1829. General Napier suppressed it in the Punjab in the 1840s. According to tradition, when told that it was the Hindu custom, he replied, 'My nation also has a custom. When men burn women alive, we hang them. . . . Let us all act according to national customs.'[1]

slave trade – *see* Appendix A.

Spice Islands: Modern Indonesia.

swadeshi: (Literally 'of one's own country'.) The name given to the movement which started in Bengal in 1905 to buy Indian, and reject foreign, goods. Although inspired by the American Embargo Acts at the time of the American Revolution, it was intended to have a great deal more moral content, re-affirming the value of all things Indian.

systematic colonisation: The phrase was popularised by Edward Gibbon Wakefield and the Colonial Reformers, although the concept had already been applied by Colbert. The settlement of a colony should not be a haphazard process but the migrants should be a balanced community of men and women, capitalists, professional men, artisans and labourers. In Wakefield's version, land in the colony should be sold at a 'just' price.

---

1. P. Woodruff, *The Founders* (1953), p. 327.

Terra Australis Incognita: In the eighteenth century, scientists hypothesised that there must be a great southern continent to balance the land masses of the northern hemisphere. A number of expeditions were despatched to look for it. But, insofar as it existed, it consisted of the barren wastes of Antarctica, not the populous land they hoped to discover.

Ticonderoga, Fort: A key point at the southern end of Lake Champlain on the route between New York and Montreal, which featured in many of the struggles for the control of North America.

Tordesillas, Treaty of (1494): A treaty between Spain and Portugal which modified the papal Bull *Inter Caetera*. It had the effect of leaving to Portugal the route to the East via the Cape of Good Hope and to Spain the vast majority of the American continent, but, since the dividing line came to be interpreted as lying on the longitude 54.37 West, it gave Brazil to Portugal.

Townshend Duties: Duties (named for the British Chancellor of the Exchequer, Charles Townshend) on glass, lead, paper and tea when imported into the American colonies. They were rejected by the Americans on the grounds that they were revenue duties (taxation intended to pay for defence), not for the control of trade, and so breached constitutional precedent.

transportation: The sending overseas of criminals (including occasionally political offenders). It was regarded as both cheaper and more constructive than imprisonment. The French made some use of it but it was best known in the British empire. Criminals were sent to both the West Indies and the North American mainland, prior to the American War of Independence. After the loss of the American colonies, Australia became the new destination, the 'First Fleet' arriving in 1788. Cape Colony refused to have convicts and the Australian colonies too gradually rejected them (New South Wales, 1840; Tasmania, 1852). Because of a labour shortage, Western Australia accepted them up to 1868. In all, over 130,000 convicts were sent to Australia.

Uitlander: Afrikaans term for foreigner. Applied to white residents in the Transvaal who were not Boers and were refused citizenship.

utilitarians: The disciples of Jeremy Bentham, prominent among them James and John Stuart Mill. Utilitarians wished to reform society on rational grounds, having little patience with Edmund Burke's theories of the organic nature of society. They exercised significant influence in British India, especially during the Governor-Generalship of Lord William Bentinck (1828–35).

viceroy: Literally the King's deputy. It was a term widely used in the Spanish empire. In the British empire it was used only for the Governor-General of India after 1858 when the East India Company finally surrendered its rights to the British Crown.

viceroyalties: The term for the main divisions of the Spanish empire in South and Central America.

203

Vijayanager: Hindu kingdom in the south of India. The Portuguese, seeing the Muslim Mughal empire as their natural enemy, made overtures to it. Mysore was its most important successor state.

Virginia: The name (in honour of Queen Elizabeth I) originally given to a large tract of the eastern coast of North America from Cape Breton to modern Georgia.

Virginia Association: Established in 1606 by merchants who acquired Sir Walter Ralegh's patents after his disgrace. The Virginia Company of London was to colonise the southern, the Virginia Company of Plymouth, the northern, part of the then vast territory of 'Virginia'. The London Company established Jamestown. The Plymouth Company made several attempts at settlement but it was pre-empted by the Pilgrim Fathers (who escaped from its jurisdiction) and the Massachusetts Bay Company.

VOC – *see* East India Company, Dutch.

Xhosas: African peoples who lived on the eastern border of Cape Colony. The 'suicide of the Xhosas' was a tragic event on 18 February 1857 when they obeyed the call of a 'prophetess', Nongqawuse, to destroy their cattle and crops in the belief that a whirlwind would sweep the white man into the sea and new crops and herds would appear. In the resulting famine, the tribal structure was destroyed and the British took direct control of the Ciskei region.

Zimbabwe (Great): Remarkable ruins in what in colonial times became Southern Rhodesia. When Europeans first discovered them in 1868 they could not believe that they had been built by Africans and attributed them to the Phoenicians, thus strengthening their belief that the Queen of Sheba's gold had come from the region. In fact radio-carbon dating places them between the fifth and the fifteenth centuries AD and they are now understood stylistically within the African architecture of the period.

APPENDICES

APPENDIX A

Slavery and the slave trade

Atlantic slave trade

1440s	Portuguese brought home Africans almost as trophies from early exploring voyages.
1448	Fort and warehouse built on Arguim Island, in modern Mauritania, for the reception of slaves. Slaves were bought from African traders. Lagos on the southern coast of Portugal became the European slave market.
1482	Elmina became the centre of Portuguese trade, including slaves.

Slaves were at first obtained mainly from Senegambia and the Niger region, later from the Congo and Angola. The Europeans never ventured inland to capture the slaves themselves but always bought them from African middlemen and kept them in barracoons on the coast until they had a ship ready to transport them. Those sold as slaves in the early days were probably criminals or prisoners of war from other tribes. But as the trade became more lucrative, some African states grew powerful by waging wars to ensure a plentiful supply of slaves for the European merchants.

1502	Spanish settlers in Hispaniola turned to the cultivation of sugar. Began to import a few African slaves.
1542	The Spanish government forbade the enslavement of the Amerindians.
1550	Portuguese began cultivation of sugar in Brazil and needed ever-expanding labour force.
1562	John Hawkins carried a few African slaves to the West Indies.
1564	Hawkins began trading in slaves as a commercial operation.
1570	The Portuguese government forbade the enslavement of the Amerindians in Brazil.
1586	*Asiento* system introduced into the Spanish colonies, by which contractors undertook to deliver a specified number of slaves annually.
1612	Virginia began to require slaves to work in the new tobacco plantations.
1663	Royal Adventurers of England trading into Africa formed. Undertook to supply 3000 slaves a year to the English colonies.

1672	Royal Adventurers superseded by the Royal African Company.
1717	Boers in South Africa began to import slaves, some from West Africa.
1720	An incidental result of the South Sea Bubble scandal was that control of the slave trade passed from London to Bristol and Liverpool.
Later 18th cent.	Humanitarian feeling in Europe, and especially in Britain, began to turn against the slave trade as the horrors of the 'Middle Passage', the voyage across the Atlantic, became known. Objections to slavery as an institution developed rather more slowly. The thinkers of the French Enlightenment turned against it. Montesquieu condemned it, as did Raynal in his *Histoire des deux Indes* (1772). The *Amis des Noirs* was founded.
1772	Somersett case. The Chief Justice, Lord Mansfield, ruled that a man (Somersett) who had been brought to England by his master could not be a slave in England whatever his status elsewhere. In fact by the late eighteenth century there were a number of free Africans in Britain conducting their business, especially in Bristol and Liverpool.
1781	*Zong* case. Particular horror when it became known that a slaver captain had thrown 132 slaves overboard to claim the insurance.
1787	The Society for the Abolition of the Slave Trade brought together Quaker and non-Quaker campaigners. The leading members were Granville Sharp, Thomas Clarkson and William Wilberforce.
	Captain James Taylor established a homeland for freed slaves in Sierra Leone.
1791	Slave rising in Santo Domingo.
1807	Britain and the United States in independent moves declared the slave trade to be illegal. The Society for the Abolition of the Slave Trade became the African Institute, with the objectives of seeing that the new legislation was enforced, to encourage legitimate commerce to replace the slave trade and to persuade other countries to give up the slave trade.
1814–15	Congress of Vienna. All the leading European nations agreed to outlaw the slave trade.
After 1815	Britain kept warships (the West Africa Squadron) on the African coast to intercept vessels carrying slaves. Britain tried but failed to equate slave trading with piracy, which, under international law, gave any naval vessel the right to act.

Consequently British warships had no jurisdiction over vessels flying foreign flags unless such a right was conceded by treaty. Most of the smaller maritime nations were prepared to sign such treaties. But France and the United States were incurably suspicious of British intentions.

1822   American Colonisation Society established a home for freed slaves in Liberia.

1823   The African Institute was replaced by the Anti-Slavery Society (again with Quakers in the forefront) to work for the abolition of slavery itself. (In 1839 it became the British and Foreign Anti-Slavery Society, in 1909 the Anti-Slavery and Aborigines Protection Society and, in 1945, the Anti-Slavery Society for the Protection of Human Rights.)

1833   An Act of parliament abolished slavery throughout the British empire. Emancipation was to take place through a system of 'apprenticeship' over a period of four years. Compensation was to be paid to the slave owners for their loss of property rights. A sum of £20,000,000 was set aside for the purpose, of which £6,161,927 went to Jamaican planters. The Boers were left with a particular grievance because they did not have agents in London and frequently failed to obtain their compensation. But the West Indies too felt that they had been ruined. The Southern States of America suspected that subsequent British campaigning for the abolition of slavery was intended to ruin them so that they would not have a trading advantage over the West Indies.

1841   Niger experiment. A group of British philanthropists, of whom Thomas Fowell Buxton was the best-known, tried to establish legitimate commerce on the Niger in the hope that it would drive out the illegal slave trade. It failed disastrously because the would-be traders succumbed to disease, mainly malaria. But it attracted British attention to the area and helped to found what became the very flourishing trade in palm oil (an important raw material in the nineteenth century).

1848   The Second Republic abolished slavery in the French West Indies.
Denmark abolished slavery in its colonies.

1853   Brazil ceased to import slaves.

1861   Britain annexed Lagos (Africa), one of the few remaining centres of the slave trade.

1861–5   American Civil War. Preliminary Emancipation proclamation issued in 1862. Slavery finally abolished 1865.

1863	The Dutch abolished slavery in their possessions.
1865	Cuban slave trade finally ceased.
1870	Spain began to free slaves in Cuba. The process was completed in 1886.
1888	Brazil abolished slavery.

Numbers

It is impossible to establish with any certainty how many slaves were shipped across the Atlantic between the mid-fifteenth and the late nineteenth centuries, but 13 million is a plausible figure.[1] Many others probably died in the wars engendered among African people in procuring the supply of slaves.

At the time of the abolition in the British empire numbers of slaves were estimated as – British empire, 800,000; United States of America, 2,750,000; Brazil, 2,500,000; Spanish colonies, 600,000; French colonies, 265,000; Dutch colonies, 70,000; and Danish colonies, 30,000.

The Arab slave trade on the east coast of Africa

Slaves had always formed one item in the trade between east Africa, the Ottoman empire, Arabia and the Persian empire, but in the nineteenth century, numbers seem to have risen. The Sudan was a particular source. Arab slavers, unlike European merchants on the west coast, frequently went inland to capture the slaves for themselves. A man known to the westerners as Tipu Tip was a particularly notorious example of this in the 1870s.

Once feeling had turned against slavery and the slave trade in the West, strenuous efforts were made to persuade East African states to eliminate them too.

The Sudan

Egypt had gained control of the (Egyptian) Sudan from the time of Mehemet Ali (1805–48). In 1869 the ruler of Egypt, Ismail, appointed an Englishman, Sir Samuel Baker, to suppress the slave trade there. In 1874 Baker was succeeded by General Sir Charles Gordon (who became Governor of the Sudan in 1877). Both men had some success.

Zanzibar

Zanzibar was the key entrepôt for East African trade and, because of its important trade with India, Britain had long maintained consular relations there. Much diplomatic effort was expended to persuade its Sultans to suppress, first, the sea-borne and, later, the land trade in slaves. In 1822 and 1845 the Sultan Said agreed to sign treaties. Much pressure was put on his successor, the Sultan Majid, and a British squadron, similar to the West Africa Squadron, was maintained off the coast, 1856–73. In 1873 the Sultan Barghash signed a new treaty.

---

1. P.D. Curtin, *The Atlantic Slave Trade: A Census* (1969).

(It has been estimated that about 1870, the slave trade was causing losses – enslavement or death – of 80–100,000 East Africans every year.[2])

The suppression of the slave trade was a useful argument in favour of the take-over of East Africa by the European powers during the Scramble period. In fact the building of railways and the opening up of the region to commerce did stamp out the remnants by 1914.

2. R. Coupland, *The Exploitation of East Africa, 1856–1890: The Slave Trade and the Scramble* (2nd edn, 1968), p. 234.

APPENDIX B

British colonies and protectorates on the eve of the First World War (Constitutional Status)

(As stated in the Colonial Office List, 1913. List does not include India or Burma, which came under the India Office)

I   Colonies possessing responsible government now known as self-governing Dominions in which the Crown has only reserve powers of disallowing legislation and the Secretary of State has no control over any public office except that of governor. Canada: New Zealand: South Africa: Newfoundland: Australian Commonwealth and its six component States.

II   Colonies not possessing responsible government.

i.   Colonies with elected House of Assembly and nominated Legislative Council.
Bahamas, Barbados, Bermuda.

ii.   Colonies with partly elected Legislative Council, the constitution of which does not provide for an official majority.
British Guiana. Cyprus has a similar constitution. [Cyprus, although governed by Britain, was not technically a British colony at this time, being still part of the Ottoman empire.]

iii.   Partly elected Legislative Council but with an official majority.
Fiji, Jamaica, Leeward Islands, Malta, Mauritius.

iv.   Nominated Legislative Council.
British Honduras, Ceylon, East African Protectorate, Falkland Islands, Gambia, Gold Coast, Grenada, Hong Kong, Nyasaland Protectorate, St Lucia, St Vincent, Seychelles, Sierra Leone, Southern Nigeria, Straits Settlements, Trinidad.

v.   No Legislative Council.
Ashanti, Basutoland, Bechuanaland Protectorate, Gibraltar, Northern Nigeria, Northern Territory of the Gold Coast, St Helena, Somaliland, Swaziland, Uganda, Weihaiwei, Islands under the Western Pacific high Commission.
[The list does not include the territories of the British South Africa Company, i.e. the Rhodesias.]

APPENDIX C

Governor-Generals and Viceroys of British India, 1773–1921

(The Governor-General was styled the Viceroy after 1858, but the older title remained in force and was still used for certain legal purposes.)

1773–85	Warren Hastings
1786–93	Marquis Cornwallis
1793–8	Sir John Shore
1798–1805	Marquis Wellesley
1807–14	Lord Minto (1st Earl)
1814–22	Marquis of Hastings
1823–8	Lord Amherst
1828–35	Lord William Bentinck
1835–42	Lord Auckland
1842–4	Earl of Ellenborough
1844–8	Lord Hardinge (1st Viscount)
1848–55	Marquis of Dalhousie
1856–62	Viscount Canning
1862–3	Lord Elgin (8th Earl)
1863–9	Sir John Lawrence
1869–72	Lord Mayo
1872–6	Lord Northbrook
1876–80	Lord Lytton
1880–4	Lord Ripon
1884–8	Lord Dufferin
1888–94	Lord Lansdowne
1894–8	Lord Elgin (9th Earl)
1898–1905	Lord Curzon
1905–10	Lord Minto (4th Earl)
1910–16	Lord Hardinge (Baron Hardinge of Penshurst)
1916–21	Lord Chelmsford

APPENDIX D

The British empire: Colonial Secretaries and Secretaries of State for India

Secretaries of State for War and the Colonies, 1794–1854

1794–1801	Henry Dundas (later Viscount Melville)
1801–4	Lord Hobart (later Earl of Buckinghamshire)
1804–5	Lord Camden
1805–6	Viscount Castlereagh
1806–7	William Windham
1807–9	Viscount Castlereagh
1809–12	Earl of Liverpool
1812–27	Lord Bathurst
1827–8	F.R. Robinson (later Viscount Goderich and subsequently Earl of Ripon) William Huskisson
1828–30	Sir George Murray
1830–3	Viscount Goderich (later Earl of Ripon)
1833–4	E.G. Stanley (later Lord Stanley)
1834–5	Thomas Spring Rice (later Lord Mounteagle) Earl of Aberdeen
1835–9	Charles Grant (later Lord Glenelg)
1839–41	Marquis of Normanby Lord John Russell
1841–5	Lord Stanley (later 14th Earl of Derby)
1845–6	W.E. Gladstone
1846–52	3rd Earl Grey
1852–4	Sir John Pakington Duke of Newcastle

Secretaries of State for the Colonies, 1854–1922

1854–5	Sir George Grey Sidney Herbert Lord John Russell Sir William Molesworth
1855–8	Henry Labouchere

1858–9	Lord Stanley (later 15th Earl of Derby) Sir Edward Bulwer Lytton
1859–64	Duke of Newcastle
1864–6	Edward Cardwell
1866–7	Earl of Carnarvon
1867–8	Duke of Buckingham & Chandos
1868–70	Earl Granville
1870–4	Earl of Kimberley
1874–8	Earl of Carnarvon
1878–80	Sir Michael Hicks-Beach
1880–2	Earl of Kimberley
1882–5	Earl of Derby
1885–6	Sir F.A. Stanley (later Lord Stanley and subsequently Earl of Derby)
1886–7	Edward Stanley
1887–92	Sir Henry Thurston (created Baron Knutsford, 1888)
1892–5	Marquis of Ripon
1895–1903	Joseph Chamberlain
1903–5	Alfred Lyttelton
1905–8	Earl of Elgin and Kincardine
1908–10	Earl of Crewe
1910–15	Lewis Harcourt
1915–16	Andrew Bonar Law
1916–19	Walter Hume Long
1919–21	Alfred (1st Viscount) Milner
1921–2	Winston Spencer Churchill

Presidents of the Board of Control of India, 1784–1858

1784–90	Thomas Townsend, Lord Sydney
1790–3	William Wyndham Grenville, Lord Grenville
1793–1801	Henry Dundas (later 1st Viscount Melville)
1801–2	George Legge, Viscount Lewisham
1802–6	Lord Castlereagh
1806	Gilbert Ellice (later 1st Earl of Minto) Thomas Grenville
1806–7	George Tierney
1807–9	Robert Dundas (later 2nd Viscount Melville)
1809–12	Dudley Ryder, 1st Earl of Harrowby

1812–16	Robert Hobart (4th Earl of Buckinghamshire)
1816–21	George Canning
1821–2	Charles Bathurst
1822–8	Charles Watkin Williams Wynn
1828	2nd Viscount Melville
1828–30	Edward Law, Lord Ellenborough (later 2nd Earl of Ellenborough)
1830–4	Charles Grant (later Lord Glenelg)
1834–5	Lord Ellenborough
1835–41	Sir John Cam Hobhouse (later 1st Lord Broughton)
1841	Lord Ellenborough
1841–3	William Vesey-Fitzgerald, 1st Lord Fitzgerald
1843–6	Lord Ripon (1st Earl)
1846–52	Sir John Hobhouse
1852	Fox Maule, 2nd Earl Passmore (later 11th Earl of Dalhousie) John Charles Herries
1852–5	Sir Charles Wood (later 1st Viscount Halifax)
1855–8	Robert Vernon Smith (later 1st Lord Lyvedon)
1858	Earl of Ellenborough Edward Henry Stanley, Lord Stanley (later 15th Earl of Derby)

Secretaries of State for India, 1858–1922

1858–9	Edward Henry Stanley (as above)
1859–66	Sir Charles Wood (later 1st Viscount Halifax)
1866	George Frederick Robinson, 2nd Earl of Ripon
1866–7	Robert Arthur Talbot Gascoyne-Cecil, Lord Cranborne (later 3rd Marquess of Salisbury)
1867–8	Sir Stafford Northcote (later 1st Earl of Iddesleigh)
1868–74	George Douglas Campbell, 8th Earl of Argyll
1874–8	3rd Marquess of Salisbury
1878–80	Gathorne Gathorne-Hardy, Viscount Cranbrook (later 1st Earl of Cranbrooke)
1880–2	Spencer Compton Cavendish, Marquess of Hartington (later 8th Duke of Devonshire)
1882–5	John Wodehouse, 1st Earl of Kimberley
1885–6	Lord Randolph Churchill
1886–92	Earl of Kimberley Sir Richard Assheton Cross, 1st Viscount Cross
1892–4	Earl of Kimberley

1894–5	Henry Hartley Fowler, 1st Viscount Wolverhampton
1895–1903	Lord George Francis Hamilton
1903–5	William St John Fremantle Brodrick (later 1st Earl of Midleton)
1905–10	John Morley (later 1st Viscount Morley)
1910–15	Robert Crewe-Milnes, 1st Earl of Crewe
1915–17	(Joseph) Austen Chamberlain
1917–22	Edwin Samuel Montagu

APPENDIX E

The French empire: Colonial Ministers

Under-Secretaries for the Colonies, 1881–94

1881–2	Félix Faure
1882–3	A. Berlet
1883–5	Félix Faure
1885	A. Rousseau
1886–7	De La Porte
1887–8	Eugene Étienne
1888	Félix Faure
1888–9	De La Porte
1889–92	Eugène Étienne
1892–3	E. Jamais
1893	Théophile Delcassé
1893–4	André Lebon

Ministers for the Colonies, 1894–1924

1894	Georges Boulanger
1894–5	Théophile Delcassé
1895	Émile Chautemps
1895–6	Pierre Gieuysse
1896–8	André Lebon
1898	Gabriel Hanotaux Georges Trouillet
1898–9	A. Guillain
1899–1902	Albert Decrais
1902–5	Gaston Doumergue
1905–6	Étienne Clemental
1906	G. Leygues
1906–9	Raphael Millies-Lacroix
1909–10	Georges Trouillet
1910–11	Jean-Baptiste Morel
1911	Adolphe Messimy

1911–13	Albert Lebrun
1913	René Besnard
	Jean-Baptiste Morel
1913–14	Albert Lebrun
1914	Étienne Raynaud
1914–17	Gaston Doumergue
1917	André Maginot
	René Besnard
1917–20	H. Simon
1920–4	Albert Sarraut

APPENDIX F

Resistance movements

The European conquest of the rest of the world did not go unopposed, but the growing disparity between Euopean technology and that of most of the world meant that military resistance rarely succeeded by the nineteenth century. Increasingly, successful resistance came from political movements (which sometimes grew out of military resistance).

Military resistance (examples)

The early Portuguese empire

The expansion of Portuguese trade into the Indian Ocean and the Spice Islands was vigorously contested by Arab traders. Vasco da Gama defeated an Arab fleet on his third voyage (1502) and further important naval victories followed against an Egyptian/Gujerati fleet in 1509 and against a Javanese fleet in 1513, but the Portuguese were defeated by the Chinese in 1521–2. They failed to take some important stations, including Aden. In the 1570s a number of Muslim powers combined against them and attacked Goa, Malacca and Ternate. The Portuguese held Goa in a famous siege (1571) but lost Ternate (1575).

In the end, however, the Portuguese succumbed to European rivals, not to Asian resistance.

The Spanish empire

The Spanish empire in the Americas was won by war, notably against the Aztecs in 1519–21 and against the Incas in 1531–3. Almost ridiculously small Spanish forces triumphed over great empires but with the aid of the internal divisions of their enemies.

The oppression of the Indian peasants in Latin America led to a number of risings which continued to the end of the Spanish period, e.g. those in Peru in the 1770s and 1780s, of which the most famous was that led by a *mestizo*, José Gabriel Condorcanqui (who took the Inca name of Tupas Amaru), which was suppressed with difficulty; and those in Mexico in 1810–11, led by Miguel Hidalgo.

The Dutch empire

The Dutch only gradually established themselves in the Spice Islands, often acting in co-operation with, rather than in authority over, the existing polities. Even in Java itself they acted through the Sultan of Mataram until 1677.

North America

The East Coast Indians had originally been friendly and had even helped the early settlers to survive, but they became alarmed as the newcomers encroached upon their lands, and some of the tribes of the interior were more warlike.

1609	Champlain allied with the Hurons against the Iroquois.
1622	In Virginia, Opechancanough, Powahatan's successor, attacked the settlers, killing 350. Hostilities continued until 1644, the Indians sustaining heavy losses.
1637	New England. The war against the Pequot opened up the Connecticut valley to European settlement.
1675–6	'King Philip's War' against the Wampangoags.
1711–12	Carolinas. Tuscarora war.
1715–18	Carolinas. Yamasee war.
1763	'Pontiac's Conspiracy'. Alliance of Indian tribes to prevent the colonists expanding west of the Alleghenies.

(The main battle with the Amerindians for control of North America came after the United States had become independent.)

India and adjacent regions

The over-extended Mughal empire began to break up in the eighteenth century, and men who had been governors under the Mughals sought to carve out hereditary principalities for themselves. Initially, the two European powers involved, the British and the French, were brought in as auxiliaries in local struggles. It is not until the middle of the century that one can discern a clear resistance to foreign involvement (and even then the distinction is sometimes blurred).

1757	Battle of Plassey. Siraj-ud-daula, the Nawab of Bengal, had determined to challenge the English East India Company, who, he believed, were abusing the privileges granted them by the Mughal Emperor. He was defeated at the battle of Plassey, from which the British conventionally dated their rule in India. But the British had been supported by many of Siraj-ud-daula's opponents.
1799	Tipu Sultan of Mysore defeated at the battle of Seringapatam. Tipu had been one of the most irreconcilable enemies of the British and had conducted an effective propaganda campaign against them. (See, e.g., the remarkable automatom, Tipu's Tiger, now in the Victoria and Albert Museum in London.)
1803	The Duke of Wellington defeated the Maratha confederation at the battle of Assaye. Some historians have regarded the Marathas as strong indigenous contenders to become the successors of the Mughal empire, although others have

emphasised their disunity. They were not finally defeated until the Marquess of Hastings's campaigns, 1816–18.

1843	Conquest of Sind.
1845–6, 1848–9	War with Sikhs culminated in annexation of Punjab.
1857	'Indian Mutiny', spear-headed by the Bengal army. This had xenophobic elements, as well as showing some attachment to traditional rulers, and was complicated by economic and agrarian grievances, but it was probably not, as Karl Marx supposed, the 'first Indian War of Independence', but rather the last stand of the old India, which was being displaced.

Afghanistan

1839–42	First Afghan war. British failed to depose emir, Dost Muhammad, whom they distrusted as an ally of Russia.
1878–80	Second Afghan war. As in the first, the British suffered several disasters and finally withdrew with most of their objectives not achieved.

Burma

1823–6, 1856–7, 1885–7	Britain was compelled to fight three wars to gain control of Burma.

Ceylon

Initially Portuguese, and Dutch, control was confined to the coasts. Military action was necessary to subdue the interior.

1739–65	Dutch fought against King of Kandy.
1803	British used armed force against King of Kandy.
1815	King of Kandy deposed and his kingdom formally annexed.
1818	Further rebellion, eventually subdued.

China

1839–42	'Opium war' compelled China to extend trade relations with the West. (First of 'unequal treaties'.)
1856–60	'*Arrow* war' compelled China to grant further concessions.
1900	Boxer rebellion. Western powers, including the United States, and Japan intervened when their embassies were threatened.

Indo-China

The French advance in Tonkin was strongly resisted in the 1870s and 1880s by the 'Black Flags', irregular troops, often with Chinese support.

Even after the French had completed the conquest of Indo-China, resistance continued.

1885–1913	*Can Vuong* or Monarchist movement, an umbrella name for sporadic armed resistance.

New Zealand

The British theoretically admitted the prior rights of the Maori people but encroached on their land. Maori resistance led to war in 1843–8 and a series of wars in the 1860s (1860–1, 1863–6 and 1868–70).

Africa

The Europeans were kept on the coasts until the late nineteenth century (with partial exception in the extreme south). Historians are now agreed that this was not, as was at one time believed, because of climatic conditions but because of the strength of the Africans.

The British empire in Africa (including the Boers)

South Africa

Eastern borders of Cape Colony

Long series of 'Kaffir' wars on the frontier as European colonists met advancing 'Bantu'. Some of the most important were those of 1779–81, 1789–93, 1799–1803, 1811–12, 1818–19, 1834–5 and 1850–3. There was also the 'War of the Axe' with the Xhosa people in 1846–7.

Zulus

The main challengers to European supremacy were the Zulus, a clan of the Nguni people. The Zulus were themselves advancing at the expense of other groups. Their greatest military leader was Shaka (*c.*1787–1828). He was eventually deposed and murdered by his half-brother, Dingaan. An earlier quarrel between Shaka and one of his lieutenants, Mzilikaze, led to the Matabele (Ndebele) moving north-west into the territory of the Mashona (which became Rhodesia in colonial times).

1838	Boers defeated Zulus under Dingaan at Blood River.
1879	Zulu war after British annexation of the Transvaal. Zulus wiped out British force at Isandhlwana but were defeated at Ulundi.
1906	Zulu rebellion.

Rhodesias

The British advance was resisted.

1893, 1895–6	Matabele war.
1896	Mashona war.

West Africa

The Ashanti confederation offered particularly strong resistance to European advance. They fought the British in 1823–6, 1863–4, 1893–4, 1895–6 and 1900–1.

Abyssinia

1867–8   The British defeated the Abyssinian Emperor, Theodore, after he had held European captives.

Egypt and the Sudan

1882   Egyptian army, led by Arabi Pasha, tried to seize control of the country in the nationalist cause. Defeated by British intervention at the battle of Tel-el-Kebir.

1881–96   The Mahdi, and his successor, the Khalif, drove Egyptians and British out of the Sudan. (The most spectacular incident was the death at Khartoum in January 1885 of General Charles Gordon, who had been sent to evacuate the Anglo-Egyptian forces.)

1896–8   Kitchener reconquered the Sudan in the name of Egypt and Britain.

The French empire in Africa

Algeria

The French conquest was strenuously resisted, 1830–47. The French army was commanded by Marshal Bugeaud. The Algerian leader was Abd-el-Kader, who continued to work for Arab independence after he had been exiled to Damascus.

After the French defeat in the Franco-Prussian war, there were risings in Algiers and Constantine in 1871 and further risings in 1876, 1879 and 1881–4.

Western Sudan

Here the French encountered extremely strong resistance from the Muslim states in their path.

The French advance began under General Faidherbe, governor of Senegal, 1854–61 and 1863–5. It was strenuously resisted by el-Hajj Umar, the leader of the Tukolars, who was engaged in an Islamic *jihad* of his own.

The advance was resumed under later Governors, notably Colonel Brière de l'Isle (Governor, 1879), Joseph-Simon Gallieni (1886) and Major Archinard (1888–93). They were strongly opposed by Samori Touré, a convert to Islam, who was carving out an Islamic empire of his own. But the French reached Timbuktu in 1893 and Samori Touré surrendered in 1898.

The Italian empire in Africa

Although the Italians established themselves in Eritrea and Somaliland, they were the only Europeans to meet complete disaster in Africa in the late nineteenth century, being defeated by the Abyssinians at the battle of Adowa in 1896.

The German empire in Africa

The Germans attracted an unenviable reputation for brutality in their African colonies, suppressing a number of revolts with great force.

German East Africa (Tanganyika)

1888–90	Bushiri rising.
1891–8	Hehe war.
1905–6	Maji-Maji insurrection.

South-West Africa

1891–3	Guerilla warfare by Nama people.
1904	Herero rising (resulted in 123 colonists killed and approximately 60,000 Herero dead by 1906).
1904–7	Second Nama rising.

The Portuguese empire in Africa

1890s	War in Mozambique against Gaza Nguni.

The (Belgian) Congo

Early 1890s	War against Arab slave traders in the east of the country.

Political Resistance

British India

Western-style protest developed comparatively early here.

1828	Ram Mohan Roy founded *Brahmo Sabha*. This was not itself a political organisation but was formed to compare Indian and western philosophy and, hopefully, combine the best of both. It was later developed by Debendranath Tagore as the *Brahmo Samaj*. Although small in numbers, it was influential.
1830s	'Young Bengal' modelled itself on 'Young Ireland' and 'Young Hungary'.
1837	Bengal Landholders' Society (Zemindary Association) formed to work for reform.
1853	Bombay Association formed to lobby for changes when East India Company's charter came up for renewal. Remarkable in that it crossed all usual sectarian boundaries and included Hindus, Parsis, Muslims, Portuguese and Jews. Very sophisticated in the petitions it addressed to the British parliament.
1876	Surendranath Banerjea founded the Indian Association of Calcutta, to work for 'the conception of a united India, derived from the inspiration of Mazzini'.
1883	Indian National Conference met in Calcutta.
1885	Indian National Congress met in Bombay. (The Conference disbanded itself the following year to join forces.) The Congress, initially very moderate and middle class, also showed

225

itself very sophisticated in its analysis of India's problems and in its attempts to influence British opinion.

1905–8 Protests against the partition of Bengal were sometimes crudely terrorist but others were remarkable for their sophistication and depth of thought. The *swadeshi* movement, although it had its origins in American and Irish tactics of embargo and boycott, developed into a re-affirmation of the value of Indian civilisation.

French North Africa

1900–14 *Les Jeunes Algériens* (Young Algerians) was formed among those who had a French-style education and were mainly looking for political and secular reforms. A number of other groups, often short-lived, were founded by those who wished rather to re-assert their Muslim identity. Some conflict was inherent in the situation.

1906 The 'Young Tunisians' was founded, inspired by the Young Turk movement. Maintained pan-Islamic links.

French Indo-China

1904–5 Russo-Japanese war. The defeat of a European great power by an Asian power attracted the attention of the Vietnamese.

1907–8 *Dong Kinh Nghia Thuc* or Private Schools Movement. The Vietnamese, who had previously resisted the encroachment of western ideas, now saw advantages in modern education. When the system provided by the French proved inadequate, they began, despite French disapproval, to found their own schools.

1908 Formation of 'Young Annamites'.
Demonstrations demanding tax and educational reforms.
Phan Boi Chau fled to Canton, where he founded the *Viet-Nam Quang-Phuc Hoi* (Association for the Restoration of Vietnam), which established a network of secret cells in Vietnam. He also visited Bangkok, Hong Kong and Singapore and built up the *Dong-A-Dong-Minh* (League of East Asian People).

Dutch East Indies

1908 Appearance of first nationalist movements, inspired, like those in French Indo-China, by the Japanese victory over the Russians in 1904–5.

(For the later development of these embryonic resistance movements, *see* M.E. Chamberlain (1998) *Longman Companion to European Decolonisation in the Twentieth Century.*)

Section V

BIBLIOGRAPHY

Polemical literature

The European empires generated controversy almost from the beginning, both as to whether they should have been acquired at all, and how, since they had been acquired, they should be managed. The polemic literature, written at or near the time of the events described, is not only important in the historiography of empire but is also part of the history of empire. The debates themselves influenced the formation and shaping of the empires. The following were among the most important writings and controversies. (Modern editions of the works are cited where available.)

The early empires

The legitimacy of the Spanish empire in America was the subject of much debate. The Dominican Fray Bartolomé de las Casas wrote vigorously in defence of the Indians, invoking the concept of Natural Law. His best-known polemic was *Brevísima relación de la destrucción de las Indias* (1552). This was widely translated (it appeared in English as *Casas' Horrid Massacres*) and became part of the 'Black Legend' in Protestant countries, deploring the cruelty of Spanish rule. Las Casas also wrote *Historia general de las Indias* (ed. A. Millares Carlo and L. Hanke, 3 vols, 1951) and *Apologética historia sumaria* (ed. Edmundo O'Gorman, 2 vols, 1967). The *Brevísima relación* is to be found in the *Colección de tratados de las Casas, 1552–3*, a facsimile edition published in Beunos Aires in 1924 (reprinted 1965). Las Casas was supported by the Dominican jurist Francisco de Vitorio in his *Relectiones de Indis* (ed. L. Perena and J.M. Perez Prendes, 1967). But Juan Ginés de Sepúlveda replied defending the Spanish right to conquest in *Democrates Segundo* (ed. Angel Losada, 1951).

Neither the Portuguese nor the Dutch embarked on such soul-searching. The Portuguese, strongly influenced by the Jesuits, accepted more readily than the Spaniards the automatic rights of a Christian power. Two Dutch *predik-ants* (preachers) who objected to the Dutch war in the Moluccas in 1653 were threatened with being shipped home in disgrace and no polemical literature seems to survive (C.R. Boxer, The *Dutch Seaborne Empire*, 1600–1800, p. 154). 'Gold is your god', said the West Africans to the Dutch in the seventeenth century (quoted ibid., p. 128).

The English did suffer some scruples (see A. Pagden, 'The Struggle for Legitimacy', in the *Oxford History of the British Empire*, vol. 1, *The Origins of Empire* (ed. Nicholas Canny, 1998), pp. 34–54). Their main concern was to establish that they had peacefully occupied ownerless land (*res nullius*). The most famous justification of the British position is to be found in John Locke's *Second Treatise of Government* (ed. P. Laslett, 1967). It was challenged, for example, by Roger

Williams, the founder of Rhode Island (*see* W. Cronon, *Changes in the Land*, 1988). Only in Virginia did they argue that they were there by a (legitimate) conquest, following the Powhatans' breach of agreements. See *True Declaration of the Estate of the Colony in Virginia* (1610).

Claims of prior discovery also came to be important (foreshadowing nineteenth-century disputes). See R.A. Williams, *The American Indian in Western Legal Thought: The Discourses of Conquest*, 1990) and David Armitage, 'The New World in British Historical Thought' in K.O. Kuyperman (ed.), *America in European Consciousness, 1493–1750* (1995).

The eighteenth century

In the second phase of European imperialism, the most vigorous debate took place within the British empire. It encompassed both India and the American colonies.

In India it began in the seventeenth century and was conducted on two fronts, economic and ethical, although the two eventually merged. The position of the East India Company was resented from the beginning. It was charged both with ruining British industries by the import of cheap Indian textiles and with draining bullion from the country (a heinous offence in the mercantilist era) to buy luxury goods. Famous polemics against the Company included Gerard de Malynes' *A Treatise of the Canker of England's Commonwealth* (1601) and 'J.R.''s, *The Trade's Increase* (1615), which attracted replies like Sir Dudley Digges, *The Defence of Trade* (1615) and Thomas Mun, *A Discourse of Trade from England into the East Indies* (1621). By the eighteenth century the return of the nabob to England with immense wealth threatened to overturn the constitution itself. The impeachment of Warren Hastings was in reality an attack on the over-mighty Company. It led to the great polemics of Edmund Burke, which both defended the right of the Indians to determine the nature of their own society, and set ethical standards (the concept of 'trusteeship') which should govern the rule of 'alien' peoples. See *The Speeches of Edmund Burke on the Impeachment of Warren Hastings* (2 vols, 1895).

The debate on the quarrel with the American colonies took a rather different form. It turned mainly on the right relationship between a metropolitan power and its colonies. The ideological battle which was conducted in speeches and pamphlets is well dealt with in John C. Miller, *Origin of the American Revolution* (2nd edn, 1959). The American argument reached its climax in Thomas Jefferson's *Declaration of Independence*. It attracted the support of Englishmen, notably Edmund Burke in his *Speech on American Taxation* (1774), *Speech on Conciliation with America* (1775) and *Address to the British Colonists in North America* (1777) (all these are in *Burke's Political Writings*, selected by John Buchan, Nelson Classics, n.d.). It gave rise to Richard Price's *Observations on the Nature of Civil Liberty* and Thomas Paine's *Common Sense* (both 1776).

Free trade

The dominant mercantilist ideology of the eighteenth century was overturned by a work of the Scottish Enlightenment, Adam Smith's *Wealth of Nations* (1776,

Everyman edn, 1977), which became the bible of the nineteenth-century free trade era. Free trade made empire itself seem redundant to many and led to the expression of 'separatist' views. The literature is comprehensively surveyed in G.A. Bodelsen, *Studies in Mid-Victorian Imperialism* (2nd edn, 1959). On the other side of the debate were the writings of the Colonial Reformers, including Edward Gibbon Wakefield's *Letter from Sydney* (1829) and *View of the Art of Colonisation* (1849). The Durham Report is available in full in *Lord Durham's Report on the Affairs of British North America* (ed. C.P. Lucas, 1912), with which should be read Charles Buller's *Responsible Government for the Colonies* (1840).

The new imperialism

The British empire

In the British case the turn of the tide towards renewed imperialism is well illustrated by the two editions of Charles Dilke's *Greater Britain* (1868 and 1890 respectively). Classic expressions of the new attitudes can be found in J.R. Seeley, *Expansion of England* (1883) and J.A. Froude, *Oceana or England and Her Colonies* (1886). At first the new imperialism attracted only muted criticism, as can be seen in Bernard Porter's *Critics of Empire* (1968). E.D. Morel denounced European activities in West Africa from 1899, culminating in his *Red Rubber: The Story of the Rubber Slave Trade on the Congo* (1906).

Egypt was regarded by many as the trigger which started the whole process of the new imperialism. Wilfrid Scawen Blunt opposed the British occupation of Egypt in 1882 but only published his *Secret History of the English Occupation of Egypt* in 1907, which led him into a major controversy with Lord Cromer, who published his *Modern Egypt* (2 vols) in 1908. The French Prime Minister, Charles de Freycinet, had published *La Question d'Egypte* in 1905. T. Rothstein weighed in with a powerful attack in *Egypt's Ruin* in 1910.

It was the Boer war which opened the flood gates of controversy. J.A. Hobson published his *The War in South Africa: Its Causes and Effects* (1900) and *The Psychology of Jingoism* (1901), culminating in his *Imperialism: A Study* (1st edn, 1902, 3rd edn reprinted with introduction by J. Townshend, 1988). The last, although cobbled together from various writings and not always self-consistent, proved a seminal work. It influenced V.I. Lenin's *Imperialism: The Highest Stage of Capitalism* (1917), although their analyses were in the last resort incompatible. Hobson saw imperialism as an aberration which could be corrected: Lenin saw it as the inevitable denouement of capitalism. Other critiques followed, including H.N. Brailsford, *The War of Steel and Gold* (1917) and Leonard Woolf, *Empire and Commerce in Africa* (1920).

The French empire

After France's defeat by Germany in 1870–1, French opinion was sharply divided between those who thought that France could re-assert her great power status by an imperial policy and those who considered overseas adventures as a dangerous distraction from the defence of French interests in Europe. The debate in the newspapers and in ephemeral literature can be traced in

N. Pisani-Ferry, *Jules Ferry et la partage du monde* (1962). Ferry's own views can be studied in his *Tonkin et la mère patrie* (1890) and in his collected *Speeches* (1893)

The German empire

Otto von Bismarck showed little enthusiasm for an empire, except perhaps as a pawn in European diplomacy, but a colonial movement developed in Germany. Friedrich Fabri believed (exaggeratedly) that he triggered it by his *Does Germany Need Colonies?* (1879, trans. and ed. E.C.M. Breuning and M.E. Chamberlain, 1998). W. Hubbe-Schleiden published *Deutsche Colonisation* in 1881 and Heinrich von Treitschke linked colonisation with German nationalism in his *Politics* (vol. 1, trans. B. Dugdale and T. de Bille, 1916)

The Dutch empire

The Dutch did not join in the Scramble for Africa, being content with their lucrative enterprise in what is now Indonesia, but a sharp controversy developed in the nineteenth century about the Culture System, by which the Javanese were expected to produce cash crops to meet taxation demands. The controversy is discussed in C.A. Bayly and D.H.A. Kolff (eds), *Two Colonial Empires* (1986). For a contemporary defence, see J. van den Bosch 'Advies . . . over het stelsel van kolonisatie' (1829), in D.C. Steyn Parve (ed.), *Het Koloniaal Monopoliestelsel* (1851).

General

The early empires

A good starting point is G.V. Scammell, *The World Encompassed: The First European Maritime Empires c.600–1650* (1981). This takes the story back to the Vikings, the Hanseatic League and the Venetian and Genoan Republics and shows what long roots the fourteenth- and fifteenth-century explorations had. Another stimulating book with a broad perspective is J.H. Elliott, *The Old World and the New, 1492–1650* (1970). This is consciously updated in K.O. Kuyperman (ed.), *America in European Consciousness, 1493–1750* (1995).

The best short introduction to the Age of Discovery itself remains *Europe and the Wider World 1415–1715* (3rd edn, 1966) by J.H. Parry, who combined the insights of a former naval officer with those of a distinguished historian, although it is outdated on some matters, e.g. colour consciousness in the Portuguese empire. He wrote at greater length on the same themes in *The Age of Reconnaissance* (1963). His *Discovery of South America* (1979) deals with a particular continent.

An excellent series covering this period is the 'History of Human Society' (gen. ed. J.H. Plumb), which includes C.R. Boxer, *The Portuguese Seaborne Empire, 1415–1825* (1969, pbk 1973) and *The Dutch Seaborne Empire, 1600–1800* (1965, pbk 1973) and J.H. Parry, *The Spanish Seaborne Empire* (1966, pbk 1973). Specifically on Portugal there is Bailey W. Diffie and George D. Winius, *The Foundation of the Portuguese Empire, 1415–1580* (Europe and the Age of Expansion, vol. 1, 1977). A.H. de Oliveira Marques, *History of Portugal*, vol. 1 (1972) sets it in its context. Victor W. von Hagen deals with the extraordinary European obsession with the elusive treasures of South America in *The Golden Man: The Quest for El Dorado* (1974). John Hemming gives a full and vivid account in *The Conquest of the Incas* (1974), parallelled by Hugh Thomas, *The Conquest of Mexico* (1993). For a concise discussion of the Spanish practice and philosophy, see J.H. Parry, *The Spanish Theory of Empire in the Sixteenth Century* (1940). The same author provides a detailed description of Spanish government in one province in *The Audiencia of New Galicia in the Sixteenth Century* (1948, reprinted 1968). On France, there is R. Cook, *The Voyages of Jacques Cartier* (1993).

C.M. Cipolla, *Guns and Sails in the Early Phase of European Expansion, 1400–1700* (1965) deals with a particular aspect. There are a number of modern studies of Christopher Columbus, including Felipe Fernandez-Arnesto, *Columbus* (1992), W.D. and C.R. Phillips, *The Worlds of Christopher Columbus* (1992) and J. Cummins, *The Voyage of Christopher Columbus* (1992). There is also S. Greenblatt (ed.), *New World Encounters* (1993) and, most polemical of all, David E. Stannard, *American Holocaust: Columbus and the Conquest of the New World* (1992)

As history becomes less Eurocentric it is possible to study the societies into which the Europeans erupted, more objectively considered. A good introduction to South and Central America is C.A. Burland, *Peoples of the Sun: The Civilisations of Pre-Columbian America* (1974).

The Times *Atlas of World History* (1978 and later updates) deals with the Age of Discovery in a very clear graphic form. A technical but fascinating survey of the cartography of exploration by the former Superintendent of the British Museum Map Room is R.A. Skelton, *Explorers' Maps* (1958).

The European empires in general

(See also under the 'early empires'.) Only a few books attempt a comprehensive coverage. The best is D.K. Fieldhouse, *The Colonial Empires: A Comparative Survey from the Eighteenth Century* (2nd edn, 1982). See also his *Economics and Empire, 1830–1914* (1973). J.H. Parry's *Trade and Dominion* (1971) deals with the eighteenth century. Interesting comparisons between the British and Dutch empires are made in J.S. Bromley and E.H. Kossman (eds), *Britain and the Netherlands in Europe and Asia* (1968). *The World of Empires* (gen. ed. Douglas Johnson, 3 vols, 1973) is straightforward and well illustrated. Also comparative in treatment is Jean-Louis Miège, *Expansion européene et décolonisation de 1870 à nos jours* (1973).

Africa in general

Since 1976 the very important volumes of the *Cambridge History of Africa* have been appearing. The most relevant for this study are: vol. 3, *1050–1600* (ed. R. Oliver); vol. 4, *1600–1790* (ed. R. Gray); vol. 5, *1790–1870* (ed. J.E. Flint); vol. 6, *1870–1905* (eds R. Oliver and G.N. Sanderson); and vol. 7, *1905–1940* (ed. A.D. Roberts). These are essential to put European colonisation in its context.

To counteract the idea that Africa had no history apart from the history of European colonisation, there is still no better starting point than the numerous writings of Basil Davidson, beginning with his seminal study, *Old Africa Rediscovered* (2nd edn, 1970) or his *Africa in History: Themes and Outlines* (1966) or *The Africans: An Entry into Cultural History* (1969). Books like J. Fage, *History of Africa* (3rd edn, 1995) also put European colonisation into a much wider context. An interesting study of an African participant is L. Farrant, *Tippu Tib* (1975).

The Scramble period is covered at a popular level in T. Pakenham, *The Scramble for Africa* (1991) and, more definitively, in H.L. Wesseling, *Divide and Rule: The Partition of Africa, 1880–1914* (trans. A.J. Pomerans, 1996). Comparisons of two empires in Africa can be found in P. Gifford and W.R. Louis, *Britain and Germany in Africa* (1967) and P. Gifford and W.R. Louis, *France and Britain in Africa* (1971). An older book but still useful is R. Coupland, *East Africa and Its Invaders* (1938). S.E. Crowe, *The Berlin West Africa Conference, 1884–5* (reprinted, 1970) is still interesting as a diplomatic interpretation, but more up to date is S. Forster, W.J. Mommsen and R. Robinson (eds), *Bismarck, Europe and Africa: The Berlin Africa Conference 1884–1885 and the Onset of Partition* (1988). Bruce Vanderwort's *Wars of Imperial Conquest in Africa, 1830–1914* (1998) looks at the military side. Christopher Hibbert's *Africa Explored: Europeans in the Dark Continent, 1769–1889* (1982) is a very readable account of the exploration period.

Asia in general

Richard Hall's *Empires of the Monsoon: A History of the Indian Ocean and Its Invaders* (1996), which includes East Africa, provides a lively introduction. The multivolume *New Cambridge History of India*, now underway, will provide encyclopaedic coverage of the sub-continent. Volumes so far published include: P.J. Marshall, *Bengal: The British Bridgehead: Eastern India, 1740–1828* (1987); T.R. Metcalf, *Ideologies of the Raj* (1994); C.A. Bayly, *Indian Society and the Making of the British Empire* (1987); and B.R. Tomlinson, *The Economy of Modern India, 1860–1970* (1993); as well as S. Gordon, *The Marathas, 1600–1818* (1993) and J.F. Richard, *The Mughal Empire* (1993). Another lively introduction to India when the Europeans arrived is Bamber Gascoigne's *The Great Moghuls* (1971). A thoughtful approach from the Asian side is K.M. Panniker, *Asia and European Dominance* (1953). See also Rudolf von Albertini, *European Colonial Rule, 1880–1940: The Impact of the West on India, South East Asia, and Africa* (1982)

The British empire

The fashionable pendulum has swung very far on writings on the British empire. Those written in Victorian and Edwardian times were almost invariably adulatory, those written since the 1960s have more often been iconoclastic, sometimes concentrating almost exclusively on the dirty underbelly of empire with as much appetite for scandal as their predecessors had for heroes. Neither approach is strictly historical, although each is interesting as an historiographical study in itself.

A number of important studies were written between the world wars and immediately after the Second World War which assume that the British Commonwealth would be a permanent and important international grouping. Although their underlying assumptions would often not be acceptable today, they had every interest in presenting detailed and accurate political, legal and economic analyses and their work will therefore remain of permanent value to the historian. A prime example of that are the eight volumes of the *Cambridge History of the British Empire* (ed. J.H. Rose, A.P. Newton and E.A. Benians, 1929–63); to which might be added the *Surveys of British Commonwealth Affairs*, published by the Royal Institute of International Affairs (Chatham House) from 1937 onwards, under the editorship first of W.K. Hancock and later of N. Mansergh.

The most authoritative up-to-date survey of research, which in many ways supersedes older studies, is the *Oxford History of the British Empire* (gen. ed. W. Roger Louis): vol. 1 (ed. Nicholas Canny), *The Origins of Empire* (1998); vol. 2 (ed. P.J. Marshall), *The Eighteenth Century* (1998); vol. 3 (ed. A. Porter), *The Nineteenth Century*; and vol. 4 (ed. J.M. Brown and W.R. Louis), *The Twentieth Century* (both 1999). Vol. 5 (ed. Robin Winks) (Histography 1999) provides the bibliography. Many contributors, however, assume a fair degree of knowledge on the part of the reader and it can be a tough introduction for the newcomer to the subject. A gentler introduction is the *Cambridge Illustrated History of the British Empire* (ed. P. Marshall, 1996).

Single-author studies of the British empire include: T.O. Lloyd, *The British Empire, 1558–1983* (Oxford Short History of the Modern World series, 1984); L. James, *The Rise and Fall of the British Empire* (1994); D. Judd, *The British Imperial Experience from 1765 to the Present* (1996); and N. Mansergh, *The Commonwealth Experience* (1969, revised in two vols, 1982). Among older books still worth consulting for their distinctive points of view are P. Knaplund, *The British Empire, 1815–1939* (1942), C.E. Carrington, *The British Overseas: The Exploits of a Nation of Shopkeepers* (1950) and John Bowle, *The Imperial Achievement: The Rise and Transformation of the British Empire* (1974). A. Koebner's important *Empire* (1961) looks mainly at the British empire, although tracing the imperial concept back to classical times.

Constitutional issues used to loom large and are best followed in detail through A.B. Keith's numerous studies, ranging from *The First British Empire* (1930) to *The Constitutional Law of the Dominions* (1933). E.A. Walker, *The British Empire, Its Structure and Spirit* (2nd edn, 1953) is a less technical approach.

The most up-to-date economic study is P.J. Cain and A.G. Hopkins, *British Imperialism*, vol. 1, *Innovation and Expansion, 1688–1914* (1993).

A good deal more than atlases in the old sense are C.A. Bayly, *Atlas of the British Empire: A New Perspective on the British Empire from 1500* (1989) and A.N. Porter (ed.), *Atlas of British Overseas Expansion* (1991).

Books which cover shorter periods of the empire in some detail include: A. Calder, *Revolutionary Empire: The Rise of the English-Speaking Empire from the Fifteenth Century to the 1780s* (1981); P.D. Curtin, *The Rise and Fall of the Plantation Complex: Essays in Atlantic History* (1990); C.A. Bayly, *Imperial Meridien: The*

British Empire and the World, 1780–1830 (1989); V. Harlow, *The Founding of the Second British Empire* (2 vols, 1952, 1963); C.C. Eldridge, *Victorian Imperialism* (1978) and *England's Mission: The Imperial Idea in the Age of Gladstone and Disraeli, 1868–1880* (1973); R. Hyam, *Britain's Imperial Century, 1815–1914: A Study of Empire and Expansion* (2nd edn, 1993); J. Morris's trilogy, *Heaven's Command* (1973), *Pax Britannica: The Climax of an Empire* (1968) and *Farewell the Trumpets: An Imperial Retreat* (1978); B. Porter, *The Lion's Share: A Short History of British Imperialism, 1850–1983* (2nd edn, 1984); and M. Beloff, *Imperial Sunset*, vol. 1, *Britain's Liberal Empire, 1897–1971* (2nd edn, 1987). Anthony McFarlane's *The British in the Americas, 1480–1815* (1994) provides an interesting comparison with the Spanish empire.

J.C. Miller, *Origins of the American Revolution* (2nd edn, 1959) is still a useful introduction to the ideas of the American War of Independence. More recent studies include S. Conway, *The War of American Independence, 1775–1783* (1995) and Jeremy Black, *War for America* (1991). G.S. Wood, *The Radicalism of the American Revolution* (1992) challenges interpretations which have become orthodox.

A number of books consider nineteenth-century attitudes to empire (some of them old but still useful), among them: K.E. Knorr, *British Colonial Theories, 1570–1850* (reprinted 1964); C.A. Bodelsen, *Studies in Mid-Victorian Imperialism* (reprinted 1960); A.P. Thornton, *The Imperial Idea and Its Enemies* (1959); B. Semmel, *Imperialism and Social Reform* (1960); and R. Koebner and H.D. Schmitt, *Imperialism . . . A Political Word, 1840–1960* (1964). B. Farwell's *Queen Victoria's Little Wars* (1972) is lively and often shrewd.

Important for the structure of the empire are J.E. Kendle, *The Colonial and Imperial Conferences, 1887–1911* (1967), J.E. Tyler, *The Struggle for Imperial Unity* (1938) and F.A. Johnson, *Defence by Committee: The British Committee of Imperial Defence, 1885–1959* (1960)

India

An attractively written and splendidly illustrated introduction to the East India Company is Anthony Wild's *The East India Company: Trade and Conquest from 1600* (1999). Older but still important studies of the Company are: Holden Furber, *John Company at Work* (1951); L.S. Sutherland, *The East India Company in Eighteenth-Century Politics* (1952); and C.H. Philips, *The East India Company, 1784–1834* (2nd edn, 1961). Sudipta Sen's *Empire of Free Trade: The East India Company and the Making of the Marketplace* (1998) focuses on Bengal in the eighteenth century. The best general introduction is J.M. Brown's *Modern India: The Origins of an Asian Democracy* (Oxford Short History of the Modern World, 1985). Older but perceptive is *The British Impact on India* (1965) by a former member of the Indian Civil Service, Percival Griffiths. Another study, anecdotal but shrewd and entertaining, by a former member of the service writing under the pseudonym Philip Woodruff, is *The Men who ruled India*, vol. 1, *The Founders*, and vol. 2, *The Guardians* (2nd edn, 1963).

On the eighteenth century there are Mark Bence-Jones, *Clive of India* (1974), Keith Feiling, *Warren Hastings* (1954) and P.J. Marshall, *The Impeachment of Warren Hastings* (1965).

On the early nineteenth century see E. Stokes, *The English Utilitarians and India* (1959), N. Mukherjee, *The Ryotwari System in Madras, 1792–1827* (1962) and B. Stein, *Thomas Munro: The Origins of the Colonial State and his Visions of Empire* (1989).

J.A.B. Palmer gives a straightforward account of the 1857 insurrection in *The Mutiny Outbreak at Meerut in 1857* (1966). The official centenary history was S.N. Sen, *Eighteen Fifty-Seven* (1957). See too R.C. Majumdar, *The Sepoy Mutiny and the Revolt of 1857* (2nd edn, 1963). A more recent study is E. Stokes (ed. C. Bayly), *The Peasant Armed: The Indian Revolt of 1857* (1986).

For the later nineteenth cetury, including the genesis of Indian nationalism, see: T.R. Metcalf, *The Aftermath of Revolt: India, 1857–70* (1964); R.J. Moore, *Liberalism and Indian Politics, 1872–1922* (1966); Anil Seal, *The Emergence of Indian Nationalism* (1968); and S.R. Mehrotra, *A History of the Indian National Congress*, vol. 1, *1885–1918* (1995).

For the government from London, see A.P. Kominsky, *The India Office, 1880–1910* (1986).

A very important study, this time by an Indian former member of the Indian Civil Service, is R.C. Dutt, *The Economic History of India*, vol. 1, *Under Early British Rule* (2nd edn, 1906) and vol. 2, *In the Victorian Age* (1903). It is interesting to compare this with N. Charlesworth, *British Rule and the Indian Economy, 1800–1914* (1982). See too P. Harnetty, *Imperialism and Free Trade: Lancashire and India in the Mid-Nineteenth Century* (1972).

Asia (other than India)

There are a number of studies of the establishment of British power, among them: C.D. Cowan, *Nineteenth-Century Malaya: The Origins of British Political Control* (1961); C.N. Parkinson, *British Intervention in Malaya, 1867–77* (1960); J.F. Cady, *A History of Modern Burma* (1958); and W.P. Morrell, *Britain in the Pacific Islands* (1960). W.D. McIntyre's *Imperial Frontier in the Tropics, 1865–75* (1967), which deals with West Africa as well as Asia, shows how little difference there was between the Gladstone and Disraeli governments in their approach to empire.

Africa

R. Robinson and J. Gallagher, *Africa and the Victorians: The Official Mind of Imperialism* (2nd edn, 1981) was a seminal but controversial book when it first appeared in 1961. A much older book but still relevant is Lord Lugard's *The Dual Mandate in British Tropical Africa* (1922, reprinted 1965).

Studies of individual regions or countries include: R. Anstey, *Britain and the Congo in the Nineteenth Century* (1962); K.O. Dike, *Trade and Politics in the Niger Delta, 1830–1885* (1956); J.E. Flint, *Sir George Goldie and the Making of Nigeria* (1960); D. Kimble, *A Political History of Ghana: The Rise of Gold Coast Nationalism, 1850–1928* (1963); C. Fyfe, *A History of Sierra Leone* (1962); J. Hargreaves, *Prelude to the Partition of West Africa* (1963) and *West Africa Partitioned* (1974); J.S. Galbraith, *Mackinnon and East Africa, 1878–1895* (1972); K. Ingham, *The*

Making of Modern Uganda (1958); P. Mason, *The Birth of a Dilemma: The Conquest and Settlement of Rhodesia* (1958); R. Oliver, *Sir Harry Johnston and the Scramble for Africa* (1957); P. Mansfield, *The British in Egypt* (1971); J. Marlowe, *Anglo-Egyptian Relations, 1800–1953* (1954); G.N. Sanderson, *England, Europe and the Upper Nile, 1882–1899* (1965); P. Holt, *The Mahdist State in the Sudan, 1881–1898* (1958); and D. Bates, *The Fashoda Incident of 1898* (1984).

The dominions

K.M. McNaught, *The Penguin History of Canada* (new edn, 1988) provides a short introduction. Fuller and more up to date are J.M. Bumsted's two volumes, *The People of Canada: A Pre-Confederation History* (1992) and *The People of Canada: A Post-Confederation History* (1992). P.C. Newman's *Company of Adventurers and Caesars of the Wilderness* (1987) tells the story of the Hudson Bay Company. On the Durham Report and its significance, J. Azjenstat, *The Political Thought of Lord Durham* (1988) is judicious.

The bi-centenary of the sailing of the First Fleet saw the publication of many histories of Australia, some of them massive. More manageable is John Molony, *Penguin History of Australia: The Story of 200 Years* (1988). Deservedly famous is Robert Hughes, *The Fatal Shore: A History of the Transportation of Convicts to Australia, 1787–1868* (1987).

K. Sinclair (ed.), *Oxford Illustrated History of New Zealand* (1990) is an attractive introduction to the history of New Zealand. On the Maori wars there is E. Holt, *The Strangest War: The Maori Wars in New Zealand, 1860–1872* (1962) and J. Belich, *The New Zealand Wars and the Victorian Interpretation of Racial Conflict* (1986). C. Orange deals with a crucial issue in *The Treaty of Waitangi* (1987).

Because of its turbulent later political history, South Africa has attracted much study and interpretations of its history have changed greatly in recent years. A very good short introduction is Nigel Worden, *The Making of Modern South Africa: Conquest, Segregation and Apartheid* (3rd edn, 1999). On a rather larger scale, there is R. Davenport, *South Africa: A Modern History* (1991). C.W. de Kiewiet's *The Imperial Factor in South Africa* (1937) is still worth reading. D.R. Morris, *The Washing of the Spears* (1966) first attracted the attention of Europeans to the African movements which went on quite independently of European intervention in the nineteenth century and is still very readable, although outdated on details. The controversy is still being conducted through articles, but see John Guy, *The Destruction of the Zulu Kingdom: The Civil war in Zululand* (1979). See also D.M. Schreuder, *The Scramble for Southern Africa, 1877–1895: The Politics of Partition Re-appraised* (1980). On the Anglo-Boer war of 1899–1902, Thomas Pakenham's original research in *The Boer War* (1979) will stand the test of time and is also very readable. Iain Smith's *The Origins of the South African War, 1899–1902* (1995) is an excellent and balanced study.

The Spanish empire

J.H. Parry, *The Spanish Seaborne Empire* (pbk 1973) remains the best introduction in English. See also the books listed under 'early empires'.

Various aspects of the loss of the Spanish empire are covered in: R.A. Humphreys, *Liberation in South America, 1806–1827* (1952); J. Lynch, *Spanish Colonial Administration, 1782–1810* (1958) and *The Spanish American Revolutions, 1808–1826* (1973); I. Nicholson, *The Liberators* (1969); and S. de Madariaga, *The Fall of the Spanish American Empire* (1947) and *Bolívar* (1952). R. Harvey's, *Liberators: Latin America's Struggle For Independence, 1810–1830* (2000) is a good modern account.

The best modern introduction to the Spanish–American war of 1898 is Joseph Smith, *The Spanish–American War: Conflict in the Caribbean and the Pacific, 1895–1902* (1994).

The Portuguese empire

C.R. Boxer's *The Portuguese Seaborne Empire, 1415–1825* (pbk 1973) is the most comprehensive introduction in English. See also his *Race Relations in the Portuguese Colonial Empire* (1963) and *Brazil* (1953). Studies of particular areas include: N.M. Pearson, *The Portuguese in India* (New Cambridge History of India, 1987); E. Axelson, *The Portuguese in South East Africa, 1488–1600* (1963) and *The Portuguese in South East Africa, 1600–1700* (1960); and D. Birmingham, *The Portuguese Conquest of Angola* (1965).

The Dutch empire

C.R. Boxer's *The Dutch Seaborne Empire, 1600–1800* (pbk 1973) provides a good general introduction but there are a number of modern studies in English such as J.I. Israel, *Dutch Primacy in World Trade, 1585–1740* (1989). A detailed study of a neglected subject is G.F. Jones *The Georgia Dutch: From the Rhine and the Danube to the Savannah, 1733–1783* (1992). The Dutch in South Africa are covered in two studies which go beyond the ending of Dutch rule: G.H.L. Le May, *The Afrikaners: An Historical Interpretation* (1995) and W.A. de Klerk, *The Puritans in Africa: A Story of Afrikanerdom* (1975). There are some interesting comparative studies of the heart of the Dutch empire, Indonesia: C.A. Bayly and D.H.A. Kolff (eds), *Two Colonial Empires* (1986) and J.S. Furnivall, *Colonial Policy and Practice: A Comparative Study of Burma and Netherlands India* (1948). Also C. Day, *The Policy and Administration of the Dutch in Java* (reprinted 1966) and R.E. Elson, *Javanese Peasants and the Colonial Sugar Industry* (1984).

The French empire

Comparable to the older British studies of empire, detailed, factually reliable, but outdated in interpretation, is S.H. Roberts, *A History of French Colonial Policy, 1870–1925* (1925, reprinted 1963). See also A. Murphy, *The Ideology of French Imperialism* (1948) and T.F. Power, *Jules Ferry and the Renaissance of French Imperialism* (1944).

More up-to-date studies are H. Brunschwig, *French Colonialism, 1871–1914: Myths and Realities* (1966) and J. Cooke, *New French Imperialism, 1880–1910: The Third Republic and Colonial Expansion* (1973). C.M. Andrew and A.S. Kanya-Forstner's *The Climax of French Imperial Expansion, 1914–1924* (1981) deals with the very end of the period.

An important study of a particular area is A.S. Kanya-Forstner, *The Conquest of the Western Sudan: A Study in French Military Imperialism* (1969). On North Africa there is C.A. Julien, *Histoire de l'Algérie contemporaine*, vol. 1, *La Conquête et les débuts de la colonisation* (1964); J. Ganiage, *Les Origines du protectorat français en Tunisie* (1959) and J.L. Miège, *Le Maroc et l'Europe*, vol. IV (1963).

The best introduction to the French in Indo-China is still J.F. Cady, *The Roots of French Imperialism in Eastern Asia* (1954). Many books on the Vietnam war devote some space to the French period but more specifically on it are: T.E. Ennis, *French Policy and Developments in Indochina* (1956); M.E. Osborne, *The French Presence in Cochinchina and Cambodia: Rule and Response, 1859–1905* (1969); and D.G. Marr, *Vietnamese Anticolonialism, 1885–1925* (1971).

The German empire

M.E. Townsend proposed an essentially domestic origin for Germany's colonial empire in her *Origins of Modern German Colonialism, 1871–1885* (1921) but the idea then became unfashionable as major diplomatic historians saw the German colonies as by-products of Bismarck's European policy. This was most trenchantly argued in A.J.P. Taylor's *Germany's First Bid for Colonies* (1938) but it also underlies W.O. Aydelotte's *Bismarck and British Colonial Policy* (1937), S.E. Crowe's *The Berlin West Africa Conference* (1942) and W.L. Langer's *Alliances and Alignments* (2nd edn 1950) and *The Diplomacy of Imperialism* (2nd edn 1950). But after the Second World War left-wing historians began to see the German colonies rather as the by-products of the attempts of the German establishment to maintain their power and domestic interpretations were revived. See, e.g., H.U. Wehler's *Bismarck und der Imperialismus* (1969).

Studies representing various points of view include: H. Brunschwig, *L'Expansion allemande d'outre-mer* (1957); W.O. Henderson, *Studies in German Colonial History* (1966); W.D. Smith, *The German Colonial Empire* (1978); and H. Stoecker, *German Imperialism in Africa* (1986). K.J. Bade has an interesting study in *Friedrich Fabri und der Imperialismus in der Bismarckzeit: Revolution, Depression, Expansion* (1975). Some of the forces driving German colonialism are examined in M. Walker, *Germany and Emigration, 1816–1885* (1964). An individual region is studied in H.R. Rudin, *The Germans in the Cameroons* (1938).

The Belgian empire

A journalistic but basically accurate account of Leopold II's activities is given in N. Ascherson, *The King Incorporated* (1963).

Section VI

MAPS

Map 1 The Portuguese Empire *c.*1600

N

Madeira
(1420)

Arguim Is
(1448)

Cape Verde Is
(1456)

El Mina (1482)

Fernando Po

São
Thomé Is
(1493)

São Paulo
de Luanda
(1575)

1530–1650 Maskat

Ormuz (1515–1622)

Diu (1535)

Surat (1540–1615)

Aden
(1524–38)

Bombay
(1530)

Goa
(1510)

Cochin
(1503)

Malindi (1498)

Mombasa (1593)

Pemba (1593)

Zanzibar (1503)

(1502)

Kilwa

Mozambique
(1508)

Sofala
(1505)

Masulpata
(1570–1605)

Atjeh
(1514–1641)

Colombo
(1518)

Macao
(1555)

Malacca
(1517–1641)

Manado
(1540)

Bantam
(1512–96)

Amboina
(1511–99)

Ternate
(1522–74)

Moluccas
(1512–1621)

Timor
(1520)

0   3000 miles

0   4000 km

243

Map 2 The French Empire on the eve of the Seven Years War (1756)

Hyderabad
(French influence)

Carnatic
(French influence)

St Louis

Goree

Assini

Pondicherry

Ile de France (Mauritius)

Réunion

0   3000 miles

0   4000 km

Map 3 The 'first' British Empire on the eve of the American War of
Independence (1776)

Minorca

Gibraltar

St Louis (Senegal)

The Gambia

Bombay

Bengal

Madras

Cape Coast
Castle

St Helena

0   3000 miles

0   4000 km

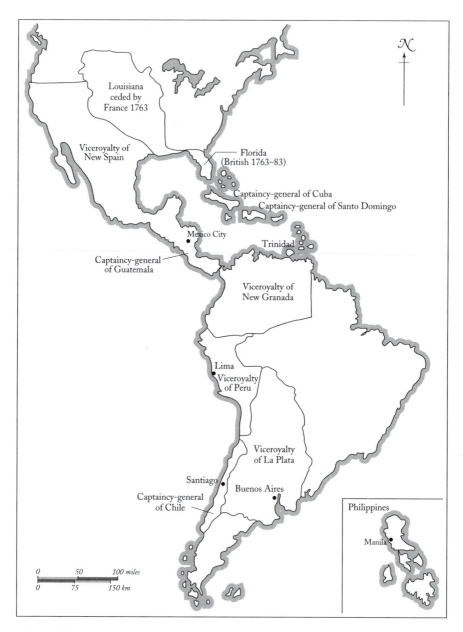

Map 4 The Spanish Empire in the Americas and the Pacific in the late
eighteenth century

Map 5 The European Empires in 1914

Iceland

Faroe Islands
(Dan.)

Gibraltar (Br.)

Spanish
Sahara

Morocco

Algeria

French
West
Africa

Sierra
Leone

Liberia

Ascension Is (Br.)

The Gambia

St Helena (Br.)

Malta
(Br.)

Libya

French
Equatorial
Africa

Nigeria

French
West
Africa

Cameroon

Cyprus (Br.)

Egypt

Sudan

Belgian
Congo

German
East
Africa

Angola

German
Southwest
Africa

South
Africa

Aden

Trucial
States

Goa (Port.)
(Fr.) Somaliland
(Br.) Somaliland
(Ital.) Somaliland

Kenya

Uganda

Zanzibar

Nyasaland

Northern Rhodesia

Madagascar

Mozambique

Southern Rhodesia

Bechuanaland

INDIA

Burma

Pondicherry
(Fr.)

Ceylon

Mauritius (Br.)

Réunian (Fr.)

Macao (Fr.)

Hong Kong (Br.)

INDOCHINA

Malaya

Borneo

DUTCH EAST INDIES

New Guinea

Timor
(Port.)

AUSTRALIA

Tasmania

0   3000 miles

0   4000 km

INDEX